THE CAMPAIGN IN BULGARIA
1877—1878

THE
CAMPAIGN IN BULGARIA
1877—1878

BY

F. V. GREENE

CORPS OF ENGINEERS, U.S. ARMY
FORMERLY MILITARY ATTACHÉ TO THE UNITED STATES LEGATION
AT ST. PETERSBURG

The Naval & Military Press Ltd

Published by

The Naval & Military Press Ltd
Unit 5 Riverside, Brambleside
Bellbrook Industrial Estate
Uckfield, East Sussex
TN22 1QQ England

Tel: +44 (0)1825 749494

www.naval-military-press.com
www.nmarchive.com

*In reprinting in facsimile from the original, any imperfections are inevitably reproduced
and the quality may fall short of modern type and cartographic standards.*

NOTE

Greene's "Russian Campaigns in Turkey" is universally recognised as being by far the best work in the English language on the Russo-Turkish War of 1877-78. As it has been out of print for some time, we have obtained the permission of the Publishers, Messrs. D. Appleton & Co., to reprint the most instructive part of this work, viz., "The Campaign in Bulgaria."

We have undertaken this in the hope that it will prove useful to officers who are preparing for the Staff College and Promotion Examinations, and also to those desirous of studying a Campaign, preparatory to writing a critical memoir, as laid down in "Combined Training," 1903 (par. 192).

THE PUBLISHERS.

December 1903.

CONTENTS

	PAGE
INTRODUCTORY—Declaration of War—The Theatre of Operations—Plan of Campaign	1

CHAP.
- I. First Period of the War, April 24th to June 27th—The Concentration in Roumania and Passage of the Danube . . . 9
- II. Operations of the Advance Guard under Gourko, July 12th to August 6th 27
- III. Operations of the Right Wing, under Lieutenant-General Baron Krüdener 50
- IV. General Condition of Affairs at the beginning of August—Battle of Shipka Pass, August 21st to 26th—Operations on the Lom in August and September 69
- V. Operations on the Right Flank in August and September—Battles of Lovtcha, September 3rd, and Plevna, September 11th 94
- VI. The Investment of Plevna—Battle of Gorni-Dubnik, October 24th, 1877 136
- VII. Events on other portions of the Theatre of War from September to December, 1877—Shipka—The Lom—The Lower Danube—Gourko's Advance to Orkhanie . . 157
- VIII. The Fall of Plevna 177
- IX. The Passage of the Balkans near Sophia by Gourko's Column 201
- X. Gourko's Advance to Philippopolis, and the Battles near that point, January 15th to 17th, 1878 219
- XI. Capture of the Turkish Army at Shipka Pass . . . 230
- XII. The Advance to Constantinople—Remarks on the Winter Campaign 241

LIST OF MAPS

Theatre of War in Europe	*To face page*	1
Progress Map No. 1. First Period of the Campaign	,,	9
The Crossing at Galatz	,,	19
The Crossing at Zimnitza-Sistova	,,	21
Progress Map No. 2. Second Period of the Campaign	,,	27
Relative Positions of the Russian and Turkish Armies, August 5th, 1877	,,	71
Plan of the Topography around Plevna	,,	107
Progress Map No. 3. Third Period of the Campaign	,,	201
Scene of Operations at Shipka Pass	,,	231

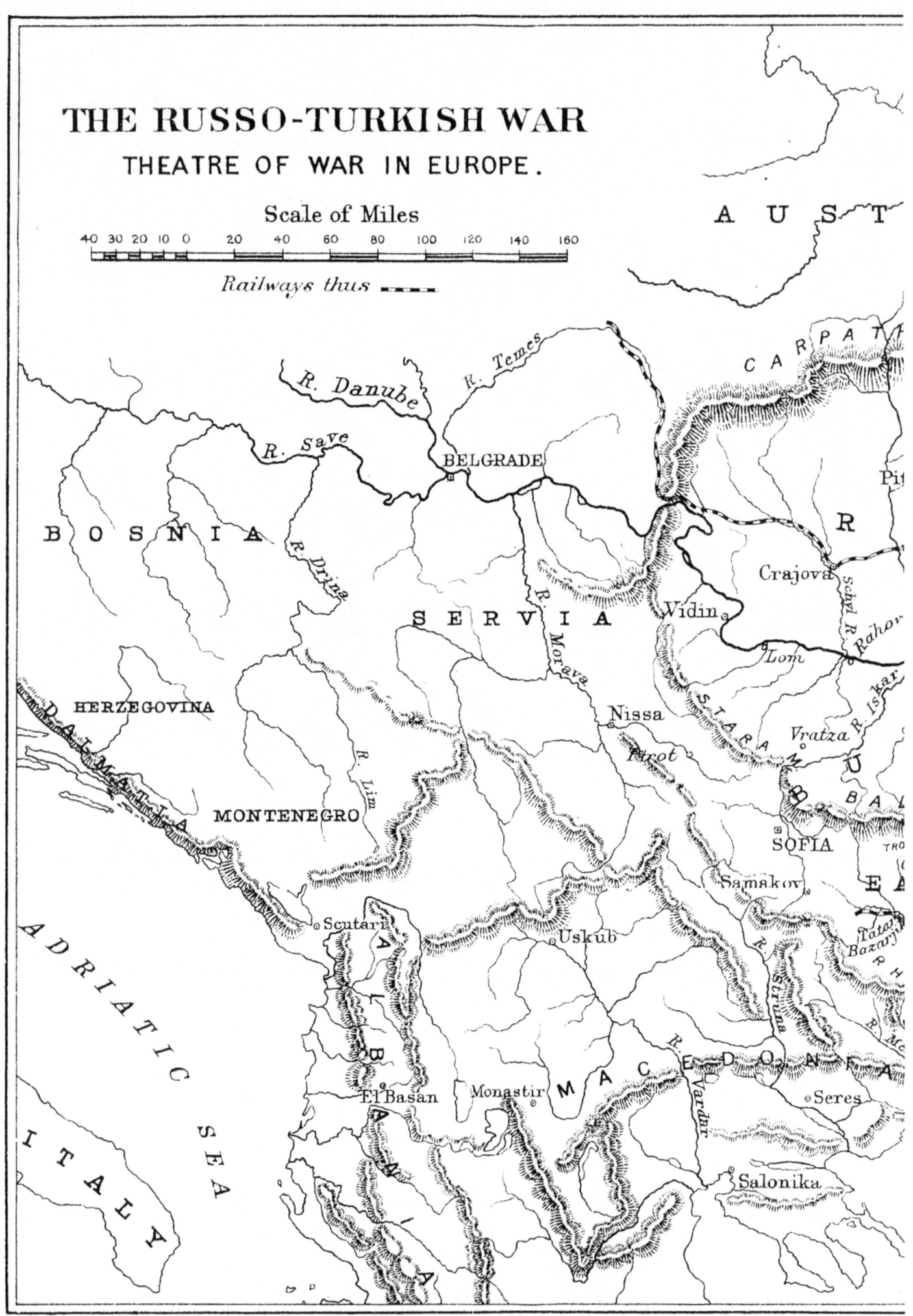

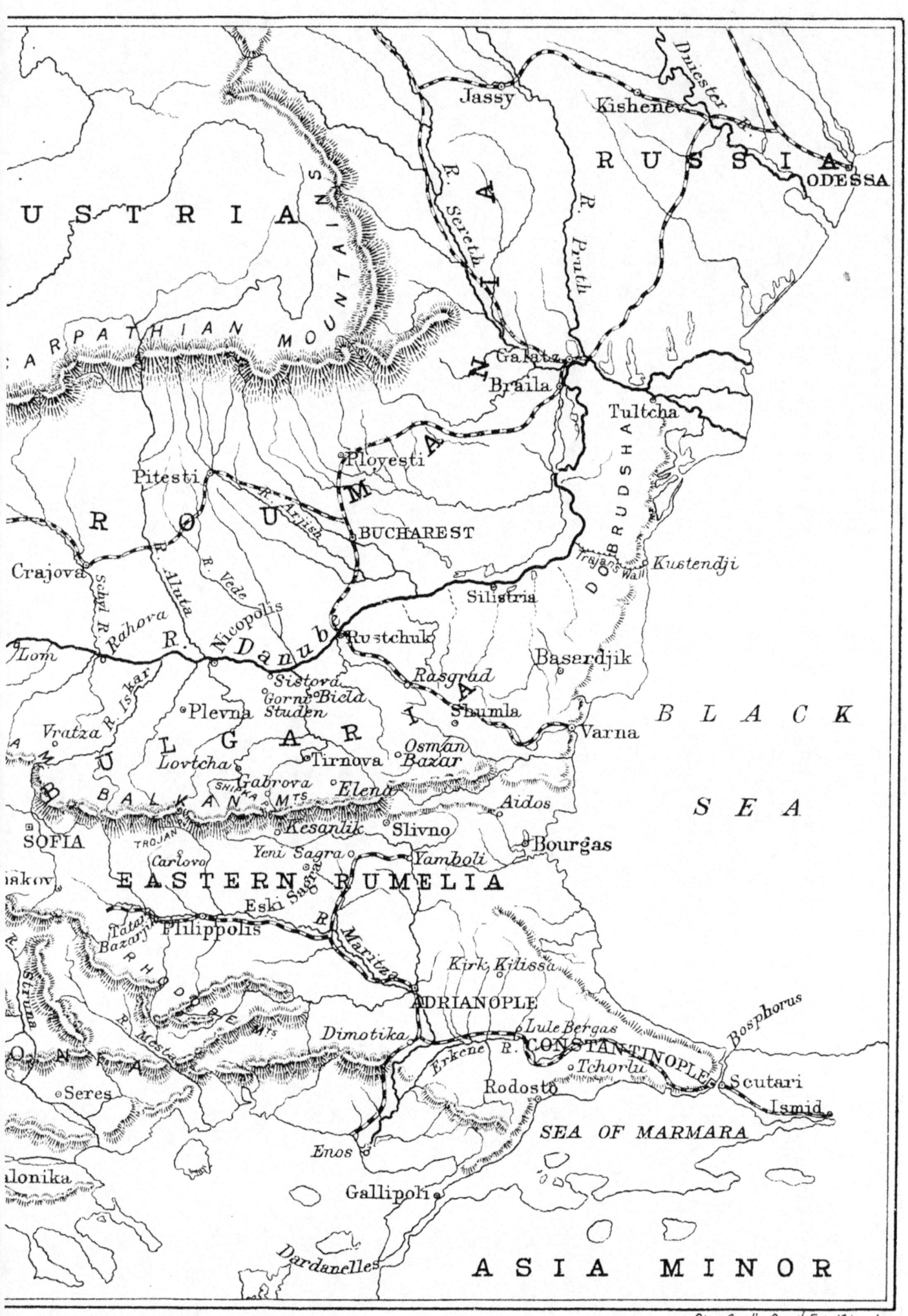

INTRODUCTORY

DECLARATION OF WAR.—THE THEATRE OF OPERATIONS.—
PLAN OF CAMPAIGN.

ON the 24th of April, 1877, the Emperor of Russia promulgated at Kishineff his manifesto, reciting his warm interest in the welfare of the oppressed Christian races in Turkey and his desire to ameliorate their condition, which desire was shared by the whole Russian people, and stating that for two years—ever since the disturbances in Bosnia—he had constantly striven, in concert with the other European Powers, by peaceful negotiations, to induce the Porte to introduce those reforms to which it was solemnly bound by previous engagements, and by which alone the Christians in Turkey could be protected from local exaction and extortion; that these negotiations had all failed through the obstinacy of the Porte; and now, all peaceful methods being exhausted, the moment had arrived for him to act independently and impose his will on the Turks by force; and therefore the order had been given to his army to cross the Turkish frontier.

In the previous month of November the six army corps (VII., VIII., IX., X., XI., and XII.), occupying the districts nearest the Roumanian frontier, had been mobilised, and four of them had been concentrated in the vicinity of Kishineff, the other two remaining near Odessa and in the Crimea. Later in the winter the IV., XIII., and XIV. Corps had also been mobilised, but had remained in their respective districts in the interior, at a distance by rail of from 400 to 800 miles.

The "Army of the South," under the command of the Grand Duke Nicholas, which was ordered to cross the frontier on the 24th of April, consisted of the four corps at Kishineff and two rifle brigades. A few days later (May 8) the IV., XIII., and XIV. Corps were also placed under his orders, and moved forward to the frontier by rail. The organisation of the Russian army corps consists of two divisions (24 battalions) of infantry, two brigades (96 guns) of artillery, and one division (18 squadrons) of cavalry, with two batteries (12 guns). With seven army corps and two rifle brigades, therefore, the force which was thought sufficient for the invasion of Turkey consisted of about 180 battalions, 200 squadrons, and 800 guns—in all, about 200,000 men, which the usual casualties in the way of sickness, detachments, &c., at the beginning of a campaign, would reduce to 180,000 effectives by the time they reached the Danube. From this great defect of insufficiency of numbers more than from any other cause came the checks and reverses which Russia met with after crossing the Danube.

The exact number of troops which Turkey had under arms in Europe at the outbreak of the war it is not possible to state; but in round numbers she had about 360 battalions, 85 squadrons, and 450 guns—an effective force of about 250,000 men of regular troops (*nizam* and *redif*), distributed as follows:

In the western provinces from Bosnia to Thessaly, including the army operating against Montenegro	85,000
On the Upper Danube, at Widdin	60,000
In the quadrilateral of fortresses, Rustchuk, Silistria, Varna, Shumla	50,000
In detachments at minor points along the whole length of the Danube	15,000
South of the Balkans, at Sophia, Philippopolis, Adrianople, and Constantinople	40,000
Total	250,000

Of these, 165,000 were immediately available for operations in Bulgaria.

During the month of July the Egyptian contingent, 12,000 men, arrived at Varna, and Suleiman's Montenegrin army of about 40,000 men was brought by sea to Enos, and thence to Adrianople, thus making a total of 217,000 on the theatre of war in Europe in the month of August. In Asia there was a vast recruiting-ground which supplied recruits during the whole war, but the number of them it is not possible to state. But in general terms it may be said that Turkey had 225,000 men on the theatre of operations in Europe; and, until the collapse in the month of January, she replaced her losses by recruits, and maintained her army at about that strength.

From the above statement it will be seen that in artillery the Turks had only something more than half of that possessed by the Russians, and that their regular cavalry was lamentably deficient in numbers. But, on the other hand, they were far superior in the quality of their armament; their artillery was all composed of Krupp's steel breech-loaders, of 8 and 9 centimetres calibre, which, in quality of metal, in range, accuracy, and lightness, were superior to the bronze pieces of the Russians. In small arms, the great majority of the troops were armed with the Peabody-Martini gun, calibre ·45, made by the Providence Tool Company of Rhode Island—an arm which has no superior among modern breech-loaders; there were over 300,000 of these guns on hand at the beginning of the war, and about 200,000 were subsequently received. The rest of the troops were armed with the English Snider, calibre ·50, a gun superior to the Russian Krenk. Only the cavalry on the Turkish side was inferior in armament to the cavalry of the Russians; the latter had the short Berdan, while the Turks had the Winchester, which, although a repeating arm, has such a small charge and short range as to make it a very inferior weapon.

In order to make up their deficiency in cavalry, the Turks had recourse to the irregular troops known as Bashibozouks.* These were principally composed of the Tcher-

* The Turkish words *bashi bozouk* mean simply irregular soldier, or, as we would say," guerilla "—*i.e.*, a man who is a farmer one day and a soldier the next.

kesses who were brought from Circassia in 1866 and settled in Bulgaria and Roumelia; they furnished their own horses, and the Government supplied them with arms and ammunition. These troops were insubordinate and unruly, occupied in marauding and pillaging instead of reconnoitring, cowardly and disobedient in battle, and of no military service whatever to the Turks.

THE THEATRE OF OPERATIONS

The Carpathian Mountains or Transylvanian Alps, coming from Galicia in a southerly direction, form the boundary between Hungary and Moldavia for a distance of about 150 miles; then they suddenly turn due westward for another 150 miles, forming the northern boundary of Wallachia; here they again turn southward, are cut through by the Danube at the Iron Gates, and then lose their identity in the confused mountains of Servia. From these latter runs a small range known as the Etropol Balkans, in a south-easterly direction, until it joins the main chain of the Balkans, which goes due east into the Black Sea. Between the Carpathians and the Balkans is the valley of the Danube, about 200 miles broad. On the north-eastern slope of the Carpathians begins a region stretching far away across Russia, known as the "Steppe," and similar in every respect to the plains of Kansas and Colorado. In Galicia rises the Dniester, which flows south-easterly through these plains for 500 miles, and empties into the Black Sea near Odessa. Nearer the Carpathians are two slightly smaller streams, the Pruth and the Sereth, which have a parallel course, and empty into the Danube on either side of Galatz. Along the east-and-west portion of the Carpathians the slopes of the mountains extend southerly for about 50 miles from their crest. The remaining 80 miles to the Danube is made up of the flat, treeless Wallachian plains—the counterpart of those of southern Illinois; the soil is fertile, and well watered by a great number of streams flowing south-easterly from the mountains to the Danube. The northern banks of this river from Widdin to Galatz are nowhere more than 100 feet above the level of the stream, and usually not more than 40 feet. On the other side of the Danube the country is of a totally different character; the Balkans, whose crest is from 3500 to 5000 feet above the sea, send their foot-hills to the very bank of the Danube, which is from 500 to 1000 feet above the river-bed; the country is rolling and hilly, well wooded, and has numerous rich valleys, through which streams flow from the Balkans to the Danube.

The Danube, after breaking through the Carpathians at the Iron Gates, flows in a southerly direction for 70 miles to Widdin, then keeps a generally easterly course for 250 miles, arriving within 35 miles of the Black Sea; then it suddenly turns north, and reaches the sea by going around a right angle, the total length of which is about 175 miles. The country inclosed within this rectangle is known as the Dobrudja; it has a barren and sandy soil, and is remarkable for its scarcity of wood and water; across its narrowest part are still seen the remnants of Trajan's Wall, built by that conqueror to protect his newly acquired provinces from the northern hordes.

From Widdin to Silistria the Danube bears a striking resemblance to the Missouri between Bismarck and Omaha; from bluff to bluff the distance is about three miles, and in the bed there are from two to five streams separated by islands of various sizes and constantly varying shapes; the largest stream is usually about 1000 yards in width, and it has a tortuous channel through which eight feet of draught can usually be carried at all seasons; the current is swift— two and a half to three miles an hour. On the western side of the Dobrudja the bed is over ten miles wide, and consists of an impassable swamp (broken by the bluff at Hirsova), through which the river winds its way in several streams.

In Roumania there is one main line of railway, which comes from Austria over the Galician frontier, and descends the valley of the Sereth to its mouth at Galatz; thence it goes west by a very irregular route to Bucharest; and from there again in a very winding direction it goes on to the west, reaching the Danube at Turn-Severin, near the Iron Gates—the corner of the frontiers of Austria, Roumania, and Servia. Near the Galician frontier a branch line turns off to Yassy, and thence, crossing the Pruth at the little village of Ungheni, goes on past Kishineff, and near Odessa joins the main system of Russian roads. From Bucharest another branch line goes down to the Danube at Giurgevo, and connects with a line on the other side of the Danube which runs from Rustchuk past Shumla to Varna, on the Black Sea coast. The line of Trajan's wall in the Dobrudja is followed by another railway, from Tchernavoda on the Danube to Kustendje on the Black Sea.

These are the only railroads between the Carpathians and the Balkans.* The Roumanian railroad follows such an irregular course that the distance from Kishineff to Bucharest is 425 miles by rail, though only about 250 by post-road.

In Roumania there are now excellent post-roads connecting all the larger towns; as there was no fighting on that side of the river, it is not necessary to enumerate them. In Bulgaria, on the other hand, there are very few good roads; they will be described in subsequent chapters.

RUSSIAN PLAN OF CAMPAIGN

Between the slopes of the south-eastern bend of the Carpathians and the Black Sea the distance is but 120 miles in a straight line, and through this space of course any advance from Russia to Turkey must be made; the Danube divides it into two parts, on one side the Dobrudja, on the other Roumania. By the treaty of Paris in 1856 an artificial boundary-line was created, which caused the frontiers of Russia and Turkey to be separated by a narrow strip of territory which was given to the Principalities; and by the same instrument the naval forces of Russia on the Black Sea were destroyed—both measures being aimed to hinder Russia's

---

* During the war the Russians built a railroad direct from Bender on the Dniester to Galatz, and also extended the Roumanian railroad from Giurgevo to the bridge at Zimnitza-Sistova.

future operations against Turkey. The former clause proved of no avail, for when the war was declared a convention was at once concluded with Roumania allowing the passage of Russian troops through her territory; the latter clause was wholly revoked by the convention of 1871, but between that time and 1877 Russia had not been able to construct a fleet on the Black Sea which could in any way cope with the powerful ironclads which Turkey had meanwhile been buying in England.

Had Russia had control of the Black Sea, the natural plan of campaign would have been to advance by the Dobrudja, using the ports of the Black Sea as bases of supply; capturing Varna (the only fortified place on the seacoast) by a combined land and sea attack, and masking the other three fortresses, they could have crossed the eastern passes of the Balkans (which are much lower than the western), as Diebitch did in 1829, and thus have reached Adrianople, always basing themselves on the Black Sea. But, not having the control of the sea, such a plan was impossible; for they could not have maintained their long, narrow line of communications between the Danube on one side and the sea on the other, both in possession of the enemy's fleet; and the three strongest of the fortresses, Varna, Shumla, and Rustchuk, being connected by a railway, would have constituted a line of defence which it would have been hard to break, for it is well known that the Turks fight well behind fortifications.

The plan therefore adopted was to seize the railway bridge at the mouth of the Sereth, thus securing the line of the Roumanian railway; to send one corps across the Danube at Braila into the Dobrudja in order to protect their rear against any attack by that route, and to march the bulk of the army through Roumania and cross the Danube at Nikopolis or at some point between that and Rustchuk; then to post a strong force along the line of the Yantra or the Lom, in order to mask the Quadrilateral; another force on the Vid or Isker to act against the army at Widdin, and, the flanks being thus protected as by two walls, to advance over the Balkans to Adrianople. Had the campaign been begun (as it was ended) by 375,000 instead of 200,000 men, it is quite possible that this plan might have been carried out with very little deviation (until checked by foreign intervention); but, with the insufficient force at hand, having crossed the Danube, seized a pass in the Balkans, and posted the sufficient portions on either flank, there were no troops left to send over the Balkans; and, by the time the reinforcements arrived, affairs had taken quite a different turn.

The campaign, as it resulted, lasted forty-five weeks, and naturally divides itself into three distinct portions, as follows :

1st. Ten weeks, from April 24th to July 3rd—the concentration in Roumania, passage of the Danube, and establishment on its southern bank.

2nd. Twenty-three weeks, July 4th to December 10th—the operations in Bulgaria up to the fall of Plevna.

3rd. Twelve weeks, December 11th to March 3rd (Treaty of San Stefano)—the passage of the Balkans and march to Constantinople.

In the first period the line of march (from Kishineff to Sistova) was by the road 370 miles; in the second period, for one column (Sistova to Shipka) 80 miles, for the other column (Sistova to the Orkhanie Pass) 150 miles; in the third period, for the Shipka column (Shipka to San Stefano *via* Adrianople) 300 miles, for the Sophia column (Orkhanie Pass *via* Sofia, Philippopolis, and Adrianople to San Stefano) 450 miles. The total line of direct march was therefore, for the Shipka column 750 miles, for the Sophia column 970 miles.

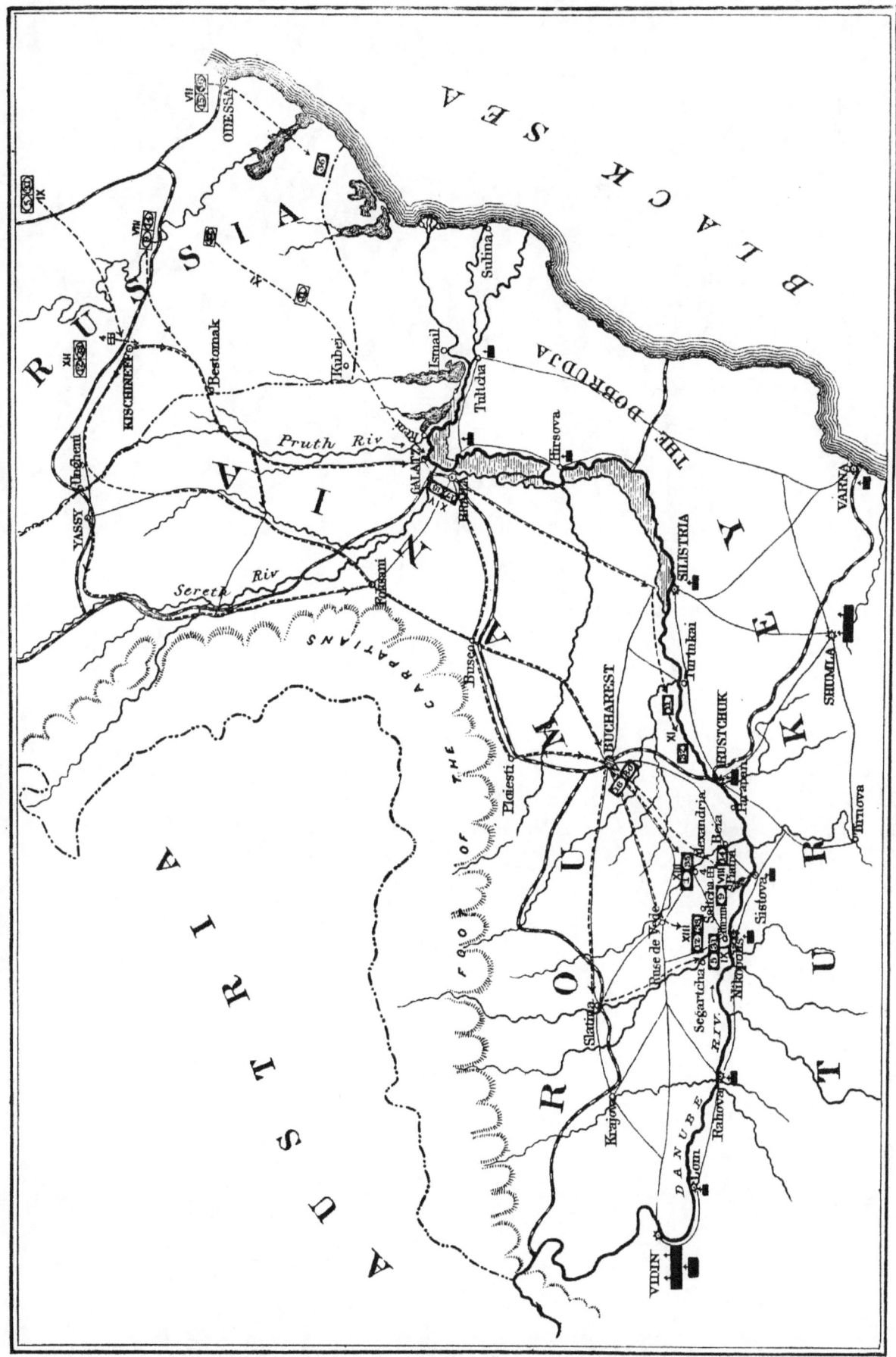

CHAPTER I

FIRST PERIOD OF THE WAR.—APRIL 24TH TO JUNE 27TH.—THE CONCENTRATION IN ROUMANIA AND THE PASSAGE OF THE DANUBE.

AT the declaration of war the *Army of the South* was composed as follows:*

	Battalions.	Foot Guns.	Squadrons.	Horse Guns.	
VIII. Corps, Lt.-Gen. *Radetzky*.					Commander-in-Chief,
9th and 14th Infantry Divisions	24	96	—	—	General H.I.H.
8th Cavalry Division	—	—	18	12	Grand Duke *Nicholas*.
IX. Corps, Lt.-Gen. Baron *Krüdener*.					
5th and 31st Infantry Divisions	24	96	—	—	Chief of Staff, General
9th Cavalry Division	—	—	18	12	*Nepokoitchitsky*.
XI. Corps, Lt.-Gen. Prince *Shakofskoi*.					
11th and 32nd Infantry Divisions	24	96	—	—	Chief of Artillery,
11th Cavalry Division	—	—	18	12	Lt.-Gen. Prince
XII. Corps, Lt.-Gen. *Vannofsky*.					*Massalski*.
12th and 33rd Infantry Divisions	24	96	—	—	
12th Cavalry Division	—	—	18	12	Chief of Engineers,
3rd Rifle Brigade, Major-Gen. *Dobrovolski*	4	—	—	—	Major-Gen. *Depp*.
4th Rifle Brigade, Major-Gen. *Zviazinski*	4	—	—	—	
United Cossack Division, Lt.-Gen. *Skobeleff* 1.					
Caucasian Cossack Brigade	—	—	10	⎫	
Terek Cossack Regiment	—	—	4	⎬ 6	
Don Cossack Regiment No. 30	—	—	6	⎭	
Unattached Cossacks of the Don.					
Reg'ts Nos. 21, 23, 26, 29, 31, 34, 35, 37, 40	—	—	54	46†	
Total	104	384	144	100	

* The VII. and X. Corps also formed part of the Army of the South, but they were formed into a separate detachment for the "defence of the coasts," and were stationed in the Crimea and along the coast near Odessa. A portion of the 7th Cavalry Division joined Zimmermann's Corps in the Dobrudja during the month of July, and one infantry regiment of the same (VII.) corps advanced against Sulina in the month of October. But the rest of them never crossed the Russian frontier, and have therefore been omitted in the above table. † Including 16 mountain guns.

This force was posted along the Russian frontier, its right flank at the village of Ungheni on the railroad, and its left flank at the village of Kubei, which is situated at the angle of the frontier 50 miles north-east of Galatz.

The headquarters were at Kishineff.

The auxiliary, or technical troops, were as follows:

1. *Engineers.*

3rd Engineer Brigade, Major-General Richter, composed of—
- 5th Sapper Battalion,
- 6th Sapper Battalion,
- 5th Pontonier Battalion,
- 6th Pontonier Battalion,
- 5th Field Telegraph Park,
- 6th Field Telegraph Park,
- 2nd Field Engineer Park,
- 2nd Siege Engineer Park,
- 6th Railroad Battalion;

in all about 5000 men, with the tools and appliances of their special arms.

Portions of 2nd and 4th Engineer Brigades, viz.:
- 3rd Pontonier Battalion,
- 4th Pontonier Battalion,
- 7th Sapper Battalion;

about 2000 men.

With these troops were 4 pontoon trains, each consisting of 26 iron boats and all their appurtenances, making in all 104 boats, or the material for about 900 yards of bridge.

2. *Heavy Artillery.*

A siege artillery park of 400 guns, as follows:
- 200 6-inch (24-pdr.) siege guns (bronze), ⎫
- 80 4-inch (9-pdr.) siege guns (cast steel), ⎬ all breech-loading.
- 40 8-inch rifled mortars (bronze), ⎪
- 40 6-inch rifled mortars (bronze), ⎭
- 40 4-inch smooth-bore mortars,

and their train, platforms, tools, &c.

The total number of men serving this park was about 10,000. It was divided into 12 divisions, of which Nos. 1 and 2 were for investment, 3 to 10 for bombardment (as at Braila, &c.), 11 and 12 for reserve.

3. *Naval Troops.*

2 companies of the "Crew of the Guard,"
2 companies of "Crew No. 1 of the Black Sea."

These men were destined for the service of torpedoes, guards of bridges, &c. Their material included 24 steam torpedo-launches, divided into sections for transportation, and the necessary torpedo material.

4. *Hospital Department.*

42 Field Hospitals, each with tents, clothing, medicines, surgical apparatus, train, &c., for from 600 to 1000 patients.

These were in addition to the Division Hospitals accompanying the troops on the field.

The personnel of these hospitals numbered in all about 5000 men.

5. *Intendance Department.*

14 Divisions of Intendance Transport, each consisting of 350 wagons.

These were in addition to the Intendants (Chief Quartermaster and Commissary) of the Corps and Divisions, and their clerks, &c.

6. *Gendarmerie* (Provost-Marshal's Department).

3rd and 4th Squadrons of Field Gendarmes, about 500 men.

The troops which by imperial order of May 6th were added to the "Army of the South," and ordered to the frontier by rail, were as follows:

	Battalions.	Foot Artill'y Guns.	Squadrons.	Horse Artill'y Guns.
XIV. Corps, Lieutenant-General *Zimmermann*.				
17th and 18th Infantry Divisions	24	96	—	—
1st Don Cossack Cavalry Division	—	—	24	12
IV. Corps, Lieutenant-General *Zotof*.				
16th and 30th Infantry Divisions	24	96	—	—
4th Cavalry Division	—	—	18	12
XIII. Corps, Lieutenant-General Prince *Korsakoff*.				
1st and 33rd Infantry Divisions	24	96	—	—
13th Cavalry Division	—	—	18	12
Total	72	288	60	36
To this must be added the Bulgarian Militia, formed partly during the previous winter and partly during the month of May, consisting of	6	—	—	—
GRAND TOTAL of *Army of the South*	182	672	204	136

i.e., about 200,000 combatants of all arms.

On the morning of the 24th of April the troops crossed the frontier in four columns, viz.:

Right Wing. Fifty squadrons of cavalry (8th and 12th Divisions, 21st, 26th and 37th Regiments Don Cossacks), under Lieutenant-General Baron Driesen, which crossed the frontier at Ungheni and bivouacked that night at Yassy. Their route thence lay along the base of the mountains to Ploiesti, and thence to Bucharest, the 8th Cavalry Division going on to the Danube opposite Nikopolis.

Centre (XII. Corps, 5th Infantry Division, 34th Regiment Don Cossacks), which crossed a few miles south of Ungheni, and then took a road parallel to the Pruth and about 20 miles from it, as far as Foksani, and thence followed the cavalry column to Bucharest.

Left Wing, composed of (*a*) advance guard under Lieutenant-General Skobeleff, 1st Brigade of Caucasian Cossacks, 23rd Regiment Don Cossacks, two sotnias of plastounes, 4th Rifle Brigade and all the mountain artillery; (*b*) 11th Cavalry Division and (*c*) VIII. Corps, the whole under command of Lieutenant-General Radetzky—which crossed the frontier at the village of Bestamak, 50 miles south-west of Kishineff. Late that evening, after a ride of 65 miles, the cavalry reached the Sereth and took possession of the railroad bridge near Galatz; it subsequently moved on to Bucharest, and the detachment of Skobeleff came down to the Danube opposite Rustchuk; the 11th Cavalry Division took the road arriving on the Danube opposite Silistria; the VIII. Corps followed Skobeleff's detachment as far as Bucharest.

Column of the Lower Danube, composed of the infantry of the XI. Corps, under Lieutenant-General Prince Shakofskoi, which crossed the frontier at Kubei, and proceeded to Galatz and Braila, relieving the cavalry which had previously arrived there, and then sending detachments to occupy all the principal points on the left bank of the Danube as far as Ismail. The 11th Infantry Division of this corps was then sent forward, and reached the Danube at Oltenitza, opposite Turtukai.

The portion of the IX. Corps which had not marched on with General Vannofsky was sent forward as soon as opportunity offered by rail from Ungheni to Slatina, 80 miles west of Bucharest.

On the 24th of May, one month from the date of crossing the frontier, the army was concentrated opposite the portion of the Danube selected for the passage; the bulk of it ($2\frac{1}{2}$ corps) being at Bucharest, with a detachment ($\frac{1}{2}$ corps) on its right flank at Slatina, and a strong line of cavalry pickets with infantry supports along the river bank from Nikopolis to Silistria, where the swampy section of the river begins. The headquarters were at Ploiesti. The date set for the passage was the 6th of June, but this was found to be an impossibility because the bridge materials could not arrive by that time. The spring was an unusually wet one, and on the 1st of June the level of the Danube at Galatz was 15 feet above the ordinary level of that date; and the floods on the smaller streams had carried away several railroad bridges, thus greatly delaying matters. This railroad was totally unequal to the task demanded of it; it was a single track line with a small quantity of rolling stock and insufficient terminal facilities in the way of switches and sidings. Moreover, the Russian railway having a gauge of 5 feet, while the Roumanian had the ordinary gauge of 4 feet $8\frac{1}{2}$ inches, it was not only not possible to supplement the rolling stock by that from Russia, but it necessitated a complete transfer of all freight and passengers at Yassy. In addition to the greater part of the IX. Corps (which might just as well have been marched by road), this single-track railway was required to transport the siege guns and material and ammunition for the batteries at Braila and Galatz, and those opposite Silistria, Rustchuk and Nikopolis, the four pontoon trains attached to the army (104 boats and their wagons and materials), a large number of wooden pontoons built at Galatz, more than 25 steam torpedo-boats and the torpedo materials, and all the hard bread and a few other articles of the rations for the army.

As a result of these various causes of delay, the army remained stationary in the positions previously described for the next month (May 24th to June 24th). The XIV. Corps as it arrived was directed (June 13th) on Galatz, where it relieved the portion of the XI. Corps which was guarding the Lower Danube, which portion then proceeded to join the rest of the corps opposite Turtukai. The XIII. Corps was ordered to be at Alexandria (60 miles south-west of Bucharest) by the 27th of June; the IV. Corps to come on by rail to Bucharest and await further orders.

While the army was waiting the arrival of the bridge material, great activity was displayed by the Russians in endeavouring to neutralise the action of the Turkish flotilla by means of torpedoes. At the beginning of the war the Turks had in the Lower Danube below Braila a fleet of 8 large ironclads, with armour of not less than 4 inches in thickness, and carrying altogether about 30 guns. Far from preventing the capture of the bridge over the Sereth or destroying it, these ships retired down the river at the approach of the Russians. Higher up on the river, from Hirsova to Widdin, they had 7 light iron-plated gunboats and 18 wooden ships, carrying in all about 1000 men and 60 guns. Within a week from the time war was declared the Russians succeeded in placing a line of torpedoes across the river at Reni, which cut off the fleet of large ironclads and restricted them henceforth to the Sulina mouth of the river. A few days later they succeeded in placing another barricade of torpedoes across the river opposite Braila.

These two barricades protected the mouths of the Pruth and Sereth, as well as the town of Galatz. They consisted of the ordinary submarine mines, anchored in two rows; their mechanism was so arranged as to explode automatically on contact, as well as by electricity from the shore. They were anchored in the night by means of steam torpedo-boats (ten of which had already arrived by rail), protected by the 9-pdr. field batteries on shore. On the 6th of May a portion of the up-river flotilla, consisting of five monitors and two wooden ships, approached Braila and opened fire upon the Russian batteries and the town; but by this time the Russian batteries at this point were partially armed (viz. with ten 24-pdr. siege guns and four 6-in. rifled mortars); and on the 10th a shell from one of the mortars penetrated the deck of one of the largest monitors, the Lufti-Djelil, and exploded in the powder magazine. She blew up and sank instantly, with all her crew of 17 officers and 200 men. The ship was a twin-screw, ironclad, sea-going monitor, carrying four 150-pdr. Armstrong guns.

On the 25th of May Lieutenant Dubassoff, of the Russian Navy, obtained permission to try to blow up one of the Turkish monitors by means of a torpedo from an open boat, in which he was as completely successful as was Cushing against the Albemarle, and under very similar circumstances. He took four steam-launches, carrying in all 6 officers and 40 men, and rigged with spars for torpedoes. Leaving the port of Braila at midnight of a dark rainy night, he arrived about half-past two in the morning in the midst of a fleet of two Turkish ironclads and one wooden ship, anchored in the Matchin channel. He was discovered by the sentinel, and all their ships opened fire on him with musketry. He immediately put on full steam and went straight at the largest monitor, and exploded his torpedo under her port quarter. The ship began sinking by the stern, but slowly, and he then called out to Lieutenant Shestakoff, who commanded the launch just behind him, to "come on." This officer then came forward with his launch at full steam, and exploded a second torpedo under the monitor amidships; the ship sank in the course of a few minutes. Meanwhile Dubassoff's launch had been filled with water by the first explosion; Shestakoff's boat had got some of the *débris* of the monitor tangled in her propeller; the third boat had been pierced by a shell; and only the fourth was not disabled, and was endeavouring to assist the other three. It was a considerable time before the little fleet of boats could repair damages, pump out, and retire. During all this time the Turks kept firing at them with artillery and musketry; but, owing to the darkness and general confusion, the Russians finally managed to escape, *without a single man being hurt*.

The Turkish ship was the *Seifé*, which is described in the Turkish Navy List of 1876 as a light-draught river gunboat, protected with two inches of armour, 115 feet long, armed with two 80-lb. breech-loading Armstrong guns placed in a battery on the fore part of the deck, and two smaller guns near the stern; her crew was about 120 men.

On the 10th of June the Russian steamer *Constantine* put out from Odessa with six torpedo-launches in tow, bound for Sulina. She arrived in that vicinity during the night, and at two o'clock in the morning sent the launches in toward the shore; they found three Turkish ironclads at anchor, and one under steam in the roadstead outside the jetties, which they immediately attacked; but the torpedo of the leading launch exploded before reaching the ship's side (the officer of the boat claimed that the monitor was protected by a wire netting). This gave the alarm to the whole fleet, and the launches were obliged to escape as best they could back to the *Constantine* and out to sea. One of them was disabled and captured with her crew, including one officer.

On the 20th of June ten steam-launches which had been carried overland were launched in the Danube at a point about ten miles above Rustchuk, and at 4 o'clock in the morning Commander Novikoff began placing a barricade of torpedoes across the river at Parapan, in order to isolate the monitors at Rustchuk. He was discovered at 5 o'clock by the Turks, who sent out a monitor, which opened on the launches with shrapnel. Commander Novikoff immediately sent a launch to attack the monitor with a torpedo. The torpedo was disabled before reaching the monitor, owing, as it is claimed, to the wire being cut by bullets; but nevertheless the monitor retreated to Rustchuk, and the operation of placing the torpedoes was successfully finished. Nearly every one in this launch was wounded. Just after the launches had finished their work and regained the shore, a Turkish battery came into position on the opposite bank and opened on them. Five of the launches turned up stream and five down, and after steaming a few miles they reached points where they were hauled out of water and carried overland to Turnu; three of them, however, were so damaged as to be temporarily useless.

On the night of the 23rd of June, Commander Novikoff succeeded in placing a barricade of torpedoes at Karabia, five miles above Nikopolis, by means of rowboats; he did not use his steam-launches for fear that they might be injured, and they would be so greatly needed in the passage of the river a few days later. On the same day a Turkish monitor from Nikopolis got up steam and came down the river, and was immediately attacked by two launches and by four light guns on the shore. There was here, as at Parapan, a failure to explode the torpedo successfully; but the audacity of the attack, combined with the very accurate fire of the guns on shore, compelled the monitor to retire hastily to Nikopolis. On the 24th of June another monitor put out from Nikopolis, and endeavoured to escape up stream, but she was turned back by the siege guns of the battery on the Russian shore.

After this date no Turkish gunboats ever left the shelter of their fortresses, and the history of the Turkish fleet on the Danube may be summarised as from first to last a complete failure. Two of their river ironclads were sunk, two more were captured subsequently at the surrender of Nikopolis, and the other three remained at Rustchuk till the close of the war. Of the large ironclads on the lower river, one was sunk by a stationary torpedo near Sulina in the month of October; the others remained idle in the port of Sulina. The only damage the whole fleet ever did was in wounding five or six men in one boat at Parapan and in inflicting some slight injuries on three of the launches, which were subsequently repaired. It was not that opportunities were lacking for the flotilla to act. On the breaking out of the war, they could have made an effort to prevent the capture of the bridge over the Sereth, and, failing in this, they might at least have destroyed it, and thereby greatly delayed the Russian operations. Later on, if they had been vigilant and skilful, they might have destroyed a portion at least of the Russian flotilla of small launches; they might have protected their own ships with nettings, and used their small boats to drag for torpedoes, if they could not prevent them from being placed. But they did none of these things; and at the end of two months they found themselves isolated in sections by means of the torpedo barricades, and so alarmed by the loss of two of their ships that the idea of a torpedo became a bugbear to them, and a few launches moving over the water with the motions of planting torpedoes were enough to make them retire under the guns of their forts.

The only means which the Russians used against them were small steam-launches and torpedoes, aided somewhat by the batteries on shore. Of these launches the Russians had about 25 at various points on the river at the time of the passage; later on they had 54, engaged in policing the river and guarding the various torpedo barricades. Some of them were of the Thornycroft pattern, attaining a speed of 15 knots; others were ordinary ship's launches, with the engine covered with bullet-proof boiler-plate iron; the largest of them were not longer than 30 feet, and the most numerous crew 15 men. Their operations were all planned under the general direction of Captain Rogouly of the Russian Navy.

When we remember the brilliant achievements of the gunboat flotillas improvised under the orders of Commodore Foote and Admiral Porter on our Western rivers during the Civil War, the complete failure of the fine Turkish navy in this instance becomes all the more apparent. The Navy List of Turkey for 1876 gives its strength at 132 vessels and 18,292 officers, seamen, and marines. This force

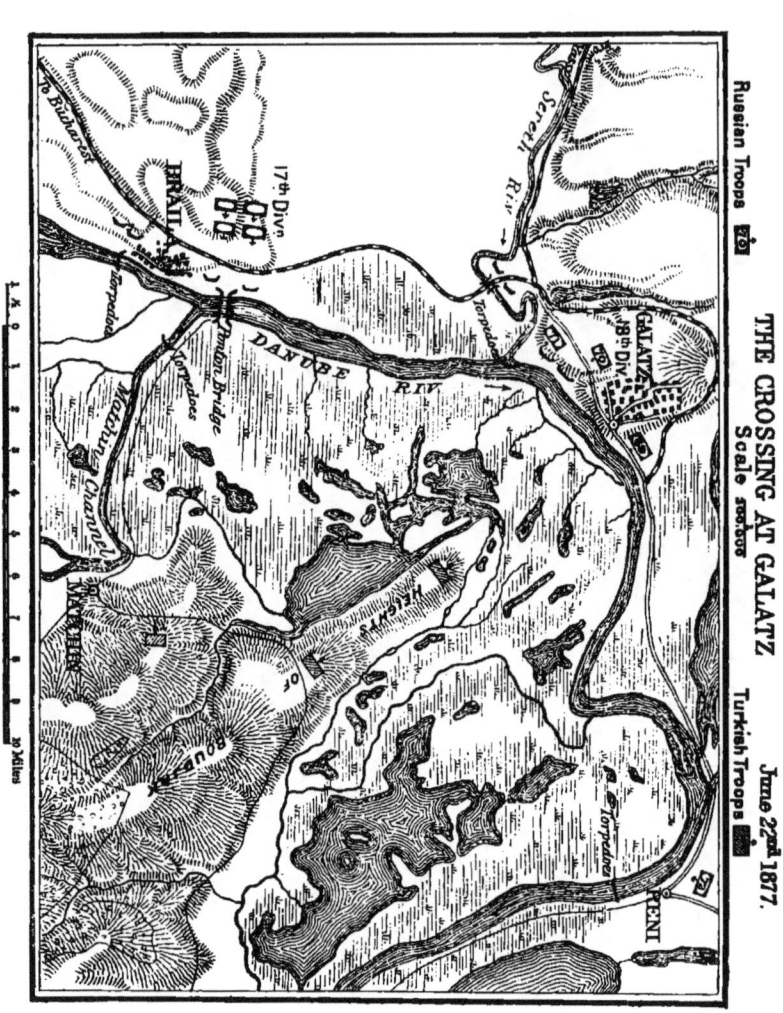

was composed of 15 sea-going ironclads, procured in England at great cost, 5 wooden steam frigates, 11 wooden corvettes, 7 armoured river gunboats, and the rest of transport ships, dispatch-boats, yachts, and small wooden craft. The river flotilla accomplished nothing, as just explained, and the sea-going ships did no more; they never penetrated to Odessa or any of the Crimean ports, and their only achievements were the bombardment of a few helpless villages on the Caucasian coast.

The operations of the navy were under the general control of Admiral Hobart Pasha, an ex-officer of the English service.

As previously stated, the Russian plan of campaign involved the passage of the Danube at two points—on the lower river and on its middle course. The first was accomplished without any difficulty whatever. As soon as the river had been cleared of gunboats between Reni and Hirsova, a bridge was thrown across, without opposition, between the 12th and 16th of June, at Braila; but a rise in the water immediately afterward rendered it for the time being useless, as its end on the Turkish shore as well as the opposite country was completely submerged. For this reason General Zimmermann asked permission to delay the passage of his troops until the water was lower; but the Grand Duke replied that it was imperatively necessary for him to pass not later than the 22nd. On that day, therefore, two regiments were thrown across the river at Galatz, by means of boats, rafts, and steam-tugs; and after a short struggle, in which the Russians lost 5 officers and 138 men, they gained possession of the opposite heights of Boudjak. Thereupon the Turks abandoned the whole of the lower river, and retired up the Dobrudja, behind the line of Trajan's Wall. As soon as the water was low enough to use his bridge, General Zimmermann crossed his whole force, and advanced slowly in the same direction.

On the middle section of the river the operation was much more difficult. The concentration of the army in front of Bucharest during the last week in May warned the Turks that a passage would be attempted somewhere in that vicinity. They therefore began strengthening the works at Nikopolis, Rustchuk, and Silistria, by the construction of detached earthworks, and they also posted small forces in observation at Sistova and other points, and constructed batteries on the river bank.

The Russians meanwhile had been occupied, as previously explained, in transporting their siege guns and bridge material, and in placing lines of torpedoes across the river, which separated the different parts of the Turkish flotilla from each other, and caused them to retire under the guns of the fortresses. By the 20th of June these operations were nearly completed, and the forward movement was ordered as follows :

IX. Corps to Segartcha.

XII. Corps to Saltcha.

VIII. Corps and 4th Rifle Brigade to Piatra.

XIII. Corps in reserve at Alexandria.

XI. Corps to remain in observation between Giurgevo and Oltenitza, opposite Rustchuk and Turtukai.

The original intention had been to make the passage at Zimnitza-Sistova; but when the army arrived along the Danube, it was reported that the level of the water at Zimnitza was so high that a passage there was impossible. On this information it was determined to cross near Nikopolis, and the forward movement just mentioned was in accordance with that plan, and with the intention of making the passage on the 24th. But just after the order had been issued it was found that a new delay on the railroad would prevent a number of pontoons from reaching the river by the 24th. The army was therefore halted on the line of the river Vede, from Ruse de Vede to Beia, in a position about equidistant from Nikopolis, Sistova and Rustchuk. While waiting for the pontoons, the Grand Duke and the Chief of Staff made a personal reconnaissance, between the 20th and 24th, of the river bank from Turnu to Sistova, and became convinced that it would be very difficult to force the passage in face of the strong works at Nikopolis; and also that the water had fallen sufficiently at Zimnitza-Sistova to allow the passage. At the last minute, therefore,

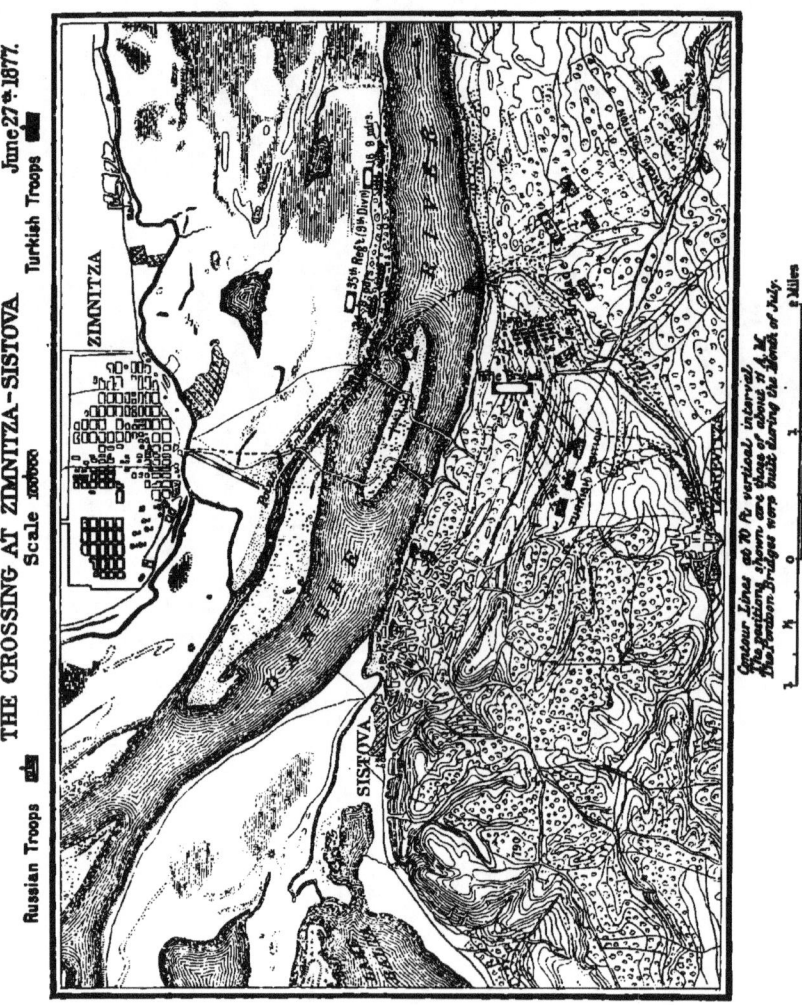

it was decided to cross at this point; and on the 24th the previous orders were modified as follows :

1. 14th Infantry Division (VIII. Corps), 4th Rifle Brigade, 16 mountain guns, and all the army pontoon trains, to proceed at once from Beia to Zimnitza, with secret order to pass the river at that point.

2. 9th Infantry Division (VIII. Corps) to continue its march on Piatra; but by special order of the following day it was brought to Zimnitza.

3. XII. Corps to change its march from Saltcha to Piatra.

4. XIII. Corps to move from Alexandria to Piatra.

5. IX. Corps to pass through Segartcha to Siaka, and prepare to pass the river at Flamunda, just below Nikopolis (this latter being a mere feint).

The siege batteries opposite Rustchuk and opposite Nikopolis were ordered to begin the bombardment of these places on the 24th and 25th respectively, and to continue it until further orders.

On the 26th the detachment of General Dragomiröff, consisting of the 14th Division and the troops attached to it, arrived at Zimnitza. At dark that evening the pontoons were launched in the creek which runs past the village of Zimnitza, and were then hauled out into the main river and down to the point of embarkation. There were 104 boats of the regular pontoon train, 100 boats and rafts which had been constructed in the neighbourhood, and four battalions of pontoniers to manœuvre them. The troops numbered in all about 15,000 men, and were divided into six detachments of 2500 men each, the plan being to cross by detachments in a body; but after the first detachment had crossed this was found to take too much time, and as soon as enough boats returned to take one company they were immediately loaded and sent back.

While the boats were being launched, five batteries (40 guns) of 9-pdrs., supported by regiment No. 35 (of the 9th Division), were established on the northern bank of the main river, to cover the passage, and silence the enemy's batteries on the south bank, as well as the monitors, should they venture down from Nikopolis. The troops began embarking at midnight, and about 1 o'clock in the morning they put out from the shore and began rowing toward the Turkish bank, aiming to reach it at a point about three miles below Sistova, at the mouth of a small stream known as the Tekir-Dere. Just as they were approaching the shore they were discovered by the Turkish outposts, who opened fire upon them and gave the alarm; but the boats, although somewhat dispersed by the wind, reached the shore and landed their men in the vicinity of the point designated. The twelve companies composing this first detachment formed on the bank and climbed up the steep bluff, driving before them the line of Turkish skirmishers. By 2 o'clock they had gained possession of the banks of this little stream, and of a neighbouring hill, about three-quarters of a mile from the shore and east of the Tekir-Dere. Soon after this the day began to dawn, and the Turks were thoroughly aroused by the noise. They had in this vicinity one camp on the heights south-east of Sistova, counting perhaps 5000 men, with one battery of 6 guns, and another camp about 6 miles from Sistova on the road to Rustchuk, in which there were probably about the same number of men; but these numbers cannot be stated with any accuracy. The little creek Tekir-Dere was about equidistant from these two camps. As soon as the Turks were fully aroused they reinforced their skirmish line near the river bank between Sistova and the point of landing, and they also took position in front of the Russians on the heights, which rise behind each other in terraces parallel to the river. They also had a battery in Sistova; and from the whole line they opened a very hot fire on the pontoon boats which continued to arrive, and they succeeded in sinking five of them and killing and wounding in all about 100 men in the boats.

About 5 A.M. General Dragomiroff, accompanied by Major-General Skobeleff II. as a volunteer, arrived on the southern bank and took command. He immediately sent about 15 companies of the 1st brigade of his division on the left of the Tekir-Dere to attack the troops coming from the camp in that direction; meanwhile forming the rest of his troops as they arrived in the valley of this little creek, and then advancing them gradually on both sides of it. By 8 o'clock in the morning the 1st brigade had gained possession of some small heights in its front, which secured the passage from any attack on that side of the little stream. Soon afterward the troops began to arrive more rapidly, thanks to the assistance of a steamboat which had run past the batteries at Nikopolis during the night. By 11 o'clock the 2nd brigade of the 14th Division, as well as the 4th Rifle Brigade, had arrived and formed on the right of the Tekir-Dere. General Dragomiroff then ordered the principal movement of the day, which was an advance against the heights behind Sistova by the 2nd brigade, supported on its right flank by the Rifle Brigade, which took the direction of the road toward Sistova, the 1st brigade remainig on the ground it had taken. This advance was covered by the Russian batteries on the other side of the river, which succeeded in silencing the Turkish batteries; the Turks made but a feeble resistance, and at 2 o'clock the Russians gained possession of the heights behind Sistova, and at 3 o'clock entered the town itself. The Turks abandoned all their positions and retreated by the high road to Tirnova, a portion of those nearest Sistova retreating to Nikopolis. Their losses are not known; those of the Russians were as follows:

	Officers.	Men.
Killed	9	291
Wounded	22	446
Missing	—	53
Total	31	790

of whom over 600 belonged to the two regiments (Volhynia No. 53 and Minsk No. 54) of the 1st brigade, which had done the fighting on the east of the creek early in the morning.

About 3 o'clock in the afternoon General Radetzky, commanding the VIII. Corps, crossed to the Turkish side, and immediately afterward the troops of the 9th Division, which had arrived at Zimnitza during the day, also began coming over. By 9 o'clock in the evening the whole of the VIII. Corps as well as the 4th Rifle Brigade, 25,000 men in all, were established in good defensible positions on the Turkish shore. The passage was therefore secured, after 20 hours of labour and a loss of 800 men.

During the next day, June 28th, the 35th Division (XII. Corps) was ferried over on pontoons, and at the same time the construction of a bridge was commenced, which was finished on the 2nd of July.

In ten weeks from the opening of hostilities, therefore, the Russians had established themselves on the southern bank of the Danube, and with a loss which, in comparison to the importance of the success, was totally insignificant.

The question naturally arises, what were the Turks doing all this time? And it is difficult to give a satisfactory answer to this question, as no official reports or other trustworthy data have ever been published on the Turkish side. It may be said, however, that their defence had been by no means an energetic one. The mobilisation of six Russian army corps and their concentration along the Pruth in the months of November and December, 1876, were as well known to the Turks as to the rest of the world; it was also perfectly apparent that if war did break out the Russians had the choice of only two plans, either to cross the lower Danube into the Dobrudja or to advance through the narrow space between the Danube at Galatz and the Carpathians, toward some point on the middle Danube. As they had no navy to cover any operations on the Black Sea, a landing on the coast at Kustendje or Varna, or other point, was not to be feared. If, therefore, the Turks meant to oppose an energetic resistance to the Russian advance, it was very plain that their most advantageous position from which to do so was the Dobrudja. An army of 100,000 men posted behind the river in the north-west corner of this rectangle could oppose the crossing of the lower river, or, if the Russians attempted to march past, could strike them on the flank *en route*. On the declaration of war it could seize the towns of Braila, Galatz, Reni and Ismail, on the northern bank, and fortify them as *têtes-de-pont*, and get possession of the railway bridge at Galatz, over which passes the one railway of Roumania. For their own supplies they had the harbour of Kustendje and the Kustendje-Tchernavoda Railroad, which is only 70 miles from the Danube at Galatz; they also had the Danube itself by which to bring supplies.

But instead of taking positions from which they could strike the Russians as soon as they crossed the frontier, the Turks passed the winter preceding the declaration of war with an army of 50,000 to 60,000 men in the quadrilateral, another of about the same size 200 miles away at Widdin, and a few weak garrisons along the Danube. Whether it was Oriental procrastination, or because, as has been pretended, they had a deep plan of luring the Russians across the Danube and then overwhelming them, or, as is more likely, because they had no very definite plan of campaign beyond simply waiting, according to their traditional mode of warfare, behind fortifications to be attacked, it is hardly possible to state; but the fact is certain that they allowed the Russians to make their preparations for war without taking proper steps to meet them; that when war was declared they opposed only the most feeble resistance to the passage of the lower river; and, when the passage of the middle course was threatened by the concentration of the Russian army to the south-west of Bucharest, they made no movements to oppose it beyond a slight increase of the Danube garrisons and the construction of a few batteries on the river bank. They made no *active* defence. Although the Russians remained near Bucharest for nearly a month waiting for their bridge and siege material, yet the Turks pushed no reconnaissances to develop their strength, position, and movements; and more than all, they did not assemble a mobile army at some central point behind the threatened line, ready to move at once to the point where the real passage should begin, and attack the invaders before they got a firm footing on the southern bank.

Von Moltke, in his account of the campaign of 1828 (which was a campaign of sieges), remarks that "the Turks usually began their resistance at that point where in other sieges it usually terminates; *i.e.*, after the crowning of the covered way and the opening of a breach." In the campaign of 1877 there were no regular sieges, but the Turks fought a purely defensive campaign, in which the resistance began only after the Russians were well over the Danube and the first line of Turkish defence was wholly lost.

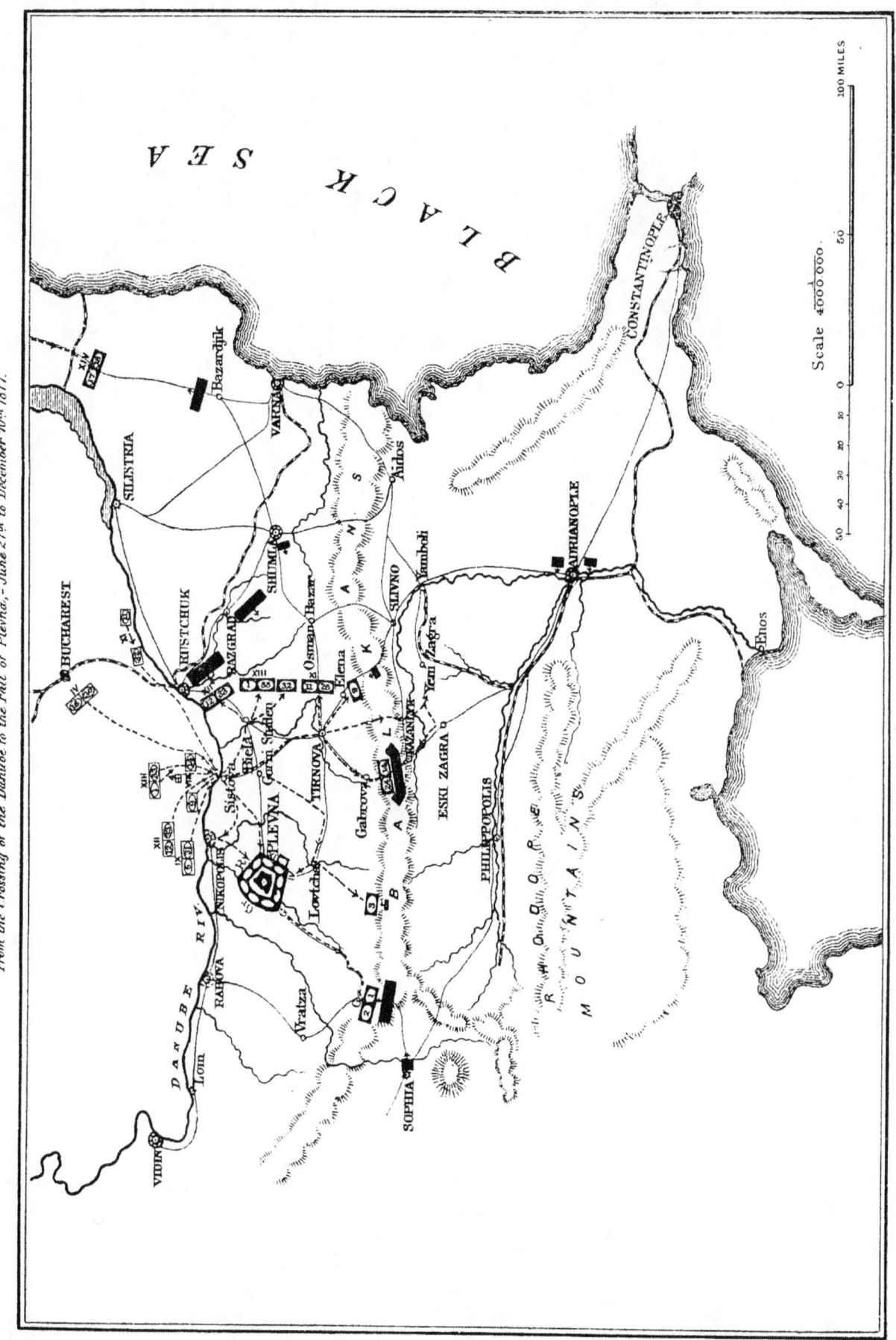

CHAPTER II

OPERATIONS OF THE ADVANCE GUARD UNDER GOURKO, JULY 12TH TO AUGUST 6TH.

BETWEEN the Balkans and the Danube there are but two short lines of railway, viz. that from Rustchuk to Varna, 140 miles, and that along the line of Trajan's Wall, 40 miles. Both these roads were in possession of the Turks. In that portion of Bulgaria which became the theatre of the principal military operations, the chaussées are as follows:

1. From Rustchuk, *via* Razgrad, to Shumla and Varna.
2. From Rustchuk, *viâ* Razgrad, Eski-Djuma, Osman-Bazar, Kazan (the Kazan Pass), Slivno, and Yeni-Zagra, to Hermanli, and thence to Adrianople.
3. From Sistova, *viâ* Tirnova, Gabrova, Shipka Pass, Kazanlyk, and Eski-Zagra, to Trnova, and thence to Adrianople.
4. From Rahova, *viâ* Vratza, to Orkhanie and Sophia.
5. From Lom Palanka, *viâ* Berkovitza, to Sophia.
6. From Widdin, *viâ* Pirot, to Sophia.
7. From Rustchuk, *viâ* Biela, Plevna, Lukovitza, and Orkhanie, to Sophia.
8. From Shumla, *viâ* Osman-Bazar, Trnova, Selvi, and Lovtcha, to Plevna.

All these were good, hard, macadamised roads, and were in excellent condition at the beginning of the campaign, and remained so until they had been ruined in some places by the passage of immense artillery and transport trains, and the failure to promptly repair the damages made by them.

Besides these chaussées there were common country roads connecting all the larger villages. During the summer, when there was no rain, these roads were always passable, barring slight delays at the small bridges crossing the various streams. When the autumn rains came on in September they soon became wholly impassable.

The bridge at Sistova was finished, as previously stated, on the 2nd of July, five days after the passage had been made, and the bulk of the army began passing over in the following order :

1. Advance Guard, under Gourko, July 3rd.
2. XIII. Corps (except the 35th Infantry Division, which had been ferried over in boats June 28th), July 3rd–4th.
3. XII. Corps, July 5th–8th.
4. IX. Corps, July 8th–10th.
5. XI. Corps, July 10th–15th.
6. IV. Corps, July 20th–30th.

In accordance with the general plan of campaign previously explained, Gourko was to push forward rapidly to the Balkans by the main road passing through Tirnova; the VIII. Corps was to follow the same road; the XIII. Corps, followed by the XII., was to take the line of the Yantra on the left flank; the IX. Corps was to attack Nikopolis and the line of the Vid on the right flank; the XI. and IV. Corps were for the present to be held in reserve.

On the 5th of July the cavalry of the XIII. Corps captured the town of Biela, after a short skirmish with some Tcherkesses, and the next day it was occupied by the infantry. On the 7th of July Gourko captured Tirnova. The possession of these two points gave the Russians the control of the two high-roads leading westward from the Quadrilateral, and threw the whole defensive line of the Yantra into their power. The XIII. and XII. Corps were combined into the "Left Wing," under the command of the Cesarevitch, and took post on the Yantra, and then gradually moved forward toward the Lom. This was strictly in accordance with the plan of campaign, which contemplated a purely defensive *rôle* for the left wing; but it is quite probable that a vigorous attack of these two corps upon Rustchuk at any time before the 20th of July might, in the panic which prevailed at that time and in the general unreadiness of the Turks, have been successful. It was not,

ADVANCE GUARD UNDER GOURKO

however, attempted; the left wing moved forward with the utmost caution, and took post along the Lom only about the 1st of August.

The Headquarters of the Army (Grand Duke Nicholas) were moved forward to Tirnova on July 12th, and of the Emperor to Biela on the 20th. Meanwhile Gourko executed his brilliant move over the Balkans (July 12th–18th), and Krüdener, with the IX. Corps, captured Nikopolis (July 16th) and was defeated at Plevna (July 20th). Each of these movements needs to be described in detail.

OPERATIONS OF THE ADVANCE GUARD UNDER LIEUTENANT-GENERAL GOURKO

On the 30th of June, three days after the passage of the Danube, the Grand Duke gave orders for the formation of a detachment, under the orders of Lieutenant-General Gourko, which was directed to push forward rapidly to Tirnova and Selvi, reconnoitre the surrounding country, and be prepared upon the receipt of subsequent orders to gain possession of a pass in the Balkans by which the army could cross; at the same time sending his cavalry south of the mountains to cut the railroads and telegraph, and to do what other damage they could.

This detachment was made up as follows:

Infantry.—4th Rifle Brigade, Bulgarian legion (6 battalions), half battalion of plastounes, and two mountain batteries (14 guns).

Cavalry.—1. 8th and 9th Regiments of Dragoons and 16th horse battery, under Duke Eugene of Leuchtenberg.

2. 9th Regiment Hussars, 30th Regiment Don Cossacks, and 10th (horse) battery of Don Cossacks, under Duke Nicholas of Leuchtenberg.

3. 21st and 26th Regiments Don Cossacks and 15th (horse) battery of Don Cossacks, under Colonel Tchernozouboff.

4. Half squadron of Volunteers from the Guard.

5. Detachment of mounted pioneers, under Colonel Count

de Roniquères, composed of Cossacks of the Caucasus, Don and Ural, who had been previously instructed in engineering duties.

In all, $10\frac{1}{2}$ battalions (8000 men), $31\frac{1}{2}$ squadrons (4000 men), and 32 guns (18 field and 14 mountain pieces).

The Sistova bridge being completed on the 2nd of July, this detachment crossed on the 3rd and began its march southward. On the 6th, without having met any opposition, it arrived in the villages just north of the Tirnova-Selvi chaussée. Here Gourko made his dispositions for a reconnaissance of Tirnova from the west on the 7th, and from the east on the 8th, the bulk of his detachment meanwhile remaining near the village of Madrego, 18 miles north-west of Tirnova.

Tirnova has a population of 40,000 to 50,000 people, and is the most important town of northern Bulgaria; from it roads lead to the Shipka, Travna, Elena, and Slivno passes in the Balkans, and to Selvi and Lovtcha on the west, Sistova and Rustchuk on the north, and Osman-Bazar and Shumla on the east. The town is situated in a bend of the river Yantra and on its bank, while perpendicular rocky bluffs over 500 feet high surround it on every side; the roads enter the town from four directions through narrow defiles. Its natural capacity for defence was very great; hence Gourko's caution in approaching it.

For his reconnaissance of the 7th, Gourko took the brigade of dragoons, with which he approached the town from the west over the heights of Kajabunar. Sending two squadrons forward to skirmish with the Turks and make them develop their strength, he soon became convinced that the Turks were not in great force; and he descended from the heights and, about 4 P.M., advanced toward Tirnova with the whole brigade. The Turks retreated before him and crossed to the other side of the river just above the town, where they took up a position commanding the approach by the road. Gourko then brought his light battery into action, and sent back an order directing that the four sotnias of Cossacks, which were acting as his reserve and keeping up communication with the bulk of his detachment at Madrego, should come forward. As soon as they arrived he sent them through the town (on his left and front) with orders to cross the river and threaten the rear of the Turks. Meanwhile, with the brigade of dragoons he advanced directly against the Turks in front of him. The Turks abandoned everything and retreated very hastily by the road to Osman-Bazar. Their strength was five battalions of regular infantry (about 3000 men), 400 irregular cavalry, and 6 guns. The force with which Gourko converted his reconnaissance into an attack numbered about 1400 cavalry and 6 guns; his losses were 2 men and 8 horses wounded.

The rest of the detachment came to Tirnova the next day, July 8th, and remained there till the 12th, the bulk of the troops at the edge of the town and small detachments in observation on the principal roads. These four days were occupied in collecting all possible information from the Bulgarians about the various paths over the mountains, in reconnoitring them, and in organising a pack-train and making preparations for the forward movement.

According to the information which Gourko thus gathered, all the Turkish authorities and population had left Tirnova, most of them going to Shumla; the troops had left behind them in their retreat a considerable quantity of forage and wheat (which was confiscated by the Russians). There were no troops in any of the passes except the main one at Shipka, where there were about 3000 infantry, a few mountain guns, and some bands of bashi-bozouks; some earthworks had been constructed for the defence of this pass, but it was not known whether they had yet been armed with cannon or not.

Upon this information Gourko drew up the following plan, which was approved by the Grand Duke:

1. To cross the Balkans with the whole of his detachment except one regiment of Cossacks (No. 30) and 2 guns, by a blind trail about half-way between the Elena and Travna passes—first sending his pioneers ahead to make the trail passable for his light artillery if possible.

2. The 30th Regiment of Cossacks to leave 4 squadrons at Tirnova, and send the other 2 squadrons and 2 guns

to Gabrova to watch the northern outlet of the Shipka Pass. A small detachment of Cossacks at the moment of starting was to reconnoitre the Elena Pass, and be sure at the last moment that there were no Turks there.

3. To leave at Tirnova all the baggage on wheels, and take nothing with the troops but pack-animals, which should carry five days' hard bread and three days' forage; but the men and horses were to live on the country as much as possible, and keep their regular rations and forage till absolutely required.

4. On issuing from the mountains on the south, Gourko would at once proceed to Kazanlyk and attack the Shipka Pass from the south, while the Cossacks of the 30th Regiment should make a demonstration against this pass from the north—this to take place on July 17th.

This plan was approved by the Grand Duke, and the pioneers were sent forward on the 10th of July to clear the road. On the 12th the whole detachment moved forward; and on the same day the Grand Duke as well as the head of column of the VIII. Corps arrived at Tirnova. Of this latter a detachment under Major-General Darozhinsky, composed of the 36th Infantry Regiment, the rest of the 30th Don Cossscks, and 10 guns, was at once sent forward to Gabrova, with orders to attack the Shipka Pass from the north on July 17th (the two squadrons which Gourko had detailed being rather weak for this purpose).

On the night of the 12th Gourko and his detachment bivouacked near the village of Voinis, 18 miles from Tirnova. On the morning of the 13th he moved on 15 miles to the village of Parovtchi, and there halted to rest his troops from 1 to 5 o'clock. During the evening he crossed the divide and bivouacked on the southern slope, at a point about 9 miles from the village of Hainkioi, which is at the mouth of the defile. At 2 o'clock in the morning of the 14th he continued his march, and about 10 o'clock surprised the little garrison (300 regular infantry and some Tcherkesses) at Hainkioi; and captured the place after a slight skirmish, in which he lost six men. Had the outlet of this narrow defile been energetically defended, even by the small force that held it, it would have cost the Russians a very considerable loss. But, as it was, they debouched in the valley of the Tundja, without having met any difficulties except those of the road, which, however, were not slight. The ascent of the mountain began at the village of Parovtchi, elevation about 1800 feet, and in the next 8 miles the road ascended 1900 feet, crossing the summit at an elevation of 3700 feet. On the southern slope in 12 miles the road descended 2300 feet, the elevation of Hainkioi being about 1400 feet. Over the greater part of the road from Parovtchi to Hainkioi the guns were dragged by the infantry, the grades being much too steep for the horses to be of any use. Considering that this trail was previously nothing but a footpath, great credit is due to the pioneers, under Major-General Rauch of the Engineers, for having in two days made a road over which it was possible *by any means* to transport artillery. There was but one accident, in which two guns with their teams rolled down a ravine; they were, however, afterwards recovered.

The Turkish garrison of Hainkioi retreated by the road to Slivno, and on arriving at the outlet of the Elena pass (village of Tvarditza) was joined by the garrison of that place; and the two garrisons, numbering four battalions or about 2000 men, then turned back during the afternoon (July 14th) and attacked the Russians who were following them, viz., two battalions of the Rifle Brigade; the latter were reinforced by a third battalion, and after a short fight, in which the Russians lost 7 men, the Turks retreated toward Slivno. They were followed till nightfall by part of the Rifle Brigade, which then returned toward Hainkioi. The Russians gained possession of two Turkish camps containing a number of arms, cartridges, rations, &c.

July 15th, Gourko remained at Hainkioi, assembling his troops, which had not all passed through the defile the previous day. He also sent three squadrons of Cossacks in the direction of Yeni-Zagra. They had a skirmish in the afternoon with some Tcherkesses followed by three battalions of infantry; they called for reinforcements, and the 9th Dragoons were sent to them late in the afternoon, whereupon the Turks retreated in disorder. The Cossacks lost

8 or 10 men, and they as well as the Dragoons returned to Hainkioi during the night. The next day two squadrons of the 26th Don Cossacks succeeded in reaching Yeni-Zagra and cutting the telegraph.

July 16th, Gourko left Hainkioi and began his march toward Shipka, intending to reach the neighbourhood of Kazanlyk (20 miles) that afternoon, and attack Shipka Pass the next morning. He took with him $6\frac{1}{2}$ battalions (5000 men), $19\frac{1}{2}$ squadrons (3000 men), and 16 guns, and left the balance of his detachment, viz. 4 battalions (3000 men), 6 squadrons (500 men), and 14 guns, under Major-General Stoletoff at Hainkioi, in order to keep possession of that pass in case of retreat, but with orders to move on toward Kazanlyk on the morning of the 18th.

After Gourko had marched about 8 or 9 miles he came upon a body of Turks about 3000 strong, posted behind a little stream issuing from the mountains at the village of Uflani. With these he had a sharp fight, in which he lost 2 officers and about 60 men. There were 400 Turkish dead (according to the official report) left upon the field; the number of their wounded was not known. This affair consumed so much time that Gourko could go no farther that day than Maglis, 10 miles east of Kazanlyk. The next morning, July 17th, at daybreak, Gourko moved out with his troops in three columns; that on the right ($1\frac{1}{2}$ battalion) being ordered to follow the mountains and attack Kazanlyk from the north-east, that of the centre (5 battalions and 10 guns) to attack the town from the east, and that on the left (all the cavalry and 6 guns) to follow the valley of the Tundja and turn the enemy's right flank. But the Turks were found posted 5 miles in front of Kazanlyk, behind a little stream called Kara Dere; their strength was about 3 battalions and 3 guns, and another column was seen coming from Shipka with the intention of occupying the heights on the Russian right flank. The fight began at 7 o'clock in the morning, but it was a small affair, although it lasted for two or three hours. The cavalry turned the right flank of the Turks, who thereupon began to retreat upon Kazanlyk; the cavalry still outflanking them cut off their retreat from Karlova and turned them toward Shipka, and then converted their retreat into a rout in which they lost 400 prisoners and their 3 guns; the Russian loss was 14 men. The village of Kazanlyk was in possession of the Russians by noon, and Gourko wished to march immediately on to Shipka and attack the pass; but his men were so exhausted (the heat was very great) that he was obliged to give them several hours' rest. Meanwhile with the cavalry he went on in person to Shipka village, where the infantry rejoined him about sunset; it was then too late to attack. In this way it happened that Gourko was one day behindhand for the joint attack which he had ordered from the north and south of Shipka Pass for the 17th of July.

The attack from the north was, however, made on this day, in the following manner:

General Darozhinsky, with his detachment (36th Infantry Regiment, 30th Don Cossacks, and 6 guns), left Tirnova on the 12th and arrived at Gabrova on the 13th. He immediately sent a portion of his Cossacks to Selvi, to drive out some bashi-bozouks that were there, and the rest of them into the mountains east of Shipka Pass to reconnoitre. The latter penetrated as far as the Berdek hill (about 3 miles east of the Shipka) without meeting any resistance; here, however, they came upon a battalion of Turks intrenched in a good position, before whom of course they were obliged to retire, sending back for infantry reinforcements. Two companies were sent to them, and arrived the next day, 16th.

Prince Mirsky (Lieutenant-General, commanding 9th Division) arrived at Gabrova on the evening of July 16th, and superseded Major-General Darozhinsky in command of the troops there. From the vicinity of Gabrova it could plainly be seen that the Turks had several lines of trenches dug across the high-road leading over the Shipka Pass; their numbers were learned to be between 4000 and 5000 infantry, with some bashi-bozouks and 12 guns. To attack a mountain position thus defended, with one regiment numbering, perhaps, 2400 men and 6 guns, would have been simply folly, except that another and stronger attack was to have been made simultaneously from the other side. But, as we have seen, the troops on the other side were one day behindhand; and as a result the isolated attack on the north was a complete failure. It was made in four columns, viz.:

On the right, four companies, with four guns which were to follow a mountain path through the village of Zeleno-Drevo and attack the Bald Mountain two miles west of the main Turkish position, which was at the hill of St. Nicholas on the main road.

In the centre, four companies, which were to follow a trail which would bring them in front of the advanced positions on the main road.

On the left, two companies, which were to take a path through the woods leading to the main position at St. Nicholas hill.

On the extreme left, three companies, three sotnias of Cossacks, and two guns, which were to attack the hill of Berdek, three miles from St. Nicholas.

The remaining two companies of the regiment were left to guard the baggage at Gabrova.

The various columns, each conducted by guides, were in motion by 7 o'clock in the morning. The plan of attack shows a considerable ignorance of the Turkish position, for on the Bald Mountain there were no Turks at all, and the weakest column was directed against the strongest position of the Turks (St. Nicholas).

The result of the attack was as follows:

The *column on the right*, after marching all day, arrived at 7 P.M. on the Bald Mountain without having met any Turks; its four guns were left *en route* at the village of Zeleno-Drevo, with orders to assist the attack of the centre column, but they were found to be out of range.

The *column in the centre* arrived in front of the Turkish advanced trenches at 3 P.M., and opened fire upon them; but, the position being too strong to assault, it simply remained on its ground till sunset, keeping up a straggling fire with the enemy.

The *column on the left* debouched from the woods at 2 P.M., and found itself only a few hundred yards from the intrenched position of the Turks; it was very warmly received, but managed to hold its ground till 4 P.M., when it began to retreat, the Turks pursuing till 6 P.M. This column lost 5 out of 6 officers and 115 out of 320 men.

The *column on the extreme left* attacked at 3 o'clock in the morning, and carried the intrenchments on the hill of Berdek, the Turks retreating to St. Nicholas.

This was the only success of the day, and it availed nothing, for it was too far away and the column was too small in numbers to assist the little detachments in the centre, one of which had been badly beaten, and in retreating had brought the Turks into a position to threaten the rear of the other. There were no reserves, and nothing had been heard from Gourko; during the night, therefore, all the columns fell back toward Gabrova. The total losses of the day were 6 officers and 205 men.

Gourko meanwhile, as previously stated, had reached the village of Shipka that same evening (July 17th), and made preparations to attack the pass the next morning. Of this he sent word early in the morning by a note taken by a Bulgarian across the mountain to Prince Mirsky, asking him to support his attack by a diversion with the 36th Regiment; but this note did not reach its destination until noon, and then it was too late, so that Gourko's attack from the south (July 18th) was isolated and unsuccessful—just as had been the one from the north the previous day,

Gourko attacked with two battalions of the Rifle Brigade and a half battalion of plastounes. They climbed through the woods on either side of the main road and deployed against the position at the hill of St. Nicholas. Just after the firing had begun the Turks sent out a flag of truce. " Cease firing " was sounded, and a party of officers [*] advanced to meet the flag, when suddenly the Turkish officers turned and retired hastily to their lines, and at a signal the Turks opened fire upon the Russian party. Fortunately none of them were hit. Excited by this treachery,

---

[*] One of these officers was Major Liegnitz, the Military Attaché to the German Embassy in St. Petersburg, who made a very full report of the whole circumstance to his Government.

the rifle battalions rushed forward and gained possession of some of the outer lines of trenches; but they were not strong enough to carry the main works on the St. Nicholas hill, and, hearing nothing of the attack from the north on which they had relied, they retired in good order down the mountain to the village of Shipka. The Turks fired at them with artillery, but did not leave their trenches; the Russian losses were something over 150 men.

Two unconcerted and isolated attacks had therefore been made on the Turkish position in the Shipka Pass, and both had been repulsed. On the morning of the 19th both detachments prepared to renew the attack, but meanwhile the Turks evacuated their positions and dispersed in small bands through the mountains to the west, finally reuniting somewhere near Philippopolis. In order to gain time for this manœuvre, they entered into negotiations with General Gourko looking to a surrender. The Turkish *Parlementaire* came to Gourko's camp at 7 in the morning, bearing a letter from the Pasha offering to surrender, in answer to a summons to that effect sent by Gourko the previous day. It was agreed that the capitulation was to take place at noon, and the Turkish officer departed in order to get the Pasha's answer concerning some details, promising to be back in two hours. Meanwhile Gourko sent some hospital attendants up to the scene of the previous day's fight in order to bring in his wounded. The two hours passed, and finally noon passed, and nothing was seen of the Turkish officer. Then Gourko, suspecting some foul play, sent forward a reconnoitring party, and got two battalions in position to support them. But, before the reconnoitring party had gone far, some of the hospital attendants returned from St. Nicholas Hill, saying that Major-General Skobeleff II. was there; and soon afterward arrived a note from that officer saying that he had occupied St. Nicholas Hill, and that the Turks had all fled. He had in fact taken nine companies of the 36th Regiment and four guns, and advanced early in the morning to attack the position by the same route as that taken the day before by the column of the centre; but he had advanced successively from one line of trenches to another, and finally to the St. Nicholas Hill, without finding any defenders. The hospital attendants found but little to do, as the Turks had mutilated all the Russian dead and wounded left on the field. On the road near the Nicholas Hill was found one heap which alone contained over twenty human heads which had been cut from their bodies. The Turks left their tents standing, and abandoned their artillery (eight guns) and a large amount of ammunition and supplies, as well as their wounded (whom, in spite of the example set before their eyes, the Russians treated in their own hospitals).

On the 19th of July, therefore, the Shipka Pass was in the hands of the Russians, and the principal objects of Gourko's expedition were accomplished. In eight days from the time of leaving Tirnova, and sixteen days from the Danube, he had gained possession of three passes (Hainkioi, Travna, and Shipka), covering a length of thirty miles in the Balkans, and one of them the great high-road from Bulgaria to Roumelia: he had dispersed various Turkish detachments, numbering in all about 10,000 men, had captured 11 guns and a large quantity of ammunition, clothing, and provisions, and had disarmed the Turkish population throughout a large part of the valley of the Tundja; and all with a loss of less than 500 men. His men and horses had lived off the country and what they captured from the Turks, and on the 19th they still had three days' rations of hard bread (out of the five they had taken with them) untouched.

By this time the whole of the VIII. Corps had arrived at Tirnova and been distributed as follows: Corps Headquarters and 14th Division at Tirnova, watching the road from Shumla; two regiments of the 9th Division in Hainkioi Pass, detachments of Cossacks in Travna Pass, one regiment at Selvi, and of the remaining regiment (No. 36) one battalion at Gabrova and the other two in the Shipka Pass. Gourko's detachment was about equally divided, one half in the village of Shipka and the other at Kazanlyk. They remained in these positions until the 22nd.

It is now necessary to cast a glance at what was transpiring on the Turkish side. The political effect of the passage of the

Danube, followed so quickly by the appearance of Gourko's detachment on the south of the Balkans, was tremendous. A panic reigned at Adrianople and at all the larger towns in the valleys of the Tundja and Maritza, the Mohammedan population of which began fleeing toward Constantinople. In that city the panic was hardly less great. Daily councils were held at the palace, and the Sultan wavered between the projects of "displaying the standard of the Prophet," thereby proclaiming a religious war, and of transporting himself and his government to Brusa, in Asia Minor. Then his whole Cabinet was overthrown, and the Commander-in-Chief, Abdul-Kerim Pasha, was dismissed in disgrace and banished along with the War Minister to one of the islands in the Ægean. Mehemet Ali Pasha was recalled from Montenegro and appointed Commander-in-Chief, and Suleiman Pasha commander of the troops between Adrianople and the Balkans; and the greatest efforts were made to get together an army to oppose the Russians, who were supposed to be marching in force toward Adrianople. At the same time England sent her fleet to Besika Bay and made other warlike preparations.

In order to follow the movements of the Turkish troops, a few topographical explanations are necessary. The Maritza River rises in the Balkans about 30 miles south-east of Sophia, and follows a course a little south of easterly for 170 miles, and then (at the city of Adrianople) turns and flows south for another 100 miles, emptying into the Ægean Sea near the town of Enos. On the south and west it receives the streams flowing from the Rhodope Mountains, the principal of which, called the Arda, empties at Adrianople; on the north it receives the drainage of a low range of hills known as the Little Balkans, which are parallel to the main range of that name and about 15 miles from it. Between these two is a very fertile valley, long famous for its culture of roses, from which "ottar of roses" is distilled, through which flows the Tundja River past Kazanlyk to Slivno, where it turns south and empties into the Maritza at Adrianople. Between the Tundja and Maritza system and the waters of the Black Sea there is a range of hills rising in places to the height of 2000 feet, nearly parallel to the coast and about 12 miles from it.

In this section of the country is the principal railroad of Turkey, which, coming from Constantinople, unites near Adrianople with a branch coming from Enos. From Adrianople the railroad follows the valley of the Maritza to about 30 miles above Philippopolis (the grading of the road is complete as far as Sophia). At the little station of Trnova (which must not be confounded with the large town of Tirnova north of the Balkans) a branch railroad turns off and follows the valley of a stream called Sasli to Yeni-Zagra, and thence turns east to the town of Yamboli in the valley of Tundja. This road was intended to cross the Balkans and unite near Shumla with the Rustchuk railroad, but it has never been built beyond Yamboli.

The principal high-roads are:

1. Shipka — Kazanlyk — Eski-Zagra — Trnova — Adrianople.
2. Philippopolis — Haskioi — Hermanli (the great road from Sophia to Adrianople).
3. Kazanlyk — Slivno — Yamboli — Adrianople.
4. Philippopolis — Karlova — Kazanlyk.
5. Philippopolis — Tchirpan — Eski-Zagra — Yeni-Zagra — Yamboli.

At the beginning of July the Turks had in the region from Philippopolis to Slivno about 10,000 men and 60 guns, which were then sent forward to the Balkans in the neighbourhood of Shipka. Soon after (about July 5th–10th) 10,000 to 12,000 men with 40 guns, under command of Reouf Pasha, were sent from Adrianople by rail to Yamboli, and thence into the Balkan passes about Slivno. It was the western portion of this latter detachment that Gourko drove away in his skirmishes near Hainkioi; the first detachment he destroyed at Kazanlyk and Shipka.

When the news of the passage of the Danube reached Constantinople it was decided to recall the greater part of Suleiman's army from Montenegro, and a fleet of 20 transport ships was sent to bring it. On the 16th of July 49 battalions, 18 guns and 2000 cavalry (about 30,000 men in all) were embarked at Antivari; they landed at Enos on the 19th, and proceeded by rail to Trnova, where they were assembled July 26th. (At this date the railroad between Trnova and Yeni-Zagra had been cut by Gourko's cavalry.)

By the last week in July, therefore, the Turks had brought together an army of about 50,000 men of regular troops for the defence of Roumelia. It was posted as follows: 35,000 men under Suleiman at Trnova, Karabuna and Gidsal—*i.e.*, at the confluence of the Maritza and Sasli rivers and the junction of the two railways; 15,000 men under Reouf at Slivno, Yamboli, and Yeni-Zagra.

We will now return to the subsequent movements of Gourko's detachment, which was resting at Shipka and Kazanlyk on the 22nd of July. On that date, at the request of a deputation of the inhabitants, the town of Eski-Zagra was occupied by the 9th Dragoons, a sotnia of Cossacks and 2 guns.

On the 23rd Gourko began to resume the offensive by sending two raiding-parties as follows:

1. Detachment of Colonel Matsioulevitch (8th Dragoons, two sotnias 21st Don Cossacks, section of 16th mounted battery), which was ordered to proceed by Eski-Zagra to the station Karabuna on the Yamboli Railroad, destroy the railroad and telegraph near this point, and gather as much information as possible about the movements of the Turks. This detachment bivouacked for the night at Eski-Zagra, and early the next morning (July 24th) moved forward in three parties, one of which was to strike the railroad above Karabuna, the other below it, while the third as a reserve moved directly on that point. The first party reached the road and destroyed it, the other two were held in check by a Turkish detachment of three or four battalions and several hundred Circassians, which they met before arriving at Karabuna. After skirmishing all day the three parties withdrew, and the united detachment retired to Eski-Zagra at night, having destroyed five bridges, three culverts, several way-stations, and the track and telegraph on a length of several miles.

2. Detachment of Colonel Korevo (9th Dragoons, one sotnia 26th Don Cossacks, section of 16th mounted battery),

which was to proceed from Eski-Zagra (July 24th) to the station of Kaiadzik on the Philippopolis Railroad, and destroy the track in that vicinity, as well as gather information about the Turkish forces. They drove off some bashi-bozouks which they found near the station, and then destroyed the building with all its contents, as well as the track and telegraph line for a considerable distance.

These two detachments, besides destroying the track and telegraph both on the Yamboli and Philippopolis lines, gathered the following information about the Turks, viz.: that there were near Karabuna, on the Yamboli Railroad, from four to six battalions and some cavalry; that troops were beginning to concentrate near the junction of the railroads, and that they were being brought there by rail from Adrianople. The same day by a small reconnaissance in the direction of Yeni-Zagra it was learned that there were Turkish troops at that place, but it could not be discovered in what strength.

Upon these data Gourko divided his detachment into two portions on July 25th, one of which, composed of the Bulgarian Legion (6 battalions), the two regiments of Dragoons, the 9th Hussars, 3 sotnias of Cossacks (in all 15 squadrons), and 12 guns, he sent to Eski-Zagra under the orders of Duke Nicholas Leuchtenberg; with the other (4th Rifle Brigade, 6 to 8 sotnias of Cossacks, and 22 guns) Gourko proceeded on the 27th eastward along the Tundja, with the intention of crossing the Little Balkans to Yeni-Zagra.

Leuchtenberg's detachment established itself at Eski-Zagra July 25th, with outposts about ten miles out on the roads leading east, south, and west, and on the succeeding days continued to send reconnaissances toward Yeni-Zagra and toward the junction of the railroads. At this latter point the Turkish troops continued to arrive every day by trains, but they had not yet advanced beyond Karabuna, where they had about seven or eight battalions. At Yeni-Zagra was a somewhat larger force.

Gourko then ordered that the Duke of Leuchtenberg with all his detachment should move eastward on July 29th from Eski-Zagra toward Yeni-Zagra (the two towns are twenty-five miles apart), while he himself with his detachment, increased by the 1st Brigade 9th Division from the Hainkioi Pass, would cross the Little Balkans on July 30th and join him, and then move against Yeni-Zagra.

Accordingly, Leuchtenberg moved out at 2 P.M. on the 29th, having sent in the morning of the same day two reconnaissances, one in advance of his own column toward Yeni-Zagra, and the other toward Karabuna. The first of these soon met a column of Turks (6 battalions, 8 guns, and some Tcherkesses) which had advanced the previous day from Yeni-Zagra. The head of Leuchtenberg's column (8th Dragoons and 2 guns) went forward at a trot to support the two squadrons of the reconnoitring party. Thus, the two columns, Leuchtenberg from Eski-Zagra and the Turks from Yeni-Zagra, met on the chaussée midway between these two places in the afternoon of July 29th. The Bulgarian Legion, which formed the infantry of Leuchtenberg's column, did not come up until about 6 in the evening; but meanwhile he held the Turks in check by his cavalry (15 squadrons), one half of which he kept on the chaussée, and sent the other half by a détour to the right to threaten the Turkish left. At nightfall the Turks retired a mile or two to the village of Karabuna. Leuchtenberg bivouacked on the stream which comes out of the hill at Dalbok. During the evening the two squadrons which had been sent in the morning to reconnoitre toward Karabuna (on the railroad) returned, and reported that Suleiman's army was advancing in force direct from Karabuna toward Eski-Zagra, and that it was only 8 miles south-east of the latter place.

This disclosed the plan of the Turks. Suleiman with a large force was moving from the railroad toward Eski-Zagra (and thence probably toward Shipka), while a portion of Reouf's troops were advancing from Yeni-Zagra to meet Suleiman at Eski-Zagra. The Russians, on the other hand, were moving in two columns, one from the valley of the Tundja south of Hainkioi, and the other from Eski-Zagra, with the intention of attacking Yeni-Zagra. On the night of the 29th of July the troops stood as follows: Gourko, with the bulk of the infantry (4th Rifle Brigade and 1st Brigade 9th Division, 10 battalions, 8 squadrons of

Cossacks, and 22 guns), was still on the north of the Little Balkans, near the village of Jasiriu. Leuchtenberg, with 4 battalions of the Bulgarian Legion, 14 squadrons, and 12 guns, was bivouacked near the village of Dalbok, facing east, and having in front of him a Turkish detachment of 6 battalions, 8 guns, and some Tcherkesses. Suleiman's head of column was 8 miles south-east of Eski-Zagra, at which place were 2 battalions of the Bulgarian Legion and 2 sotnias of Cossacks.

The town of Eski-Zagra was of the greatest importance to the Russians, as it covered their retreat to Kazanlyk and the Shipka Pass. Leuchtenberg therefore determined to fall back upon this town with his 4 battalions of Bulgarians and 6 guns, and try to hold it for a day against Suleiman, and to direct his cavalry to retreat slowly after him along the chaussée, delaying as much as possible the advance of the Turkish infantry in front of them, and keeping up the connection between Eski-Zagra and Gourko's troops which would come over the Little Balkans during the day.

The cavalry was disposed as follows: in the centre, across the chaussée, 3 squadrons in line supported by 2 squadrons in reserve; on the left, 2 squadrons near the foot of the hills; on the right, 3 squadrons in line, with 2 guns, facing south-east, near the village of Tchavlikioi. This left a general reserve of 4 squadrons and 4 guns. The Turks opened the attack about 7 o'clock in the morning (July 30th) by a demonstration against the Russian left, before which the 2 squadrons fell back slowly. Skirmishing continued until about noon without much change in the relative positions; but then the Turks began massing their infantry against the Russian right, with the evident intention of breaking past the Russians and effecting a junction with Suleiman. The Russian right was then reinforced by the 6 squadrons in reserve, making 9 in all, while 4 remained on the chaussée and 2 near the mountains. In this way the Turks continually striving to turn their right flank, the Russians fell back, contesting every step, and about 5 P.M. they reached the village of Aidinli, 3 miles east of Eski-Zagra. Meanwhile, on the left flank several attempts had been made by the Cossacks to break through the line of

Circassians and learn something of the whereabouts and movements of Gourko's troops, but they had all been unsuccessful.

Gourko had meanwhile crossed the Little Balkans during the morning (30th), and on the west and north of Yeni-Zagra had found a portion of Reouf's detachment *en route* toward Eski-Zagra. He fought with this during the greater part of the day, and drove it to the east, thus preventing its junction with the troops near Eski-Zagra. Hearing then of the desperate situation of Leuchtenberg's cavalry, he prepared to return along the chaussée to Dalbok, reunite his detachment, and retreat toward Hainkioi.

On this day (30th) Suleiman had concentrated his force in front of Eski-Zagra, but he had made no attack. On the evening of that date, therefore, the relative positions were as follows :

Suleiman, with about 40,000 men disposed in a circle of 5 miles radius around Eski-Zagra, from the Tchirpan road on the left to the village of Dzuranli on the right, his right flank being composed of the troops which had come from Yeni-Zagra.

Leuchtenberg, in possession of the chaussée from Eski-Zagra for a distance of about 6 miles east, having the 6 Bulgarian battalions and some Cossacks on his right flank at Eski-Zagra, and the rest of his cavalry at Aidinli and Hirsta.

Gourko, on the chaussée just west of Yeni-Zagra, with 10 battalions ready to march early in the morning to the relief of Leuchtenberg.

On the morning of the 31st, between 6 and 7 o'clock, the Cossacks of Gourko's advance-guard were discovered approaching on the chaussée from the east, but the road was completely under the fire of the Turks from their position at Dzuranli. To make a diversion in favour of these Cossacks, Leuchtenberg sent the 9th Hussars and 4 guns to demonstrate against the left flank of the Turks at Dzuranli; and soon afterward he sent the 8th Dragoons and 4 guns against the right flank of Suleiman's main force south of Eski-Zagra. These two regiments were thus interposed between the Turks at Dzuranli and Suleiman's main force on the south of Eski-Zagra, and prevented their junction for several hours.

Suleiman began his attack about 8 in the morning along the two roads coming into Eski-Zagra from the south and west. There was nothing to oppose him but the 6 battalions of the Bulgarian Legion, which fell back slowly toward the town. About 11 o'clock the bulk of Gourko's forces had arrived and engaged the Turks near Dzuranli. The 9th Dragoons were thereupon sent to Eski-Zagra to aid the Bulgarians, and the rest* of Leuchtenberg's cavalry (upon the order of Gourko) was marched along the chaussée under fire of the Turks at Dzuranli to rejoin Gourko's right wing. During the afternoon Gourko succeeded in driving back the Turks in front of him; but by withdrawing his cavalry from Aidinli he had lost all communication with his people at Eski-Zagra. If the Turks had had plenty of good cavalry, they would probably have cut these latter to pieces. As it was, the Bulgarians fell back slowly and in good order, and upon the arrival of the 9th Dragoons to cover their retreat, they made good their escape over the Little Balkans to Kazanlyk.

The main body of Gourko's force retreated that evening (July 31st), in the opposite direction, to the bivouac near Dolbak, the cavalry covering their rear. The next day they crossed the Little Balkans to the neighbourhood of Hainkioi.

During the 30th and 31st of July Gourko's detachment of 16,000 men had been fighting with the whole of the newly formed "Balkan Army" under Suleiman, numbering nearly 50,000 men in all. It was impossible, owing to the course of events on the other side of the Balkans, as will be subsequently explained, to send any substantial reinforcements to Gourko and continue the advance in face of this new army. Gourko was therefore ordered to retreat slowly before the Turks, post a portion of his troops in the passes, and bring the rest to the northern side of the mountains. The Bulgarian Legion retired to Shipka; the 9th Dragoons, which had covered its retreat, then made its way past the bashi-bozouks, who had swarmed into the valley of the Tundja, and rejoined Gourko at Hainkioi.

On the 3rd and 4th of August a small reconnaissance was made to Eski-Zagra, by which it was learned that Suleiman had reduced the entire town to ashes on account of the "treason" of the inhabitants in asking the Russians to come there, and had then marched his army towards Yeni-Zagra.

On the 5th of August all of Gourko's cavalry retired through the Hainkioi Pass to Tirnova, and on the 8th arrived at the village of Nikup, 18 miles north of Tirnova; there it refitted, cured up lame and sore-backed horses, and generally repaired damages, and was subsequently distributed to the various divisions of which it formed parts. The 1st Brigade 9th Division was posted in the Hainkioi and Elena passes, the 4th Rifle Brigade at Tirnova, and the Bulgarian Legion, as previously stated, in the Shipka Pass. Gourko himself proceeded to Russia to meet and resume his proper command (2nd Cavalry Division of the Guard), which had meantime been mobilised and was *en route* to the seat of war.

The losses of his detachment from the capture of Shipka Pass (July 19th) to their return to the Balkans (August 5th) were about 500 men; their total losses from the time of leaving Tirnova (July 12th) to their return to the same place (August 6th) were as follows:

	Officers.	Men.
Killed	10	181
Wounded	24	709
Missing	—	57
Total	34	947

This expedition of Gourko's was more than a mere cavalry raid: it was an admirably conducted movement of an advance-guard composed of all arms. With 8000 infantry, 4000 cavalry, and 32 guns, it had in less than a month gained possession of one of the principal passes of the Balkans, from which the Russians, though terribly attacked, never let go their hold, and which they finally used in January for the passage of a large portion of their army; it had carried a panic throughout the whole of Turkey between the Balkans and Constantinople; and its scouting-parties had penetrated to within 70 miles of Adrianople, the second city of the Empire, and had destroyed the railroad and telegraph on the two principal lines; finally, it had gathered accurate information concerning the strength and positions of the large Turkish force advancing toward the Balkans.

In this expedition alone of the whole campaign was the cavalry energetically handled. On several occasions it fought on foot; it was constantly on the move; it subsisted on the country; on the 29th and 30th of July 14 squadrons of it (1800 men) held their own against 4000 infantry and several hundred bashi-bozouks and Tcherkesses; and it finally covered Gourko's retreat before a force more than three times superior to his own. The irregular cavalry of the Turks never waited long enough to come to hand-to-hand blows; on one occasion (July 16th), while fighting on foot against infantry, the dragoons advanced with fixed bayonets, but the Turks retired without accepting a hand-to-hand struggle. The Russian cavalry, it will be remembered, is armed with the short Berdan rifle, an arm much superior to the Winchester and nearly equal to the Peabody-Martini. In artillery, however, the Turkish superiority was clearly proved, especially during the fight of July 29th on the chaussée near Karabuna; in which the Turks covered the Russian cavalry with shell, while the Russian guns (4-pdrs.), even with their greatest elevation, could not reach the Turkish battery, the distance being something over 4000 yards. During the fight of the 31st near Aidinli, one well-aimed shell killed and wounded 12 hussars and 10 horses. But the Russian inferiority in armament (as well as in numbers) was more than counterbalanced by the skill and energy with which their squadrons were handled.

CHAPTER III

OPERATIONS OF THE RIGHT WING UNDER LIEUTENANT-GENERAL BARON KRÜDENER.

As previously stated, the IX. Corps crossed the Danube by the Sistova bridge on the 10th of July, and immediately moved eastward toward Nikopolis. Two of the Cavalry regiments (9th Hussars and 9th Dragoons) belonging to this Corps had been taken to form part of Gourko's detachment. To replace them, the brigade of Caucasian Cossacks (12 squadrons), which originally had also been detailed to Gourko's detachment, was relieved from him and ordered to report to Krüdener. One of his infantry regiments (No. 124) was left near Sistova, and another (No. 19) was sent forward toward Bulgareni, on the high-road (Rustchuk-Plevna-Sophia). With the rest of his corps Krüdener advanced along the direct road to Nikopolis. He arrived in front of the Turkish positions on the 13th, reconnoitred and made his dispositions on the 14th, attacked and carried the field works on the 15th, and on the 16th the fortress capitulated.

Nikopolis is a town of some 8000 or 10,000 inhabitants. Its fortifications consisted of an old masonry fortress situated on a bluff overhanging the river, much out of repair and completely commanded by the hills in rear; the greater part of the town lies outside of this fortress. Behind the town is a plateau, about 700 feet above the river, and from 3 to 8 miles in width, between the Osma River on the west of it and the marshes of the Danube on the east; deep wooded ravines descend abruptly from this plateau to the marshy valleys on either side. About 3 miles west of the Osma River is the Vid River, and between the two is a rolling country, the top of which is about 600 feet above the Danube level. While the Russians had been demonstrating in front of Nikopolis previous to their passage of the river at Sistova, the Turks had placed several batteries in position for firing across the river and had also lined the Danube bank, as well as the bluffs of the Osma and the Ermenli ravine, with rifle-pits; but after the passage of the Danube they hastily began the construction of some work to defend the place in the rear (south). At the time of Krüdener's arrival these works consisted of five redoubts—two of them west of the town on the plateau between the Nikopolis ravine and the Osma, one just south of the town, and two east of it near the Danube—and of three batteries in the form of lunettes on the south and south-west of the town, the most advanced being near the village of Voubla; in front of these batteries were lines of rifle-pits. In these works there were about ten field guns; and there were several siege guns in batteries facing the river. The Turkish forces consisted in all of 10,000 to 12,000 men, the greater part of which were posted in the works just described, and the rest, 3000 or 4000 men, were placed on the hills between the Osma and the Vid, in an entrenched position extending from the village of Gradesti to Missilyeou.

Krüdener divided his force for the attack into two portions, one of which, under his own orders, was to advance between the Osma and the Ermenli ravine directly against the Turkish works south of the town; and the other, under Lieutenant-General Schilder-Schuldner, commanding 5th Division, was to move down the left bank of the Osma, assault the heights between that river and the Vid, cut off the Turks from Rahova and Plevna, drive them into Nikopolis, and then take the main positions in flank.

The troops were posted as follows at 3 A.M. July 15th:

In the *centre*, from Voubla to the Ermenli ravine, 5 batteries of 9-pdrs., supported by the 121st Regiment on their right and the 20th on their left; behind the centre of this line was a reserve composed of the 122nd Regiment, 3 batteries and 2 sotnias.

On the *right*, 3 sotnias of the 9th Don Cossacks observed the country between Ermenli and the Danube.

On the *left*, Schilder-Schuldner's column, composed of the 17th and 18th Regiments, 3 batteries, the 9th Lancers, and the Caucasian Brigade of Cossacks, was posted in the valley of the Osma near the village of Debo; communication between them and the main body was kept up by the 123rd Regiment, which was in the ravine of Slatina.

At 4 A.M. the batteries near Voubla opened fire, and about the same time Schilder-Schuldner began to advance along the valley of the Osma against the heights on its left bank, having on his right the 18th Regiment, which was to attack these heights forming the right flank of the Turkish position, while the 17th Regiment and the 9th Lancers were to incline to the left toward Gradesti, and thus turn the Turkish right flank—the whole attack being based on the idea of driving the Turks *into* their fortress and then compelling its surrender. The Caucasian Brigade was to cover the left and rear from any reinforcements which might arrive from Rahova or Plevna. At 7 A.M. the 18th Regiment arrived in front of the Turkish heights, and the artillery which accompanied it (one battery) opened fire, to which the Turks replied energetically; not long afterward the regiment moved forward to the assault, and after a struggle gained possession of the heights, driving the Turks back across the Osma toward Nikopolis. Seeing this, the 123rd Regiment moved forward toward the Osma, seized the bridge at Missilyeou, sent one battalion across to harass the Turks in retreat, and with the other two battalions moved forward along the road in the valley of the Osma toward the second bridge (at Djournevo). The Turks retreated in good order, delaying the advance of the Russians as much as possible, crossed the Djournevo bridge, and retired to the heights on the right bank of the Osma, between it and the Nikopolis ravine. Two battalions of the 18th Regiment then crossed to the right bank (as also the battalion of the 123rd Regiment) and joined the 123rd Regiment. These five battalions then began to climb the heights north of Djournevo under a hot fire from the Turks. Seeing them appear and reform

CAPTURE OF NIKOPOLIS

on the top of these heights, and having learned of their success on the left bank of the Osma, Krüdener then (about 2 P.M.) gave the order for the 20th Regiment and the five batteries on its right to advance—two battalions against the battery nearest Voubla, and one battalion toward the principal redoubt (No. 3) east of the Nikopolis ravine. The battery was carried, though with heavy loss, about 4 P.M., the Turks losing one gun, but retiring with the other two to battery "*b*." But the battalion advancing against the redoubt was repulsed; the 122nd Regiment was brought up to its support, but a second assault was repulsed; a part of the 121st Regiment was then brought up, and a third assault about 6 P.M. was successful, and the redoubt was carried. The 20th and 122nd Regiments then advanced along the east side of the ravine in which the town is situated, and arrived in front of the walls of the fortress.

Meanwhile the 18th and 123rd Regiments continued to advance along the Rahova road on the heights east of the Osma, and toward evening came in front of a large redoubt forming the principal defence from the direction of the west. The Turks sortied from the redoubt against their left flank, but were repulsed. Soon afterward the 17th Regiment and the remaining battalion of the 18th, which had followed the valley of the Osma through the village of Tcherkovitza, scaled the heights behind that village and opened fire on Redoubt No. 1, near the river. Darkness soon put an end to the fighting. During the night a portion of the Turkish troops tried to break through the Caucasian Brigade and escape toward Plevna, but they were repulsed.

The results of the day were therefore the capture of two of the three principal positions of the Turks on the hills outside the fortress and the investment of the place. Preparations were made for an open assault the next morning, supported by the 9-pdr. field batteries on the heights overlooking the town, and also by the siege batteries on the opposite bank of the Danube, which had kept up a very lively bombardment throughout the previous day. The troops began to move forward at 4 A.M., but immediately afterward the

Turks hoisted a white flag, and during the morning concluded negotiations for an unconditional surrender.

The Turkish losses are not known; 7000 men, including 300 wounded, surrendered as prisoners of war, and the Russian trophies included 6 flags, 110 guns, over 10,000 small arms, 2 monitors, and a great quantity of ammunition and supplies.

The Russian losses were:

	Officers.	Men.
Killed	3	273
Wounded	28	921
Missing	—	84
Total	31	1278

While these operations had been going on about Nikopolis, Osman Pasha, with an army of 40,000 men of the best troops in Turkey—those that had defeated the Servians in their campaign of 1876—was on the march from Widdin toward the east; and a force of perhaps 10,000 or 12,000 men had left Sophia and was advancing by the high road which leads through Plevna (a portion of it having been sent to Lovtcha). The exact date when Osman left Widdin is not known; the order was given by the Commander-in-Chief, Abdul-Kerim Pasha, and probably just after the Russians had effected the crossing of the Danube. The head of Osman's column was first heard of on the 17th of July, when the pickets of the Caucasian Brigade posted along the Vid reported that a strong force coming from the west was marching on the road to Plevna; but neither at the Grand Duke's Headquarters (then at Tirnova) nor at General Krüdener's does much importance appear to have been attached to this report. The Grand Duke simply telegraphed an order to Krüdener to "occupy Plevna as promptly as possible." Krüdener had in fact learned from prisoners even *before* the capture of Nikopolis that reinforcements were expected from the direction of Rahova and Plevna, but he put little confidence in the report; for otherwise he would immediately after the capture of Nikopolis (July 16th) have ordered the Caucasian Brigade, and if possible one

FIRST BATTLE AT PLEVNA

other regiment of cavalry, to advance to Plevna (which is only 20 miles south of Nikopolis) and find out what force was there. But instead of this the Caucasian Brigade remained the 16th and 17th on the Vid, and on the 18th was sent off on the left flank to Bulgareni, where the road from Sistova to Plevna comes into the high road from Rustchuk. In short, Osman Pasha with a large army arrived upon the flank of the Russians without their knowing anything about it. There has been much controversy as to who was responsible for this ignorance, but no satisfactory solution has ever been made public.

On the 18th of July, as just stated, the Grand Duke directed Krüdener to occupy Plevna; and immediately Krüdener ordered Lieutenant-General Schilder-Schuldner, with the 1st Brigade 5th Division (17th and 18th Regiments), four batteries, and the 9th Don Cossacks, to proceed by Bryslan to Plevna and occupy that town; and he placed under his orders to assist him—1, the 19th Regiment, which with one battery and two sotnias was already on the high road from Rustchuk to Plevna (one battalion with the baggage at Bulgareni and the rest at Poradim); 2, the Caucasian Brigade of Cossacks and its mounted battery, which were also at Bulgareni.

Schilder-Schuldner moved out the same day, and bivouacked about 10 miles from Nikopolis, sending word to the 19th Regiment to move forward to Zgalevitza, and the Caucasian Brigade to Tutchenitza. On the 19th he continued his march, and about 2 P.M. arrived on the heights south of Verbitza, and was halted by the Turkish artillery from the heights of Grivitza. *Schilder-Schuldner had no cavalry at all with his main column*, and, so to speak, stumbled on the Turks. The 9th Don Cossacks were marching by a road about 5 miles to his right, and at this time (2 P.M. July 19th) were quietly cooking their soup in their bivouac at Riben, 8 miles to the right *and rear* of Schilder-Schuldner. When they heard the noise of the latter's guns they emptied their kettles, mounted, and rode forward at a trot toward Plevna. On the Bukova heights, about $2\frac{1}{2}$ miles north of Plevna, they came upon a detachment of Turkish infantry, with whom they skirmished till nightfall. On the other flank, the 19th Regiment had advanced as ordered to Zgalevitza and bivouacked there, sending meanwhile two sotnias of Cossacks in reconnaissance as far as Grivitza, where they were met and driven back by the Turks. The Caucasian Brigade had marched to Tutchenitza without finding any enemy. On the night of July 19th, therefore, the little force of Schilder-Schuldner (9 battalions, 16 squadrons—6500 men—and 46 guns) was distributed over a distance of 17 miles, as follows: Near Bukova, 9th Don Cossacks; two miles south-west of Verbitza, 17th and 18th Regiments and 4 batteries; at Zgalevitza, 19th Regiment, 1 battery, and 2 sotnias; at Tutchenitza, Caucasian Brigade and 1 horse battery.

The first portion of Osman's army had arrived a few days previously (the exact day is not known), and up to the present time they had constructed some trenches near Bukova, on the site of the Grivitza redoubt which subsequently became so famous, and on the hills just east and south of the high road and commanding the approach by the latter.

Schilder-Schuldner ordered an attack on all sides at daylight the next morning (July 20th). But already at 4 A.M. the Turks came out of Plevna to attack the Don Cossacks on the extreme right near Bukova. Two companies, of the three which formed the guard of the baggage behind Verbitza, and a battery were sent to the aid of the Cossacks, and thus reinforced they held their ground until ordered to retreat about noon.

About 4.30 A.M. the other three batteries were brought into position opposite the Grivitza ridge and about 2500 yards north of the intrenchments, and opened fire; the 17th Regiment was placed with one battalion on the left, and two battalions on the right of the batteries, in two lines of company columns; on their right the 18th Regiment in two lines of company columns. After an hour's cannonade, at 5.30 A.M. the troops moved forward, crossed the ravine, and assaulted the Grivitza heights. The western extremity of the trenches was carried, and the 18th Regiment and a few

FIRST BATTLE AT PLEVNA

companies of the 17th followed the Turks down the south side of the heights to the very outskirts of Plevna, where they were brought to a halt by a very hot fire from behind the hedges and ditches on the edge of the town. This was at 7 A.M., and they remained here till 11.20, when they received the order to retreat. Meanwhile the rest of the 17th Regiment and all the artillery were two miles behind them on their left rear, making unsuccessful efforts to get possession of the main Grivitza position.

On the other flank the 19th Regiment had received at 3 A.M. its order for the attack, and by 5 A.M. had reached Grivitza; here it brought its battery into action against the trenches south of the chaussée, and after a short cannonade moved forward to the assault in columns of companies; it carried the first two lines of trenches without much difficulty, had a hard struggle for the third, but finally carried it, and followed the Turks to the edge of the town (on the east side), where they were brought to a stand-still by the heavy fire from the gardens and buildings; this was at 9 A.M.

The Caucasian Brigade had moved from Tutchenitza to Radischevo, and thence on to the heights in front of that village. Here it opened fire with its little battery on the right flank of the Turks who were opposed to the 19th Regiment; but finding its guns did not carry half of the distance, it limbered up and moved over toward the 19th Regiment, which it joined when the latter was already in retreat.

At 9 A.M., therefore, the Russian right and left flanks had carried everything before them and reached Plevna itself from the north and from the east; their centre had failed to carry the main Grivitza position; the two flanks were not in sight and not in communication except by a détour of about seven miles. Then the Turks formed their troops in the town and sallied forth in great numbers on both sides; the Russians were driven back with great loss, their right flank covered by the 9th Don Cossacks to Bryslan, their left covered by the Caucasian Brigade to Zgalevitza. The Turks pursued them only to their lines of trenches, and the fighting was all over by 5 in the afternoon. The Russians preserved their traditional firmness and did not take a panic, but they left on the field a great part of their dead and wounded, as well as 17 caissons, and all the baggage of the 19th Regiment. Their losses were: 22 officers killed and 52 wounded, and 2771 men killed and wounded. Nearly two-thirds of the officers and over one-third of the men were therefore *hors de combat;* of the three Colonels commanding regiments, two were killed; the General commanding the 1st Brigade 5th Division was wounded; of the six field officers present with the 19th Regiment, two were killed and two wounded. The Russians credit the Turks with a loss of 4000 men in killed and wounded, but this is a mere estimate, and there is no reason to suppose that their loss was any greater than that of the Russians.

The almost criminal faults of this battle on the part of the Russian commander are so apparent that they hardly need to be pointed out. Without having learned anything about the strength or position of the enemy, and without any reserves whatever of his own, his troops were led blindly to the assault in company columns, along two lines which had no communication with each other, and against an enemy which, as the official report says, was *subsequently* discovered to be more than four times their own strength! To crown all, the ammunition parks of the left wing had been left back at Bulgareni, 18 miles in rear of the field, and both the artillery and infantry ran short of cartridges during the retreat.

Immediately after this defeat Krüdener was ordered to bring the 19th Regiment, which had been so roughly handled, to Nikopolis, and leave it there together with some Roumanian troops that had just crossed the river as a garrison, and to proceed at once with the rest of the IX. Corps to the vicinity of Plevna and take command of all the troops there; and to strengthen his command, a detachment was sent to him under the orders of Lieutenant-General Prince Shakofskoi, consisting of the 1st Brigade 32nd Division (XI. Corps), the 1st Brigade 11th Cavalry Division from Tirnova, and the 30th Division (IV. Corps), which had just crossed the Danube. These troops were all on the ground by the 25th of July.

The Turks meanwhile were working with the utmost diligence upon their fortifications, confident that they would be again attacked in the course of a few days. They strengthened the Grivitza redoubt and the lines between it and Bukova, and began the construction of the group of redoubts just east of the town. By the 30th of July the Grivitza redoubt and four of those of the " middle group " were more or less completed.

Between the Lovtcha high road and the Vid there were no fortifications at this date. Osman's army on the 30th numbered about 40,000 men.

Krüdener reconnoitred carefully the ground in his front, and, on account of the natural strength of the position and the force of the enemy (who was receiving reinforcements every day), he hesitated to assume the responsibility of an assault of which the issue was doubtful. He therefore telegraphed to the Grand Duke, whose Headquarters were at Tirnova, 80 miles off, asking for instructions. The Grand Duke telegraphed somewhat sharply in reply, on the 28th, that he could not understand his hesitation in attacking as he had been previously ordered to do. Krüdener immediately gave orders for the assault, which was to take place on the 30th. On the 29th his troops stood as follows:

9th Lancers and 9th Don Cossacks, with one horse battery (10 squadrons and 6 guns), at Bryslan;

31st Infantry Division, less 124th Regiment and 1 battery (9 battalions and 40 guns), at Koioulovtsy;

5th Infantry Division, less 19th Regiment and 1 battery (9 battalions and 40 guns), at Tristenik;

2nd Brigade 30th Division, with 3 batteries (6 battalions and 24 guns), at Karagatch;

1st Brigade 30th Division, 1st Brigade 32nd Division, 1st Brigade 11th Cavalry Division, 6 foot batteries and 1 horse battery (12 battalions, 8 squadrons, and 54 guns), at Poradim;

Caucasian Brigade, with 2 horse batteries (12 squadrons and 12 guns), at Bogot.

Total, 36 battalions, 30 squadrons, and 176 guns (80 9-pdrs., 72 4-pdrs., 18 horse 4-pdrs., 6 mountain guns)—say 30,000 men in all, the losses at Nikopolis and at Plevna on July 20th not yet having been replaced.

The line from Bryslan through Tristenik to Poradim was about 15 miles long, and formed an arc of a circle whose radius was about 10 miles, and whose centre was at Plevna. From Poradim to Bogot the distance is about 11 miles.

Krüdener's orders for the 30th were as follows:

1. Cavalry on extreme right, under Major-General Loshkareff, to move forward at 6 A.M., observe the enemy, and protect the right flank.

2. Right flank (31st and 5th Divisions), under Lieutenant-General Wilhelminof, to attack the position north of the high road (Grivitza redoubt) with the 31st Division followed by the 5th Division in reserve.

3. Left flank (1st Brigade 30th Division and 1st Brigade 32nd Division), under Lieutenant-General Prince Shakofskoi, to leave Poradim at 5 A.M. and attack the position between Radischevo and Grivitza.

4. Cavalry on extreme left, under Major-General Skobeleff II., to leave Bogot at 5 A.M. and take position on the Lovtcha high road near Krishin, and prevent any reinforcements from arriving from Lovtcha.

5. Principal reserve (2nd Brigade 30th Division), under direct orders of the Commanding General (Krüdener), to be under arms at Karagatch.

6. The two regiments of cavalry (11th Dragoons and 11th Lancers) were distributed as follows: 4 squadrons to keep up communication between the right and left flanks, and 4 squadrons in the general reserve.

The key of the position was the Grivitza redoubt, which commanded all the others; and against this the largest force was directed (18 battalions and 80 guns); the two flanks were so widely separated that there was no chance that they could lend each other any aid. Krüdener's headquarters were to be on the left of the right wing, on the heights about $1\frac{1}{2}$ mile east of Grivitza.

The troops were under way by 7 o'clock in the morning.

The right wing advanced in two lines—the first line consisting of 6 battalions and 24 guns, the second of 3 battalions and 16 guns, followed by the 9 battalions and 40 guns of the 5th Division as a reserve, which came into position at 10 o'clock. Soon after 8 o'clock the first line came in range of the Turks, who opened fire. It halted and brought its batteries into position about 3000 yards east of the Grivitza redoubt. The artillery duel opened about 8.30 A.M., and continued without interruption until 2.30 P.M., the infantry meanwhile not firing a shot.

The left wing marched from Zgalevitza to Radischevo without finding any enemy, and thence to the heights in front of that village, from which the "middle group" of redoubts is in easy range (1500 to 2500 yards). These heights were occupied by the 1st Brigade 32nd Division, and 28 guns, and an artillery fight was begun which also lasted till 2.30 P.M. The results of this cannonade were about equal: two small Turkish batteries were silenced, and three Russian guns dismounted, causing the whole battery to be withdrawn and replaced.

At half-past two the infantry began to advance on both flanks. The right wing was divided into two columns for the assault, one from the north and one from the east. The first column consisted of the 121st Regiment (Penza) and the 2nd and 3rd Battalions of the 123rd (Kozloff), and was followed by the 17th and 18th Regiments as a reserve; the other column, of the 1st Battalion 123rd and the 122nd (Tamboff) Regiments, with the 20th Regiment (Galitz) in reserve. The 1st Battalion of the Penza Regiment, which had the lead, carried the first line of trenches, situated about 1000 yards north-east of the redoubt, but was checked by the second line just behind it. This, however, was carried by the 2nd Battalion, and they drove the Turks across the little ravine and began approaching the redoubt itself; three companies, led by the Major Commanding the 2nd Battalion, then rushed for the redoubt, and actually reached the parapet, where the Major was cut down and most of his followers also perished. The rest of this regiment (Penza) tried to advance in face of the terrible fire, but failed, and it fell back to the ravine; in a few minutes it had lost more than a third of its men and half its officers (29 officers and 1006 men). The Regiment of Kozloff then moved forward to the assault; as before, a few men reached the redoubt and met their death there, but the rest of them did not reach it. While they were still engaged, the 17th and 18th Regiments arrived somewhat on their right, but they were equally unsuccessful in their efforts to get into the redoubt. The fire which the Turks kept up from the redoubt and the trenches on either side of it was very severe.

Meanwhile the other column (Regiment of Tamboff and 1 Battalion of Kozloff) had moved forward across the ravines just north of the village of Grivitza, with the Regiment of Galitz on its left. The Tamboff Regiment got no farther than a little mound about 400 yards south-east of the redoubt; the Galitz Regiment was stopped abreast of the Tamboff by the fire from the trenches on the slope south of the redoubt. The two regiments remained in place and kept up a lively fusillade.

It had now come to be about 6 o'clock. Of the general reserve, one regiment had been sent to Shakofskoi, and the other was available. One battalion of this latter (No. 120) was then sent, with a squadron of Dragoons and two horse guns, to the right, where the 17th and 18th Regiments were being pressed back. With the aid of these fresh troops they managed to hold on a little longer. Finally, at sunset, Krüdener gave orders for another assault from all sides; it was made with desperation (a general officer being killed within 100 paces of the redoubt), but without success. Then Krüdener gave the order to retire, covering his retreat by the two remaining battalions of the 120th Regiment, by the 20th, which had till then lost comparatively little, and by the 124th, which arrived from Sistova during the evening. The firing continued all night, during which the troops were gradually withdrawn; it was daylight before the last of them retired. At 11 A.M. (July 31) they were all assembled at Tristenik and Kargatch, and took up position there to receive the enemy if he advanced, which however he did not do.

SECOND BATTLE AT PLEVNA

The attack of the right wing had been a total failure.

On the left wing, at half-past 2 the two regiments of the 32nd Division (Nos. 125 and 126) began descending the Radischevo ridge; as they came out of the brush at the bottom of the ravine and began climbing the opposite slope, they were received by a murderous fire from the two redoubts and from several lines of trenches in front of them. But, in spite of terrible losses, these two regiments kept pressing on, and carried one after another of the lines of trenches, and by 5 o'clock had gained possession of the two redoubts. From No. 1 the Turks withdrew 10 pieces, leaving 2 in the hands of the Russians; from No. 8 they succeeded in withdrawing all their artillery.

At 5 o'clock, therefore, Shakofskoi had gained possession of the two most southerly redoubts of the "middle group" (the other two remaining still in the hands of the Turks), his left flank had penetrated by a ravine to the edge of the town on the south-east, and his right flank was in Redoubt No. 1. Of the troops forming his second line (1st Brigade 30th Division), one regiment (No. 118) had already been brought into action (one battalion on the left flank and the other two on the right), so that he now had but one regiment in reserve; of his artillery, 8 guns had been advanced to the knoll on which was subsequently built Redoubt No. 10, and 16 guns to a position on the right of Redoubt No. 1. Four guns were with Skobeleff, 3 were disabled, and the remaining 21 were kept in reserve.

It now became a question whether Shakofskoi could hold the ground he had taken. His right flank, in Redoubt No. 1, was separated from Krüdener's troops in front of the Grivitza redoubt by a distance of about two miles in a straight line, and as the Turks occupied the intervening space, at least five miles as the troops must march. All hope of mutual support between the two wings was therefore out of the question. The Turks meanwhile were massing a large force in this interval, and preparing to advance beyond Shakofskoi's right (his line of battle faced nearly north) against his line of retreat. At the same time, 5 P.M., Shakofskoi received word from Krüdener that, of the two regiments forming the general reserve, one (No. 119) was already on the road to him, while the other (No. 120) had been directed toward his own (Krüdener's) position. This regiment (No. 119) never reached Shakofskoi's position, for the following reason: On the march between Grivitza and Radischevo it passed about 1500 yards in front of the column of Turks which was already advancing through this interval. Seeing the danger which menaced Shakofskoi's right and rear if this column continued its advance, the officer conducting this regiment, a captain on the staff at Krüdener's headquarters, who was familiar with the plan of battle, took the responsibility of halting the regiment and bringing it into action by the right flank against the advancing Turks. This partly filled up the wide interval separating the two wings, and, in conjunction with the firing from the troops near Redoubt No. 1, checked the Turkish advance.

The troops in the ravine near the town (Shakofskoi's left) were meanwhile very hard pressed by fresh Turkish reserves issuing from the town; to sustain them Shakofskoi sent in succession two battalions of the 117th, his only fresh regiment. By 6 o'clock, therefore, every man was engaged, and all hopes of a farther advance were abandoned; and, as their present position was surrounded by the Turks on three sides, it was only a question of holding their ground until dark and then withdrawing back to the Radischevo ridge, which was done in good order. The next morning the troops were marched back to Poradim.

Meanwhile, it will be remembered, there was a small force on the extreme left, under the orders of Major-General Skobeleff II. It was hotly engaged during the whole day, and, although small in numbers, was handled with such skill as to establish beyond doubt the military genius of this brilliant young general. His operations were in brief as follows: With the Caucasian Brigade (12 sotnias and 12 small guns), reinforced by one battalion of the 125th Regiment, he left Bogot at 5 A.M. and moved out to the Lovtcha chaussée, and thence up to the village of Krishin. His orders were to prevent any reinforcements from arriving

SECOND BATTLE AT PLEVNA

from Lovtcha, and in general to cover the left flank of the Russians; in case the Turks retreated, to cross the Vid and strike them in flank. At this date the Turks had not yet built any fortifications between the Lovtcha road and the Vid. Arrived at Krishin, he left there the bulk of his force in a central position, and, taking 2 sotnias and 4 guns, rode forward to the heights about 300 yards south-west of the town of Plevna. From this point he had a complete view of the whole Turkish position, and noticed that besides the troops in the redoubts the Turks had an immense camp of at least 20,000 men in the valley just north of Plevna, and a considerable force of cavalry behind them in the direction of the bridge over the Vid. When Shakofskoi's guns opened fire about 10 A.M on the Radischevo ridge, Skobeleff also opened fire with his four pieces, and thus diverted about 4000 Turkish infantry against himself. The Turks made a resolute attack, and Skobeleff with his handful of Cossacks fell back to his main force at Krishin. In this little reconnaissance Skobeleff had taken in at once the whole position of the Turks, and he saw that if they simply moved out about two miles from Plevna on the Lovtcha road, they could occupy a hill (the second knoll of the "Green Hills," on which Turkish Redoubt No. 20 was afterwards built), from which at 2500 yards' range they could enfilade the whole of Shakofskoi's line and take him in reverse as he advanced; Shakofskoi could do nothing against this position, as it was separated from his own by a rocky ravine with perpendicular bluffs. It was of vital consequence to keep the Turks away from this hill; and as the best means to accomplish this result, Skobeleff determined to *attack energetically* with his little detachment. But in order to carry out his instructions about covering the left flank of the whole force, he sent one little detachment of Cossacks to find a ford over the Vid, posted a sotnia between them and Krishin, another sotnia between Krishin and Shakofskoi's position to keep up communication, several strong pickets in the direction of Lovtcha, and finally on the hill near Krishin 3 sotnias and 12 guns. This left him 4 sotnias and the battalion of infantry with 4 guns; with these Skobeleff moved forward directly against the troops who had attacked him, and who remained on the height just south-west of the town. With them Skobeleff kept up a desperate fight all day and into the night. Until four o'clock he kept 3 companies and 2 sotnias in reserve, leaving the other 2 companies, 2 sotnias (dismounted), and 4 guns to do the fighting; then, just as his men were beginning to give way, he sent in the other 3 companies; and thus he managed to keep up the fight until dark, and also to remove all his wounded. After dark, covered by the remaining 2 sotnias, he made good his retreat to Krishin, and re-assembled there the whole of his little force, or what was left of it, for the infantry had lost over 50 per cent. But Skobeleff had gained his object, and had kept the Turks away from this hill, from which, if they had occupied it, they would have cut Shakofskoi's troops to pieces. During the night Skobeleff received orders to return to Bogot and thence to Pelishat.

Thus ended in complete failure the battle of July 30th, the second of the series of assaults upon Plevna.

The Russian loss, out of 30,000 men engaged, was 169 officers and 7136 men. Of this number, 2400 men had been killed and were left upon the field. The regiments which suffered the most were the 121st in Krüdener's Corps, and the 126th in Shakofskoi's. These two regiments had led the assaults; the latter lost 725 killed! besides some 1200 or more wounded—a total loss of about 75 per cent. of its strength.

The Turkish loss, as usual, is not accurately known, but it was estimated at between 5000 and 6000 men.

On receiving the news of this defeat, the Grand Duke hastened from Tirnova to Karagatch, and on the 2nd of July inspected the troops in the positions which they occupied from Tristenik to Poradim; they were in good spirits notwithstanding their recent rough handling. The trait which more than any other distinguishes the Russian soldier is his steadiness and solidity; he never has taken a panic, and, though he was terribly defeated, there was none now. Some of the wounded carried exaggerated tales to Sistova, and a grand stampede took place among the inhabitants and camp-followers on both sides of the bridge. But there was nothing of this kind among the troops. Had Osman followed them, he would probably have met a very stubborn opposition; the positions about Tristenik and Poradim are favourable to the defence, and the 16th Division, which had just crossed the Danube, was within one day's march, besides the rest of the XI. Corps, which might have been brought from Tirnova (three days' march) if necessary. It would appear at first sight as if Osman made a great mistake in not pursuing the force which he had so signally defeated, especially as he probably had a considerable force of fresh troops which had not been engaged at all, and as the Russians had retreated in two columns on divergent country roads totally independent of each other, leaving the great high road midway between them perfectly open. Yet it is a fact that every offensive movement of the Turks throughout the war came to naught, and it is more than probable that Osman did exactly the wisest thing; he felt sure that the Russians would come at him again as soon as they got a few more men together, and he therefore kept his troops on their own ground, and set them to work as hard as they could with their spades.

The failure of the Russians on this day gave rise to much hard feeling and recrimination. Shakofskoi complained that Krüdener had not supported him, while Krüdener complained that Shakofskoi had not obeyed his orders, which were to advance to the hill midway between Radischevo and Grivitza, and due east of Plevna, and open fire with his artillery, but not to assault without further orders. Krüdener was the senior officer present, but Shakofskoi was also a Corps Commander, though he had only one brigade of his Corps with him. Finally, the Grand Duke had given orders from a distance to attack a position of which he knew nothing, and against a partial remonstrance of the General (Krüdener) in local command.

It is none of our business to follow these controversies or try to fix the responsibility of the failure. It is enough for us foreigners to notice the plain facts:

1. That a strongly fortified position was attacked by an inferior force.

2. That the attack was made by two columns not in supporting distance, but wholly independent of each other.

3. That against the Grivitza Redoubt the regiments were sent to the assault one after the other, not at the critical moment when the regiment already engaged was beginning to waver, but after it had been wholly driven back.

4. That the tactical formation of two lines of company columns was maintained long after the troops came under fire. This close formation partially accounts for the great losses, about 25 per cent. of all the troops on the field.

The redeeming feature of the day was Skobeleff's brilliant manœuvres with a handful of troops on the left flank, whereby he saved Shakofskoi from being knocked to pieces.

CHAPTER IV

GENERAL CONDITION OF AFFAIRS AT THE BEGINNING OF AUGUST.—BATTLE OF SHIPKA PASS, AUGUST 21ST TO 26TH.—OPERATIONS ON THE LOM IN AUGUST AND SEPTEMBER.

THE decisive defeat at Plevna on the 30th of July brought the Russian advance to a standstill. The positions of the opposing armies at that time were as follows: The Russians occupied a figure nearly elliptical in shape, and extending from Nikopolis, through Poradim, Selvi, Gabrova, Shipka, Elena, Cesarevo, Katselevo, and the line of the Lom, to the Danube near Rustchuk; from Sistova to the Shipka Pass, *i.e.*, along the major axis of the ellipse, the distance, following the high road through Tirnova, is about 80 miles; from Poradim to Katselevo, the minor axis, the distance is about 90 miles by the road. The six Corps (IV., VIII., IX., XI., XII., and XIII.) occupying this space had lost about 15,000 men in killed and wounded since the beginning of the campaign. Their total strength was therefore probably about 120,000 infantry, 12,000 cavalry, and 648 guns of all kinds. There was also Zimmermann's detachment off in the Dobrudja, numbering about 25,000 men (XIV. and part of VII. Corps), but this was necessarily limited to the defensive *rôle* of covering the communications of the army from any attack from the Dobrudja, and it could not be of any assistance to an offensive movement.

The Turks were on the exterior of this ellipse, and occupied in force three points (Plevna, Yeni-Zagra, and Rasgrad) situated nearly at the angles of an equilateral triangle whose sides are from 70 to 90 miles long. Osman commanded at Plevna with 50,000 men, Suleiman at Yeni-

Zagra with 40,000, Mehemet Ali at Rasgrad with 65,000. They also had strong detachments at Lovtcha and at Osman Bazar, as well as in the Quadrilateral fortresses. Their total force in the field numbered about 195,000 men of all arms.

Two feasible plans were therefore open to the Russian Commander-in-Chief:

1. To leave small detachments at Shipka and on the Tirnova-Shumla and Biela-Rasgrad roads, and then transfer the VIII., XI., and XIII. Corps with the utmost rapidity to Plevna, and unite them with the IV. and IX. Corps already there, and overwhelm Osman; then move his army rapidly to Tirnova or Biela, according to the movements of the Turks meantime, and attack the other Turkish detachment; the united Russian army was larger than any one of the widely scattered detachments around it, and it had the advantage of short interior lines; or

2. To leave the troops on the defensive in their present positions, and quietly await the arrival of reinforcements from Russia.

All idea of carrying on the original plan of campaign with the troops actually in hand was out of the question; for the two wings posted to cover the flanks—IV. and IX. Corps on the line of the Vid, XII., XIII., and XI. Corps on the Lom —had each an enemy numerically superior in their fronts, and there was nothing left to cross the Balkans with except the VIII. Corps, which was obviously not sufficient in strength. Moreover, the right flank was, properly speaking, not covered at all; for the two most important points along that line, Plevna and Lovtcha, were in the hands of the Turks and strongly occupied. The terrible error of underestimating the enemy and beginning the war with an inadequate force was apparent to every one, and was freely acknowledged. The singular part of it is, that the same mistake was committed in 1828, and again in 1829.

To the first plan, independently of its military difficulties, requiring most active leadership and prompt movements, and resulting if unsuccessful in a retreat across the Danube, there were also the gravest political objections. It was a

RELATIVE POSITIONS OF RUSSIAN & TURKISH ARMIES AUGUST 5TH 1877

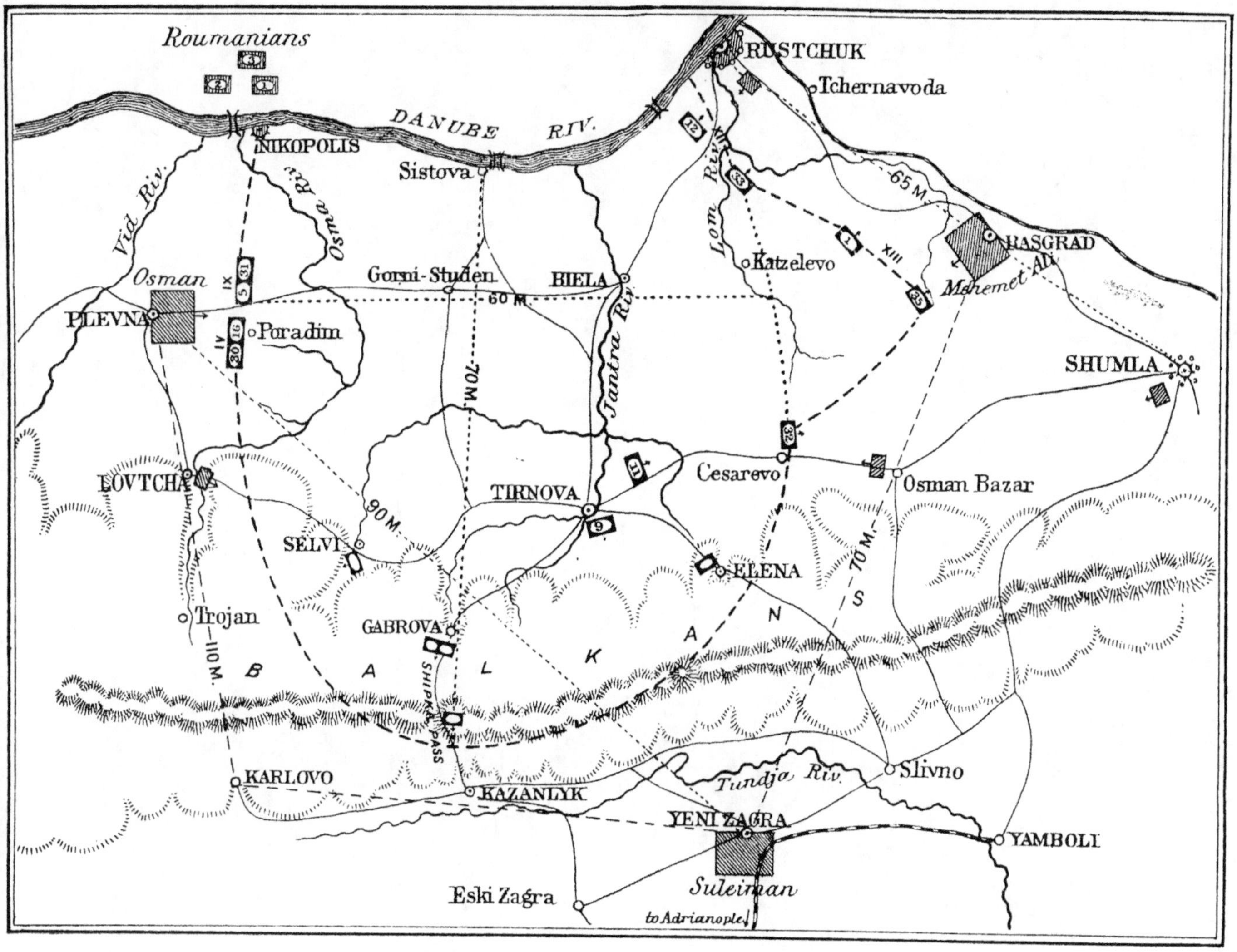

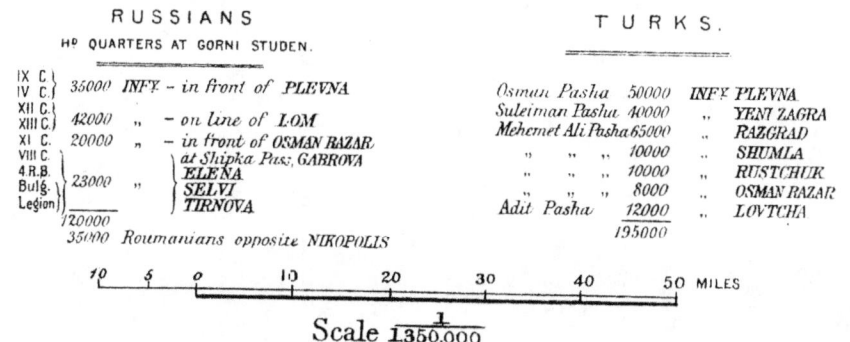

RUSSIANS

HD QUARTERS AT GORNI STUDEN.

IX C. / IV C.	35000	INFY.	– in front of PLEVNA
XII C. / XIII C.	42000	,,	– on line of LOM
XI C.	20000	,,	– in front of OSMAN BAZAR
VIII C. / 4 R.B. / Bulg. Legion	23000	,,	at Shipka Pass, GABROVA / ELENA / SELVI / TIRNOVA
	120000		
	35000	Roumanians opposite NIKOPOLIS	

TURKS.

Osman Pasha	50000	INFY.	PLEVNA
Suleiman Pasha	40000	,,	YENI ZAGRA
Mehemet Ali Pasha	65000	,,	RAZGRAD
,, ,, ,,	10000	,,	SHUMLA
,, ,, ,,	10000	,,	RUSTCHUK
,, ,, ,,	8000	,,	OSMAN BAZAR
Adit Pasha	12000	,,	LOVTCHA
	195000		

10 5 0 10 20 30 40 50 MILES

Scale $\frac{1}{1350.000}$

war which brought out the long pent-up hatreds engendered by difference of race, irreconcilable religions, and centuries of oppression and misrule on one side and suffering on the other. The two classes of the population fled in turn before the approach of the opposing armies, the Mohammedans before the Russians, the Bulgarians before the Turks. Suleiman Pasha had already burned the large town of Eski-Zagra to the ground, and had begun in the valley of the Maritza a wholesale system of hanging at the street corners every Bulgarian who had assisted (as guide, &c.) Gourko's troops during their stay south of the Balkans. As a result the Bulgarians, to the number of nearly 100,000 souls, were fleeing north over the Balkans. If the Russians now withdrew from any of the territory they had occupied, they left the Christian population to the chance of being massacred. In a war undertaken for their liberation, this was not to be thought of.

The second plan was therefore decided upon, and on the 3rd of August the Emperor signed the order for the mobilisation of the Guard, the Grenadiers, and two divisions of the Line (24th and 26th). Two other divisions of the Line (2nd and 3rd) had been ordered to mobilise just after the outbreak of the war. The strength of these troops was as follows:

	Battalions.	Squadrons.	Foot Guns.	Horse Guns.
Corps of the Guard	53	24	148	12
2nd and 3rd Divisions of Grenadiers	24	—	96	—
2nd Division of the Line	12	—	48	—
3rd " " "	12	—	48	—
24th " " "	12	—	48	—
26th " " "	12	—	48	—
1st Cavalry Division	—	18	—	12
Total	125	42	436	24

or in all about 120,000 men and 460 guns.

In addition to this, the Emperor had a few days previously (July 22nd) issued a ukase calling out a portion of the first ban of the Militia—188,000 men—to replace the losses already incurred in battle, and to be ready to replace those of the future. Of the Reserve, three Divisions (36,000 men) were ordered to be mobilised in addition to one division which had been previously mobilised; part of these were destined for garrison duty at home, and part to replace the regular troops on the line of the *étapes* in Russia and Roumania.

The effect of these measures was to call out 120,000 men for service at the front, and 220,000 more to replace losses and do ordinary duty. They arrived on the Danube as follows: the 2nd and 3rd Divisions in August, the Guard and the 26th Division in September, the Grenadiers and the 24th Division in October. The 188,000 men of the Militia began to arrive in August, and continued arriving till long after the peace of San Stefano; they came as squads of recruits destined to this or that regiment, and were immediately incorporated with it.

But as only a small portion of all these troops would be available in the course of the next few weeks, an appeal was made to the Prince of Roumania to put his army into the field, to which he promptly responded. The Roumanian Army consisted of 32,000 Infantry, 5000 Cavalry, and 84 guns, organised into 4 Divisions. They had all been mobilised and ready for active service since the month of May; a portion of the 4th Division had already crossed the Danube and gone into garrison at Nikopolis. Orders were immediately given for the passage of the remainder.

Such were the measures taken by the Russians for carrying on the struggle, and until the arrival of at least a portion of these reinforcements they were restricted to a simply defensive *rôle* in the positions which they had already gained.

This was the moment therefore for the Turks to strike a vigorous blow. Mehemet Ali had arrived at Shumla on the 22nd of July, and relieved the aged Pasha, Abdul Kerim, of the command of the Army of the Lom and the troops in the fortresses. Suleiman, after driving Gourko back into the Balkans, August 1st, had quietly encamped near Yeni-Zagra for the next 15 days. On his movements depended in a large degree the success of the Turkish offensive, and it is not too much to say that he adopted the very worst plan possible under the circumstances. There was no Turkish Commander-in-Chief at this time, the three Commanders, Mehemet Ali, Suleiman, and Osman, being independent of each other and equal in rank; and they were all directed by telegraph from Constantinople, where a " War Council " was in constant session giving orders in the Sultan's name—as bad a system as could possibly be conceived.

Suleiman had the option of joining his army to either one of the other two (a ten-days march), and then striking a vigorous blow at the Russian flank and their communications by the Sistova bridge; or of trying to force his way over the Balkan passes directly in his front. The road to Plevna by the Trojan Pass was not a good one, and it led rather dangerously near the Russian positions at Selvi; moreover, even supposing they gained a victory at Plevna, the Turks could not advance against Sistova without recapturing the fortress of Nikopolis. On the other hand, the road toward Shumla led over the Slivno-Shumla Pass, which is one of the best high roads over the Balkans, and was nowhere nearer than 30 miles to any of the Russian positions. By taking the garrisons of Shumla and Varna, the united forces of Mehemet Ali and Suleiman would have been more than 125,000 men. By throwing these upon the Russian left wing, they would have compelled the Russians to let go their hold of Shipka in order to get together even 90,000 men (VIII., XI., XII., and XIII. Corps) to resist them ; and if they beat the Russians in a decisive battle, there was nothing to prevent their reaching the Sistova Bridge, while if they were beaten they simply fell back upon the fortresses. Such was the plan which it is said Mehemet Ali urged, but Suleiman was determined to attack the Shipka Pass directly in front, and he was sustained by the War Council.

Suleiman moved forward on the 16th, and began his attack on Shipka on the 21st of August, and kept it up with more or less energy for the next four months. Without gaining the least material advantage in so doing, he sacrificed the best part of the fine army he brought with him from Montenegro.

Osman, on the 31st of August, made a lame attempt at the offensive in front of Plevna, but it resulted in nothing; and ten days later (September 11th) he was attacked by the Russians—the third and principal battle of Plevna, unsuccessful like its predecessors, but eventually followed by the investment of Osman's army and its ultimate surrender.

Mehemet Ali, after some preliminary skirmishing, began his attack on the Cesarevitch's army (Russian left wing) on the 30th of August, and drove it back from the Lom to the Yantra. Then he suddenly stopped, and a few days later, toward the end of September, returned to his old positions.

Such in brief was the result of the Turkish offensive. We will now follow these movements somewhat in detail.

SULEIMAN PASHA'S ATTACK ON SHIPKA PASS
AUGUST 20th–26th.

In the vicinity of Shipka the peaks of the Balkans are nearly 5000 feet above sea-level. The valley of the Tundja, which is parallel to the chain and only a few miles from it on the south, has an altitude of about 1300 feet; on the north the head waters of the Yantra near Gabrova are at about the same altitude. Near Shipka the chain throws out three long and nearly parallel spurs to the north, and these spurs, although shorter, are also distinguishable on the south; they are separated by deep wooded ravines, and are only united at the top by saddles in the main range of the mountains. The central one of these we may call the Shipka ridge, the easterly one the Berdek, the westerly the Bald Mountain ridge. It is a misnomer to speak of the Shipka Pass as a pass in the ordinary meaning of the word; for the road does not pass through a gorge or ravine between high peaks, but, on the contrary, it follows the whole length of the central spur and passes over its highest point. From Gabrova the road follows a small stream for about 5 miles to the south and then takes a sudden turn to the east, and in the course of a mile of very steep ascent climbs on to the ridge; it then follows the gradual slope of the ridge for about 3 miles to Mount St. Nicholas, the highest point; from here the road descends rapidly in steep zigzags to the village of Shipka. Near the summit of the central or Shipka spur are three sets of little hills or ridges about 200 feet high, running across the main ridge; the highest and most southerly of these is called Mount St. Nicholas, and for convenience we will call the other two the "Central" and "Northern" hills. The highest points of the western and eastern spurs are known respectively as the Berdek and the Bald Mountain. They dominate the whole position, and are reached by narrow paths along the mountain. The Russian position was on the three sets of little hills just mentioned. On St. Nicholas, the southern side of which is in part a perpendicular rock, the Russians had three batteries, which had originally been built by the Turks for the defence of the pass from the north, and which now, with slight alteration, served the same purpose in an opposite direction; in these the Russians had 25 guns. On the left and rear of St. Nicholas (*i.e.*, to the north-east of it) runs a little spur about 250 yards long, at the end of which the Russians had 7 steel guns, previously captured from the Turks. Connecting this steel battery with Mount St. Nicholas were some trenches hastily thrown up in the rocky soil. On the central hill were the "central" battery and "round" battery, each armed with 4 guns, and some rude trenches.

On the 15th of August the Russian troops in this neighbourhood consisted of 34 battalions, or about 27,000 men, with their proportionate artillery and a small force of cavalry, and were posted as follows:

At Tirnova, Headquarters of VIII. Corps and of 14th Division, 55th and 56th Regiments and 4th Rifle Brigade, and 40 guns;

At Selvi, Headquarters 9th Division, 35th, 53rd, and 54th Regiments, 3 sotnias of Cossacks, and 24 guns;

In Shipka Pass, 36th Regiment, 5 battalions of Bulgarian Legion, 5 sotnias of Cossacks, and 29 guns;

In Travna Pass, 1 battalion Bulgarian Legion;

In Hainkioi Pass, 33rd Regiment, 2 sotnias, and 14 guns;

In Elena Pass, 34th Regiment, 13th Dragoons, and 2 guns.

Tirnova and Selvi are each two days' march from Shipka.

On the 16th of August Suleiman's troops first made their appearance by a demonstration against the Hainkioi Pass, and on the 18th a detachment occupied Bebrova, on the Elena road, at the same time that the head of the main column appeared at Kazanlyk. General Radetzky, commanding the VIII. Corps, immediately ordered the 35th Regiment to proceed in all haste to Shipka, but he was sufficiently deceived by this demonstration against the Elena Pass to proceed thither in person with the 4th Rifle Brigade and the 55th and 56th Regiments. Finding no enemy in force, he returned to Tirnova on the 21st, and there received word from Shipka that the Turks had attacked in great force. In spite of their fatigue, he started the 4th Rifle Brigade and the 55th and 56th Regiments towards Shipka at daylight the next morning, and also telegraphed to the 2nd Division (which had just arrived and was in bivouac between Gorni-Studen and Selvi) to proceed to Selvi and relieve the 53rd and 54th Regiments, which were then to proceed to Shipka. In other words, all available troops were ordered to Shipka except the two regiments guarding the Hainkioi and Elena Passes. Radetzky himself arrived on the field in the afternoon of August 23rd.

Meanwhile Gen. Darozhinsky, who commanded the little force of about 5000 men at Shipka Pass, and who, on account of the difficulty of procuring water on the mountain, had kept his men in bivouac in the village of Shipka, noticed the approach of the Turks on the 18th, retired to the pass on the 19th, and on the 20th saw the whole force of Suleiman deploy in the plain just below him, and counted 40 battalions, probably 26,000 to 28,000 men, besides a large number of Tcherkesses. He immediately disposed his little force as follows: 1 battalion behind St. Nicholas and the

"Steel" battery; 1½ battalion of Russians and 3 of Bulgarians along the Central Hill; and 1½ battalion of Russians and 2 of Bulgarians, as a reserve, on the "isthmus," between the Central and St. Nicholas Hills.

On the morning of the 21st the Turks were visible on the Berdek Mountains, constructing a battery about 2000 yards from St. Nicholas. In spite of the Russian shells, they finished the construction of it and placed 4 guns in position. After one or two minor attacks, the Turks moved forward about noon from the Sugar-Loaf Hill, and began an assault with 20 battalions against the "Steel" battery, on the left flank of Mount St. Nicholas. They attacked with the utmost desperation, but were as desperately received, and the struggle went on from a little after noon till 8 o'clock at night. Again and again the Turks came on yelling "Allah," and rushed up the slope to within a few yards of the battery; but they could go no farther. Their last attack was made by moonlight about 9 P.M., and being repulsed they tried no more for that day; but they remained in the positions they had taken—the most advanced of which was not over 100 yards from the Russian battery—and kept up a constant fire throughout the night.

During the day the 35th Regiment had arrived from Selvi and taken position behind the "Round" battery.

The next morning, 22nd, the Turks opened a very heavy fire from Berdek, where they now had 10 guns in position; from the Bald Mountain on the opposite flank, whither they had dragged during the night 6 guns; and from the "Woody Mountain," where they had also placed 2 guns. In short, their batteries were in front, on both flanks, and in the rear of the Russian position; only by reason of intervening woods the battery at Woody Mountain could not reach St. Nicholas, but it completely commanded the "Central" and "Northern" Hills.

Throughout this day (August 22nd) a continuous fire of artillery and infantry was kept up, but the Turks made no serious attacks; a few guns were dismounted on both sides, but a far more serious danger was threatening the Russians in the lack of artillery ammunition, which was nearly exhausted. Both parties worked all day at repairing their batteries, and the Turks at covering their advanced positions by shelter-trenches. Meanwhile the Turks were withdrawing a portion of their troops in reserve behind Berdek and sending them over to the western spur (Woody Mountain) with the intention of attacking the right flank of the Russians at the Central Hill (held by the 35th Regiment), and thus cutting off their communications with Gabrova. At the same time a body of Tcherkesses descended the eastern spur and threatened the high road from that side.

On the morning of the 23rd, in fact, the Russian position was well-nigh surrounded on all sides; the narrow ridges, along which ran the high road, connecting the little hills which formed the Russian position, were wholly exposed to a cross-fire of the Turks at 1500 to 2000 yards' range.

At 6 o'clock in the morning Suleiman began his attack, and it soon became general from all sides, one column rushing at the rocks on the south of St. Nicholas, another against the right flank of the Central Hill (where the Russians faced west), and a third against the round battery on the left flank of this hill (where they faced east). A most desperate struggle continued throughout this whole day, 7500 Russians being engaged to the last man, and trying to hold their own against the 25,000 Turks who came to their assault. During the afternoon the position of the Russians became most critical; their artillery ammunition was exhausted; their losses were enormous, and the men began to lose courage under the demoralising effect of a cross-fire so long continued, and of the heat and lack of food and water.

About the same time the Turkish column from Woody Mountain reformed and began advancing along the northern slope of the Central Hill, and in rear of it, toward the high road. There were no reserves left on the Russian side to meet this column. The portion of the 35th Regiment which held the right flank of the Central Hill, having lost nearly all its officers, was broken into little groups, and toward 3 o'clock these groups began to pick up the last of the wounded, turn back to the road behind them, and move off to the rear. The number of wounded going back toward the field hospital was so great that these men, having no officers, thought it was a general retreat. The moment was the most critical of the campaign; if this Turkish column reached the high road and established itself on the Northern Hill, on the rear of the Russians and upon their one line of communication, a disastrous retreat before a largely superior force, or possibly a surrender, was inevitable. Taking a few non-commissioned officers, Colonel Lipinsky, commanding this part of the field, went back to the road, expostulated, reasoned, threatened, and drove these men back to the positions on the Centre Hill. From here they delivered their fire in volleys upon the Turks in their rear, who were just beginning to climb the slope toward the road. Stunned by this sudden reception, the Turks wavered a little; and at this very moment (about 4.30 P.M.) appeared in sight the first of the reinforcements—200 men of the 4th Rifle Brigade, trotting up along the high road on Cossack horses taken at Gabrova—and with them General Radetzky, commanding the VIII. Corps. The 16th Battalion of this Rifle Brigade came into position on the Northern Hill, and went down the hill at a run against the left flank of this Turkish column. The attack was so bold and spirited that the Turks fell back through the wood, and up on the Woody Mountain, leaving the Russians in possession of their first line of trenches at the foot of the slope. The little valley was filled with the dead of the twelve hours' struggle which had been going on at this point.

Meanwhile, throughout the day, the Russians at St. Nicholas and the "Central Hills" held on to their positions, though at the cost of terrible losses.

During the afternoon and evening the rest of the 4th Rifle Brigade arrived, and was posted along the whole line, partly relieving the men in St. Nicholas, whose physical strength was well-nigh exhausted.

At 5 o'clock on the morning of the 24th arrived General Dragomiroff with the leading regiment (No. 56) of his Division, having marched 38 miles the previous day. One battalion was sent across the ravine to climb the western spur and attack the Bald Mountain position in flank; the other two were moved along the road in reserve of the other troops. While posting his men on the Northern Hill General Dragomiroff was severely wounded in the knee about 10 A.M., and carried off the field, one of his staff officers being also wounded at the same time. A general cannonade and fusillade had been begun by the Turks at sunrise, and was in fact kept up all day, upon every one passing along the road; but it was not until noon that the Turks renewed the attack.

Noticing the arrival of Russian reinforcements, Suleiman now made a last desperate effort to get possession of Mount St. Nicholas. This time the Turks, at least those in the lead, actually got into the Russian trenches on the top of the hill, and were only driven out after a hand-to-hand struggle, in which the bayonet was very freely used. In this affair the leading Turkish battalion (about 500 men) was virtually annihilated. This was the last of the Turkish assaults.

During the day the rest of the regiments of Dragomiroff's Division continued arriving, and on the 25th Radetzky made an effort to get possession of the Woody Mountain, which commanded all the approaches to his own position; but he sent totally inadequate forces to make the attempt. They consisted of the one battalion (56th Regiment) which Dragomiroff had sent across the ravine the previous morning, and of the three battalions which held the right of the Central Hill. The former did not get across the deep wooded ravine and up the Bald Mountain spur till nearly noon on the 25th.

Hearing them engaged, Radetzky then sent the other three battalions against the right of the position—*i.e.*, against Woody Mountain. The Turks were driven out of their advanced trenches during the afternoon, and were followed in hot pursuit by the Russians, who arrived somewhat disorganised at the second line of works on top of the Woody Mountain. Here they met fresh troops of the Turkish reserves, and were in turn driven back. Two battalions of the 53rd Regiment were sent to assist them, and a very hot fight went on during the evening and most of the night. But Radetzky did not consider his main force strong enough to detach any more men to reinforce them, and consequently on the morning of the 26th they retreated down the slope and back again to the Central Hill. The Turks followed them as far as their most advanced trenches, but no farther.

Thus ended the first period of this remarkable battle. Desultory firing of both artillery and infantry continued, but no more assaults were made until the 17th of September. After five days of almost uninterrupted fighting, both sides were now substantially where they were at the beginning. Radetzky's report puts his losses at about 100 officers and 3500 men. That of the Turks was estimated at about 10,000 men; but a British naval officer, who was present with the Turks as correspondent of the *Times*, states that they had 8350 wounded and between 3000 and 4000 dead.

For three days (August 21st, 22nd, and 23rd) less than 8000 Russians and Bulgarians had held in check the Army of Suleiman, 25,000 to 30,000 strong. During this time their only food was the biscuit (about one day's ration) which they had in their pockets when the affair began; the heat was intense, but the nearest water was at a spring between three and four miles back on the road toward Gabrova, and all that the men had to drink was the little which was brought back in their canteens by the men who carried the wounded to the rear. Whenever the firing ceased for a while, they lay down on the ground they were defending and caught an hour's sleep; for it was the period of full moon, and night brought no cessation to the firing. It was not only during the assaults of the Turks that the men were under fire—it was at all times, dependent only on the pleasure of the Turks; for from behind the woods on the two spurs on either side the *Turks commanded every point of the Russian position*, excepting only a small portion of the reverse slope of the Northern Hill; and even here General Darozhinsky was shot dead on the morning of the 25th by some Turkish pickets in advance of Bald Mountain. The odour of decomposing corpses was sickening and the sight of them demoralising.

On the afternoon of the 23rd the men had just about

reached the final limit of human endurance. Then the reinforcements began to arrive, allowing the men to be relieved and have a little rest; the soup kitchens were established back near the spring, and the Bulgarian peasants were impressed at Gabrova and put to carrying water and food up to the men.

For impetuous assaults and tenacious, dogged defence, for long-continued fighting and physical endurance, this five days' battle in the mountains is extremely remarkable; but there were no skilful manœuvres of the troops on either side. Although Suleiman took possession of heights flanking and nearly surrounding the Russians, yet he persisted in dividing his forces and making his strongest attacks upon their strongest position (Mount St. Nicholas), thereby enabling them, although far inferior in numbers, to hold their ground at all points for three days until the arrival of reinforcements. Had Suleiman thrown the whole of his force into either one of his flank attacks, he would in all probability have carried the whole place. On the other hand, the Russians, during the ten days between the time the Bulgarians were driven out of Eski-Zagra and the appearance of the Turks at Kazanlyk, had remained idly at the village of Shipka, and done nothing toward strengthening their position in the pass, except to modify the original Turkish fortifications so as to turn them against the south instead of the north. The Russians, in fact, felt quite confident that Suleiman would either go through Slivno to Osman-Bazar, or else through the Elena Pass to attack Tirnova. This was a most natural supposition, but it hardly justified the Russians in failing to do their utmost to make the Shipka Pass impregnable. The little force of 5000 men was not sufficient to occupy the heights on all three of the main spurs, but they might easily have made strong lines of trenches on each of the little hills on the top of the road, and been prepared to make a good defence; whereas, on the third day of the fighting (August 23rd) the men on the Northern Hill were firing from behind rocks and piles of blankets; there was a sad deficiency of spades and other implements actually with the troops; and there were no

BATTLE OF SHIPKA PASS

engineer troops anywhere in that vicinity of the theatre of war.

Radetzky's attack on Woody Mountain (August 25th) was a very lame affair. Either he should not have made it at all, or else he should have sent more than 4 battalions to do it. He had on that morning, owing to the arrival of reinforcements, 24 battalions, viz., the 35th, 36th, 53rd, 54th, and 56th Regiments, 4th Rifle Brigade, and the Bulgarian Legion; and the 55th Regiment was expected to arrive during the day. If the possession of Woody and Bald Mountains was of great importance (and it would seem that it was so, since it commanded for a long distance the only road over which his ammunition, food, water, and reinforcements could arrive), then he might have risked holding the main position with 14 battalions, since it had been held for three days by 11 battalions, and have sent the remaining 10 to take the hill at any cost. The result of sending 4 battalions was that they were badly defeated and lost over one-third of their strength.

Suleiman had, however, exhausted his strength, and was obliged to stop and reorganise his shattered army and bring up the few battalions which he had left at Yeni-Zagra. His troops remained in their position on the two commanding spurs, and picked off the passing Russians on the high-road to the number of 40 or 50 a day. The latter dug trenches along the road to form a covered way, but still they were more or less exposed in passing.

On the 28th of August the brigade of the XI. Corps (1st Brigade 32d Division), which had fought under Shakofskoi at Plevna on July 30th, and which had subsequently been sent to Selvi, arrived at Gabrova; one regiment of it remained there, and the other was sent to Zelenodrevo, at the foot of the western spur, to prevent a descent of the Turks along the Bald Mountain ridge toward Gabrova. One brigade of the 2d Division was also sent over to Gabrova about August 28th; but, as the Turks failed to renew their attacks, it was a few days later sent back to Selvi, and thence it took part in the battles of Lovtcha and Plevna.

MEHEMET ALI'S ADVANCE ON THE LINE OF THE LOM, AUGUST 22ND TO SEPTEMBER 30TH

According to the general plan of campaign, as previously explained, immediately after the passage of the Danube the XII. and XIII. Corps were formed into a detachment under command of the Cesarevitch, and posted along the line of the Lom, to cover the left flank of the army from any attacks from the fortresses of the Quadrilateral. The XII. Corps advanced along the Biela-Rustchuk high-road as far as the Lom, and its cavalry penetrated in a reconnaissance (July 21st) as far as the station of Tchernavoda, on the Rustchuk-Varna Railroad, and destroyed a small portion of the track and telegraph there. The XIII. Corps deployed on its right in the direction of Razgrad, and on the 26th of July its scouts were within eight miles of that town. The XI. Corps meanwhile (except the brigade which was sent to Plevna for the attack of July 30th), after crossing the Danube, had been marched to Tirnova, and thence deployed westward along the high-road to Osman-Bazar and Shumla.

In the country between Osman-Bazar and Eski-Djuma are several foot-hills or spurs of the Balkans, which drain toward the Danube by means of the Yantra and Lom Rivers. The affluents of the former flow westward and reach the Yantra not far from Tirnova, and thence the river goes due north past Biela to the Danube. The head waters of the Lom are spread over a wide extent of country; on the east and west respectively of Rasgrad are the Lom and the White Lom; farther west are the Black Lom and Banitchka Lom; the two latter unite at a point about 20 miles southeast of Biela, and a few miles farther on they join the White Lom, and the united river then runs for about 12 miles more and empties into the Danube at Rustchuk.

There are high-roads leading from Rustchuk through Biela to Tirnova, from Rustchuk through Razgrad to Shumla, from Tirnova through Osman-Bazar to Shumla, and from Razgrad through Eski-Djuma to Osman-Bazar, and thence to Slivno. But in the basin of the Lom there are no high-roads; the country is very high and undulating, and the branches of the Lom flow through deep rocky gorges, in the vicinity of which are extensive tracts covered with a short scrub oak; the means of communication are few and widely separated, and it is generally a difficult country for military operations.

On the 15th of August the Cesarevitch's detachment of two corps, numbering in all about 40,000 infantry, 5000 cavalry, and 200 guns, was scattered over a length of more than 50 miles behind the White Lom, his left flank bein at the village of Pirgos on the Danube and his right facing Eski-Djuma.

The position of his troops was as follows:

XII. Corps	12th Division	One brigade at Pirgos; One brigade at Damogila; Picket line from the Danube in front of Rustchuk, along the Lom and Black Lom, to Tabashka.
	33rd Division	At Katzelevo and Ablava.
	12th Cavalry Division	Along the White Lom, in advance of Katzelevo.
XIII. Corps	1st Division	At Banitchka, forming the general reserve to the whole line.
	35th Division	One brigade at Karahassankoi; One brigade at Ayazlar.
	13th Cavalry Division	At Sarnasuftar.

The XI. Corps was established with the 11th Division on the Osman-Bazar road at Cesarevo, and one brigade (2nd Brigade 32nd Division) in the direction of the Elena pass. The Cesarevitch's right flank was somewhat in the air, as there was a wide gap (about 20 miles) between the extreme right flank at Ayazlar and the left of the XI. Corps on the Tirnova-Osman-Bazar road.

Mehemet Ali, having taken command of the troops in the Quadrilateral and reconnoitered the ground, concentrated the greater part of his mobile force (independent of the fortress garrisons) in two columns—at Razgrad and Eski-Djuma. He had in the field about 50,000 infantry, 60 guns, and several regiments of regular cavalry, besides a few thousand bashi-bazouks.* Four divisions were at Razgrad, and one Turkish division and the Egyptian Contingent, about equal to a division, at Eski-Djuma. Taking advantage of the scattered condition of the Russian force, he planned

* In "Der Orientalische Krieg," by Rüstow, pp. 332 and 333, it is stated as follows : "The field army, which now at the end of August Mehemet Ali actually had at his disposition, consisted of the 3rd and 4th Army Corps. The 2nd Army Corps, commanded by Achmet Kaiserli in place of Eshreff Pasha, who had been relieved, formed the garrison of Rustchuk, and could not be available for operations in the open field so long as the XII. Russian Corps remained immediately in front of that fortress.

"The two field army corps had, after the reorganisation effected by Mehemet Ali, the following effective strength :

   3rd Army Corps, Achmed Eyoub Pasha. Headquarters, Razgrad.
      1st Division, Fuad Pasha, Brigades Hussein and Mustapha—16 Battalions, 6 Squadrons, 4 Batteries.
      2nd Division, Asof Pasha, Brigades Osman and Mehmed—16 Battalions, 6 Squadrons, 4 Batteries.
      3rd Division, Nedjib Pasha, Brigades Ali and Hami—16 Battalions, 6 Squadrons, 4 Batteries.
      Unattached Brigade, Hassan Pasha—6 Battalions, 1 Battery.
      Flying Column, Mehmed Bey—3 Battalions Zeibeks, 6 Squadrons, one half Battery.
      Cavalry Brigade, Emir Pasha—18 Squadrons, one half Horse Battery, 2000 Tcherkesses.
      Total, 57 Battalions, 42 Squadrons, 2000 mounted Tcherkesses, 14 Batteries.
   4th Army Corps, Prince Hassan. Headquarters, Eski-Djuma.
      1st Division, Ismail Pasha—14 Battalions (including 9 Battalions of Egyptians and 2 Battalions of Riflemen) and 4 Batteries in Brigades Safvet and Reshid.
      2nd Division, Salih Pasha, Brigades Sabis and Assim—18 Battalions, 6 Squadrons, and 4 Batteries.
      3rd Division, Mehmed Salim Pasha, Brigades Salim and Hassan—16 Battalions, 6 Squadrons, and 3 Batteries.
      Reserve Division, Tahir Pasha, Brigades Tahir and Mehmed—15 Battalions and 3 Batteries.
      Flying Corps, Baker Pasha—3 Battalions, 1000 mounted Tcherkesses, one half Battery.
      Flying Corps, Ibrahim and Mustapha Beys—2 Batteries of Zeibeks, 8 Squadrons mounted Tcherkesses.
      Total, 68 Battalions, 12 Squadrons, 2000 mounted Tcherkesses, 14½ Batteries.

"The whole field arms of Mehemet Ali, according to the foregoing statement, amounted to 125 Battalions, 54 regular squadrons, 4000 mounted Tcherkesses, and 28½ batteries. Had the organisations been at their regulation strength, the battalion at 800 men, and the regular squadron at 150 troopers, then Mehemet Ali would have had 100,000 infantry, and, including the Tcherkesses, to strike a hard blow on their right flank and then on their centre, and drive them back to the Yantra. Further than that his plans do not seem to have been matured.

The movement was begun on the 22nd of August by Sahli Pasha's division, which advanced from Eski-Djuma and drove the Russians out of Ayazlar. The next day the Russians retóok the position, but were again driven out, and retired in the direction of Popkoi, a few miles to the north. In this affair the Russians lost about 400 men.

The effect of it was to bring the two brigades of the 35th Division a little nearer together, and they stood respectively at Popkoi and Karahassankoi, on opposite sides of the Black Lom and about 8 miles apart. There was a bridge just behind Karahassankoi.

There were no more movements until the 30th. On that date Nedjib Pasha's division was moved out from in front of Razgrad and threw itself upon the left of the 35th Division, thus cutting it off from the rest of the Russian troops. At the same time Sahli's division and the Egyptians were to advance from Sarnasuflar against the right of the 35th Division at Popkoi. The Russians fought hard all day, but were completely outnumbered, and were driven out of Karahassankoi and across the river, and back upon their principal position behind Popkoi. The Russian losses on this day have never been officially published, but were estimated in the Turkish camp to be about 1800 men, against 1000 on the part of the Turks.

Four days more passed in inactivity, and then, on September 3rd, the three divisions at Razgrad under Achmed Eyoub Pasha, and Nedjib's division at Karahassankoi, advanced

12,100 troopers. But even if we take the battalions as averaging only 600 men each, and the regular squadrons 100, there were still more than 85,000 combatants of infantry and cavalry, and 171 guns."

I have never heard of the publication of any official reports on the Turkish side, and do not know from what source the above detailed statement is drawn. It is stated so exactly as to have the air of coming from a trustworthy authority. The artillery is largely superior in numbers to that given by myself in the text, and the number of men is also greater. My own authority is the correspondence of the London *News* and *Times*, dated at Mehemet Ali's headquarters in August and September.

F. V. G.

jointly down the White Lom to Solenik, crossed the White Lom near that point on the 4th, and on the 5th attacked the Russian position at Katzelevo from the direction of the north.

The Russian troops, under the command of Lieutenant-General Baron Driesen, consisted of the 12 battalions of the 33rd Division, with 40 guns, and 8 squadrons and 6 guns of the 12th Cavalry Division, in all about 10,000 men. Five battalions and 8 guns were posted in front of the river on the heights of Katzelevo, and 7 battalions and 32 guns along the plateau behind the village of Ablava, on the left or south bank of the White Lom. The Turkish force numbered about 30,000 men and 60 guns. They posted their artillery in a semicircle of about 7 miles in length in front of the Russian position, and opened fire about 7 A.M. About 10 the Turks began to advance, and, seeing that they were so far superior in numbers, General Arnoldi, commanding the left flank (Katzelevo), withdrew his force in as good order as possible across the Lom, and fell back about five miles to Orendjik. About 11 A.M., 4 battalions and 1 battery of the 1st Division arrived as reinforcements at Ablava, and General Driesen then sent one regiment (No. 130) to cover the retreat of the left flank. The whole of the left flank had been got across the river by 2 P.M. The Turks, who had kept up a hot artillery fire all day, then (about 3 P.M.) began to advance their infantry; they crossed the Lom by fording, occupied the village of Ablava, and then began to attack the heights behind the village, on which the Russians were posted. But in this they were defeated and driven back again across the Lom. The fight ceased about sunset, the Russian loss being 56 officers and 1283 men. Driesen's position, however, was totally untenable, threatened as he was on both flanks by greatly superior forces; and the next day he made good his retreat to the left bank of the Banitchka Lom. The Turks followed slowly.

On the same day it appears it was intended that the left wing of the Turkish force, which under the command of Prince Hassan was at Sarnasuflar, should also attack the

Russians at Popkoi; but for some reason it was not done. The next day (September 6th) the Russians at that place began their retreat to Cerkovna, and thence behind the Banitchka Lom at Koprivca.

On the 1st of September about 5000 men of the garrison of Rustchuk moved out to Kadikioi, and crossed the river there to attack the Russian left flank. They made but little progress, however; but on the 4th they were reinforced by another 5000 men, and then they succeeded in driving the Russians out of their positions along the high-road and back a few miles toward Biela.

By the 8th of September, therefore, 15 days after Mehemet Ali began his advance by the attack at Ayazlar, he had driven the Cesarevitch's detachment back from the line of the White Lom to that of the Banitchka Lom, and had inflicted a loss upon it, in two small battles and several skirmishes, of between 3000 and 4000 men in all. Mehemet Ali had, counting the troops that had sortied from Rustchuk, not less than 60,000 men in hand along the right bank of the Banitchka Lom, viz.: 10,000 on the right flank near Kadikioi, 30,000 under Achmed Eyoub at Katzelevo, and 20,000 under Prince Hassan at Popkoi, where were also his own headquarters. From Kadikioi to Popkoi the distance is about 35 miles.

The Russians, meanwhile, had got their detachment into a more compact shape, and took up a position in front of the Yantra, their left flank being on the Danube at Batin and their right at Koprivca on the Banitchka Lom; their length of front was about 25 miles. They also hastened to fill up the gap between the Cesarevitch's right and the XI. Corps on the Tirnova-Osman-Bazar road, by sending the 26th Division, which had just crossed the Danube, to Cerkovna, and the 1st Brigade 32nd Division from Gabrova to Cairkioi.

Mehemet Ali, then, on the 10th of September, had under his orders an army composed of excellent fighting material and superior in numbers to the enemy in his front; he had already gained several small successes over the enemy, and driven him back for several miles along his whole line.

The question naturally arises, why then did not Mehemet Ali concentrate his whole force and fight a decisive battle about Biela? If successful, there was a fair chance of driving the Russians across the Danube; and if unsuccessful, he had only to retire under shelter of the forts at Rustchuk and Shumla, which now were strong enough to require a regular siege. The only reason which has ever been assigned for the inaction which Mehemet Ali displayed was that his army, though composed of good fighting men, was so badly officered as to greatly diminish its efficiency for offensive purposes; and especially was this incompetence noticeable among the chiefs of regiments and brigades, who desired to conduct their men on their own responsibility, and without subordinating themselves to the general plan of campaign, or even to the orders of the Commander-in-Chief, who on account of his foreign birth never had the confidence of his generals. It appears that Mehemet Ali began his movement simply with the idea of driving the Russians back from the vicinity of Razgrad and Eski-Djuma, which were of the first importance to the Turks, since the capture of the railroad at Razgrad would have enabled the Russians to isolate Rustchuk and invest it with a small force. A general advance formed no part of Mehemet Ali's plan; but having driven the Russians back beyond the Banitchka Lom and arrived himself in the positions explained above on the 7th-10th of September, he then received news of the capture of Lovtcha and the appearance of large bodies of Russian and Roumanian troops in front of Plevna. With the sole object of relieving Osman, whom he believed to be very hard pressed, Mehemet Ali then gave orders for another advance in the direction of Biela, with the hope that the Russians would reinforce the Cesarevitch at the expense of the troops in front of Plevna. His orders for the advance were as follows: Achmed Eyoub's corps to move from Katzelevo and Prince Hassan's corps from Popkoi, and, uniting near Osikova, advance on Biela. Achmed Eyoub was to detach one division under Asof Pasha to cover the right flank in the direction of Sinankoi.

The movement began on the 12th, and on the 14th the

OPERATIONS ON THE LOM

troops were in communication with each other on the line from Sinankoi to Voditza. Some skirmishing occurred on the two flanks near each of these points on that day, but without any definite result. The whole force then came to a halt for a week in order to reconnoitre the enemy's position. On the 21st an attack in force was made upon the Russian position near Cerkovna, with the intention of breaking through between the XI. and XIII. Corps. In this the Turks were completely defeated, with considerable loss, and two days later they began to retreat, not only on their left flank, but along the whole line.

This battle of Cerkovna took place as follows: Lieutenant-General Tatisheff, chief of the 11th Cavalry Division, occupied a position facing northeast on the hills just south of the Yordan brook, having his troops on both sides of a road running from Cerkovna through Cairkoi to Cesarevo and thence to Tirnova. He had 2 regiments (Nos. 125 and 126) of the 32nd Division (XI. Corps), 1 regiment (No. 1) of the 1st Division (XIII. Corps), and 1 regiment (No. 101) of the 26th Division—in all, 12 battalions, or 10,000 infantry, and the 102nd Regiment, on the march from Biela, and only 10 or 12 miles from his left flank. He also had 2 regiments of cavalry (11th Dragoons and 11th Lancers), 5 foot batteries (40 guns), and 1 horse battery (6 guns).

The Turks had 35 battalions—say 20,000 men—of which 20 were Egyptians, and about 50 guns. They were posted on the other side of the Yordan brook, on the heights about Cerkovna. Their plan was to demonstrate against the Russian centre and left and strike hard against their right, which was the weakest part of their line. The battle opened about 11 A.M., as usual by an artillery duel between the opposing heights, which continued for four or five hours without doing much harm, in spite of the fact that, owing to the superior range of the Turkish guns, the Russians could not reach a portion of the Turkish batteries. The Turkish detachment on the right and centre moved forward about 2 P.M.; they advanced rather too far in making their demonstration, and became very hotly engaged around the little village of Verboka in the valley of the brook; and about 4 o'clock the 102nd Regiment arrived, and, striking them in flank, drove the whole line back to Cerkovna in considerable confusion. The turning movement against the Russian right flank was intrusted to the Egyptians, and some idea of the manner in which they executed it may be obtained from the fact that the correspondent of the *Times* with Mehemet Ali states that they lost only 4 men killed and 32 wounded! Their losses were probably larger than that, but the Egyptians certainly fell back the instant the Russians opened fire upon them, and they retreated in great disorder to Cerkovna. The whole affair was over by 5 P.M. It was terribly mismanaged by the Turks; having 35 battalions in hand, the whole fighting was done by the 9 battalions who were on the centre and right. The 9 Egyptian battalions which went to attack the Russian right accomplished nothing; the 6 battalions which were in reserve were not brought into action; 10 or 12 Egyptian battalions never left their bivouacs at Voditza; and at Osikova, only 6 miles north of Cerkovna, was a whole division of Achmed Eyoub's corps which did not move a foot all day to help their comrades.

The Russian losses are given in General Tatisheff's report at 25 officers and 436 men; he also states that 800 dead Turks were buried on the field the next day. The Turks acknowledge a total loss of about 1,600 men.

On the 23rd there was a truce for the purpose of burying the dead, and on the 24th Prince Hassan's troops retreated to Sarnasuflar with such haste that they abandoned a large amount of material on the road. The conduct of his generals at Cerkovna probably convinced Mehemet Ali that the army under his orders was not one to be led against well-disciplined troops intrenched in good positions. On the 25th Achmet Eyoub's corps began falling back (without having given battle) in the direction of Razgrad, and by the 1st of October the whole of the Turkish force was behind the line of the Lom, and the Russian pickets advanced to their old positions.

Mehemet Ali's offensive movement was over, and, as he had lost more men than his enemy and had not diverted a single Russian from either Plevna or Shipka, it can only be considered a complete *fiasco*—though perhaps from causes beyond his control. On the 2nd of October he was relieved from command, and superseded by Suleiman Pasha.

CHAPTER V

OPERATIONS ON THE RIGHT FLANK IN AUGUST AND SEPTEMBER—BATTLES OF LOVTCHA, SEPTEMBER 3RD AND PLEVNA, SEPTEMBER 11TH

ALTHOUGH attacked at Shipka and threatened on the line of the Lom, the principal attention of the Russians during the month of August was directed to assembling a sufficient force to drive the Turks away from their right flank; as already stated, large reinforcements were ordered from Russia, and the assistance of the Roumanian army was solicited.

The 2nd Division was the first of the reinforcements to arrive. It passed through Gorni-Studen on the 20th of August, and was directed on Selvi in order to relieve the detachment of the VIII. Corps which was there and allow it to proceed to Shipka. A few days later one brigade of this division was sent to Gabrova, but when Suleiman ceased his attacks at Shipka on the 26th it returned to Selvi.

The 3rd Rifle Brigade and the 2nd Brigade 3rd Division, which arrived between August 25th and 28th, were also directed on Selvi. The 1st Brigade 3rd Division was retained at Gorni-Studen. The Roumanians had already crossed one division at Nikopolis during the month of July; the rest of their force began crossing, by a bridge which they built at Korabia a few miles above Nikopolis, early in August, and were all on the southern bank by the 28th. This force was constituted as follows:—

ROUMANIAN CONTINGENT

			Battalions.	Foot guns.	Squadrons.	Horse guns.
3rd Division	1st Brigade	8th Regiment Line	2	—	—	—
		10th Regiment Dorobanz	2	—	—	—
		12th Regiment Dorobanz	2	—	—	—
	2nd Brigade	2nd Regiment Line	2	—	—	—
		9th Regiment Dorobanz	2	—	—	—
		11th Regiment Dorobanz	2	—	—	—
	3rd Rifle Battalion		1	—	—	—
	4th Regiment of Artillery		—	36	—	—
Total 3rd Division			13	36	—	—
4th Division	1st Brigade	7th Regiment Line	2	—	—	—
		14th Regiment Dorobanz	2	—	—	—
		15th Regiment Dorobanz	2	—	—	—
	2nd Brigade	5th Regiment Line	2	—	—	—
		13th Regiment Dorobanz	2	—	—	—
		16th Regiment Dorobanz	2	—	—	—
	2nd Rifle Battalion		1	—	—	—
	3rd Regiment of Artillery		—	36	—	—
Total 4th Division			13	36	—	—
Reserve	1st Brigade	1st Regiment Line	2	—	—	—
		7th Regiment Dorobanz	2	—	—	—
		1st Rifle Battalion	1	—	—	—
	2nd Brigade	4th Regiment Line	2	—	—	—
		6th Regiment Line	2	—	—	—
		8th Regiment Dorobanz	2	—	—	—
	3rd Brigade	3rd Regiment Line	2	—	—	—
		5th Regiment Dorobanz	2	—	—	—
		4th Rifle Battalion	1	—	—	—
	2nd Regiment of Artillery		—	36	—	—
Total Reserve			16	36	—	—
3 Brigades of Cavalry, counting 9 Regiments (2 Line and 7 Kalarash)			—	—	36	18
Grand total			42	108	36	18

The battalions numbered about 750 and the squadrons 125 men, making the total force 30,000 infantry, 4,500 cavalry, and 126 guns.

By the latter part of August, therefore, the Russian Commander-in-Chief had available for operations on his right flank about 105,000 men, of whom the greater part were on the north and east of Plevna, and the rest between Selvi and Lovtcha. No more Russian troops could be expected to arrive till the latter part of September; the season was advancing, and the Grand Duke determined to attack at once with what troops he had.

On the 31st of August, however, Osman sallied forth from Plevna and attempted the offensive in the following manner:—At 6.30 A.M. word was received from the cavalry outposts between Tutchenitza and Grivitza that the Turks were advancing in the direction of Pelishat, and at 8 they appeared on the open ridge about a mile west of Pelishat. Here they established their artillery (about 40 or 50 pieces), and their infantry moved rapidly forward and drove the Russians out of a lunette which they had constructed about half a mile in front of Pelishat. The Russian troops in this vicinity consisted of the 62nd and 63rd Regiments, which were in front of Pelishat, and the 20th and 118th* Regiments, with 3 batteries and a company of sappers, in front of Zgalevitza. These two positions, which were fortified with trenches for the infantry and slight epaulments for the artillery, formed the advanced left flank of the Russian defensive line, which extended from Tristenik to Poradim; at the latter place were 3 regiments of the 30th Division (IV. Corps), and on their right were 6 regiments of the IX. Corps.

General Zotof, who by virtue of his seniority commanded all the troops before Plevna at this time, imagined that the attack on Pelishat was a mere demonstration, and that the attack would be made on the 4th Roumanian Division, which was upon the road from Plevna to Nikopolis, or upon the right of the IX. Corps; he therefore made no change in the disposition of his troops until the capture of the Pelishat lunette and the appearance of a dense line of Turks all along the ridge behind it convinced him that the main attack was to be in this neighbourhood. He then (about 9 A.M.) gave the following orders:—

a. One brigade of IX. Corps to move forward along the high road toward Plevna and take the Turks in flank;

* One battalion of this regiment was in front of Lovtcha.

OPERATIONS ON THE RIGHT FLANK

b. Three regiments of IX. Corps to move to a point about two miles north of Poradim, and remain there in reserve ready to move according to further orders;

c. The Roumanian division to concentrate at Kalysovat;

d. The 61st Regiment, which was on the march from Zimnitza and had bivouacked at Karagatch, to move forward at once to Poradim.

The Turks meanwhile had been driven out of the Pelishat lunette by the 62nd Regiment, but had retaken it; and while their artillery kept up a steady fire upon the Russian line, they were preparing their infantry for the assault. At 1 P.M. they moved forward to the attack across the open ground just west of the two villages. Their assaults were directed upon three points, viz., Pelishat, the trenches south of Zgalevitza, and the trenches west of that village. The column advancing on Pelishat was received by the concentrated fire of 36 guns in front, and its flank was threatened by 6 sqadrons of cavalry; it did not reach the village, and after about an hour it was wholly withdrawn. Around Zgalevitza, however, a very hot fight raged for the next three hours; at one time the Turks had possession of a battery and some trenches on the south of the village, but they were driven out by the 120th Regiment, which arrived from the reserve at Poradim. Soon after they got possession of the trenches north of the village, but here they were again driven out. They then (about 3 P.M.) renewed their attacks upon both these positions, but were repulsed; and they then definitely retired behind the ridge where their artillery was posted. The Russians who followed them were arrested by a third attack made with the Turkish reserves. This fighting about Zgalevitza was remarkable for its duration and for the close quarters at which it was carried on. Several hundred of the Turkish dead lay in and on both sides of the Russian trenches.

About 4.30 P.M. the Turks had regained the ridge, and then, opening a steady fire with their artillery, they began to retreat toward Plevna. The Russians made an effort to follow them, but soon gave it up on account of the fatigue of the troops, and because they had but two regiments of fresh troops available. The Turks therefore withdrew without molestation to the shelter of their works at Plevna. The Russian losses were:—

	Officers.	Men.
Killed	3	171
Wounded	27	708
Missing	—	66
Total	30	945

Besides carrying off a large number of their dead and all their wounded, the Turks left 400 dead on the field. They advanced over open ground, and one of their columns just before reaching Zgalevitza got into the ravine just southwest of the village, where it was subjected to a cross-fire and was very badly cut up. Their losses were estimated at 3000 in all, and it is probable that they were little if any under that number.

What purpose Osman had in making this attack has never been made clear. It was too strong for a reconnaissance and too weak for a serious attack, being made with about 25,000 men out of the 50,000 or 60,000 which he then had at Plevna. Whatever its object, it accomplished nothing beyond the loss of 1000 Russians and 3000 Turks. The Russians continued undisturbed their preparations for their great effort against Plevna. Their plan was to first gain possession of Lovtcha, and then close in around Plevna with their 100,000 men, and attack it from the north, east, and south.

Lovtcha is the principal village upon the high road leading from Plevna to Gabrova and the Shipka Pass, and from it also there are smaller roads leading over the Balkans by the Trojan Pass to Philippopolis, and by Mikren to Yablanitza on the Plevna-Sophia high road. It was therefore a point of considerable strategic importance, Plevna and Lovtcha having the same value for the defence of the right flank as Biela and Tirnova for that of the left flank, in the Russian advance.

On the 17th of July, while Gourko was advancing through the valley of the Tundja toward Shipka, and a detachment

BATTLE OF LOVTCHA.

of the VIII. Corps, as will be remembered, was operating on the north of that pass, 5 sotnias of Cossacks belonging to this latter detachment advanced east from Selvi, and had a skirmish with several hundred bashi-bozouks, whom they defeated and drove beyond Lovtcha. The town was thus occupied by a small force of cavalry, but there were no infantry troops available to send to their relief in order to occupy the place in force; and a few days later (about July 25th) the Cossacks were driven out by a strong detachment of Turks under Adil Pasha, which arrived from Sophia.

Immediately after the defeat at Plevna on the 30th of July, Skobeleff was ordered to Selvi with the Caucasian Brigade of Cossacks, and there received in addition one regiment and part of another from the newly arrived IV. Corps. With this command (5 battalions, 10 squadrons, and 2 horse-batteries) he made a reconnaissance in force against Lovtcha on the 6th of August. He conducted this with so much boldness and skill that he caused the Turks to develop their whole strength, and meanwhile gained time for his topographers to make a very accurate sketch of the whole of the Turkish position. He found that the Turkish force consisted of about 15,000 men and 25 guns, besides the usual bands of bashi-bozouks; that their position was fortified by a redoubt and some batteries on the left (west) bank of the Osma, by 4 batteries on the right bank, and several lines of trenches in front of each, but that their whole position was commanded by a ridge running across the Selvi road about 4 miles east of the village. Skobeleff, having accomplished his object, with a loss of one or two hundred men, retired behind this ridge, and thence to the village of Kakrina, 10 miles east of Lovtcha.

Lovtcha is about 20 miles from Plevna by the high road, but between the right of the Turkish position at one point and the left of that of the other the distance is only 12 miles over a good road. Lovtcha was therefore only the right flank—much extended—of the position at Plevna; and the Russians planned to first strike this flank and destroy it, or at least separate it wholly from the main force, and then proceed to the attack of this latter at Plevna. For this purpose troops had been sent to Selvi as already explained, and the command of the forces in that neighbourhood confided to Major-General Prince Imeretinsky. On the 1st of September this officer had under his orders: *a*, the detachment of Skobeleff (64th Regiment, 1 battalion 118th Regiment, 1 battery of 16th Division, Brigade of Caucasian Cossacks, and 1 battery of Don Cossack Artillery); *b*, the 2nd Division, with its 6 batteries of artillery; *c*, the 2nd Brigade 3rd Division, with 3 batteries; *d*, the 3rd Rifle Brigade; and *e*, the 30th Don Cossacks—in all, 26 battalions, or 20,000 men, with 80 guns, besides the Cossacks and their artillery. On the same day he began to advance, sending Skobeleff's detachment from Kakrina to the heights east of the town, the 2nd Brigade 2nd Division to Kakrina, the Don Cossacks off on the left flank to observe the Trojan road, and the Caucasian Cossacks on the extreme right to observe the Plevna road. During the night he began the march with the rest of his troops toward Lovtcha.

Skobeleff arrived at the foot of the ridge east of the town at 2 P.M. (September 1st), and drove the Turks out of that portion of it on the north of the road, which they were occupying with only a small force. During the night Skobeleff worked hard at entrenching his own position and constructing epaulments for 24 guns, in which he placed the 8 guns which he had with him. The next morning (September 2nd) Skobeleff opened fire at daylight with these guns upon the Turkish battery on the ridge south of the road, by which he compelled the Turks to evacuate this latter during the afternoon. Skobeleff immediately occupied it with the 64th Regiment and again worked all night entrenching his new position and throwing up epaulments for 32 guns. The result of Skobeleff's efforts was that, when Imeretinsky arrived with the bulk of the troops at the foot of the ridge on the evening of September 2nd, he had already gained possession of the dominating ridge east of the town, and had epaulments all ready for 56 guns, 24 on the ridge north of the road and 32 on the south. During the night the guns were dragged up into these positions by the infantry.

On the same day General Dobrovolsky, commanding the

3rd Rifle Brigade, which formed the right of the line, drove the Turkish picquets out of Prissiaka, and thus came into position on a line with the ridge.

On the morning of September 3rd, at 5 o'clock, the Russians opened fire with the 56 pieces established along the heights east of the town, and a short time after with 12 additional pieces (4 of which were siege guns captured at Nikopolis) on the hill just south of Prissiaka.

The line of the Turkish position was along a series of hills just east of the Osma river, the principal and commanding point of which was at its southern extremity, which the Russians called the "Red Hill"; in this line they had batteries containing about 12 guns and a series of lines of entrenchments. Their second line was on a hill behind (west of) the town, where they had a closed redoubt, some batteries containing 10 or 12 guns, and also several lines of trenches.

Besides the guns in position on the ridge, the Russians had 16 guns in reserve; their infantry was massed behind the ridge, the troops on the left under command of General Skobeleff, those on the right under command of General Dobrovolsky. The plan of attack was to bombard the Turkish positions for several hours, then attack the Red Hill, and subsequently the trenches to the north of it. But at 8 A.M. the Turks took the offensive in the vicinity of Prissiaka, and this compelled General Dobrovolsky to attack the northern end of these hills with the 3rd Rifle Brigade, supported by the 7th Regiment; he dislodged the Turks and drove them across the Osma.

After about eight hours of cannonading the Turkish batteries were nearly all reduced to silence, and the order was given (2 P.M.) for Skobeleff to attack the Red Hill. This he did with the 64th Regiment, supported by the 11th; at the same time the 1st Brigade 2nd Division (5th and 6th Regiments) advanced to the attack of the hills to the north of the Red Hill. The artillery fire had been so well directed that the Turkish lines had been very much injured, and they made but a feeble resistance. The whole of their first line east of the Osma was carried by 3 o'clock.

Placing two batteries (16 guns) on the Red Hill to fire over the town against the redoubt on the hill behind it, Skobeleff followed the retreating Turks through the town, and posted his men in the gardens in the outskirts in front of the second position of the Turks. Skobeleff had the 64th and 1 battalion of the 118th Regiment, the 11th, and the 7th and 8th Regiments (2nd Brigade 2nd Division); the 5th and 6th Regiments (1st Brigade 2nd Division) were on the edge of the river to the north of the town; the Rifle Brigade was on the right; and the remaining regiment (No. 12) was in reserve.

Besides the two batteries on the Red Hill, two more were established on the high road just beyond the town. While the troops were resting to regain their breath and strength, these four batteries kept up a continuous fire upon the redoubt. At 5.30 P.M., the attack having been sufficiently prepared by the artillery, the whole line moved forward, Skobeleff from the town and the 1st Brigade 2nd Division by fording the river, while the Rifle Brigade on the extreme right advanced in the direction of the Plevna road. The Turks withdrew all their artillery, and escaped with it by the Mikren road; but their infantry kept up a very hot fire, inflicting considerable losses on the Russians. The latter continued to advance, however, and soon the Turks abandoned all their trenches, and nothing remained but the main redoubt, which, although surrounded on three sides, kept up its fire to the very last. It was finally carried about 7 P.M. in the midst of a hand-to-hand struggle, in which all its defenders perished. At the close of the fight the bodies of the dead and wounded Russians and Turks together lay piled up in a mass six feet deep around the gorge of the work.

The Russians were thus masters of the whole position, the Turks retreating in scattered bands, which assembled on the road toward Mikren. In view of the necessity of his co-operation in the attack on Plevna, Imeretinsky could not follow them with his infantry, but he sent the brigade of Caucasian Cossacks (which had been observing the Plevna road all day), and they cut down about 3000 of the fugitives on the road.

THIRD BATTLE AT PLEVNA

Late in the night word was received from the headquarters of the IV. Corps that their picquets at Bogot had seen a strong column advancing from Plevna along the road to Lovtcha. Nothing was heard of it that evening, but the next morning Skobeleff moved out on the Plevna road with an advance guard, and soon began skirmishing with this column, which was apparently making a turning movement round toward the Russian left. Imeretinsky disposed his whole force to meet this, but after some skirmishing the Turks began moving off in the direction of Mikren. Imeretinsky did not follow them, owing to the fatigue of his troops and the necessity of arriving at Plevna. Letting his troops rest during the remainder of this day (September 4th), Imeretinsky marched the next morning by the Plevna high road toward Bogot, where he arrived in the evening. He left the 2nd Brigade 3rd Division as a garrison for the works at Lovtcha, and brought the rest of his troops to Bogot.

The losses of the Russians were:

	Officers.	Men.
Killed	6	313
Wounded	33	1112
Missing	—	52
Total	39	1477

The losses of the Turks were very great. There were 1000 buried on the 4th, and 1200 more after the departure of Imeretinsky; 3000 were cut down by the Cossacks during their retreat. Very few prisoners were taken, and the number of Turkish wounded does not appear to have been very large. In short Adil Pasha's detachment of 15,000 men was not only defeated, but it was cut to pieces; it made no attempt to retake Lovtcha, and was not again heard of until the month of November, when the Russians began moving toward Tetevan and the Trojan Pass.

On the same day that the battle of Lovtcha took place, Prince Charles of Roumania, to whom had been assigned the command of the allied troops in front of Plevna (with General Zotof as Chief of Staff), arrived at Poradim and took command, and on the same date the orders were issued for the concentration of the troops. This took place the following day (September 4th), the Roumanians between Bryslan and Riben, the IX. Corps at Zgalevitza, and the IV. Corps at Pelishat. September 5th was passed in the same positions, and on that evening, Imeretinsky's detachment having arrived at Bogot, the troops were all assembled. On the night of the 6th-7th they moved forward to their positions in front of the Turkish redoubts.

General Levitzsky, Assistant Chief of Staff of the whole army, was temporarily at Prince Charles's headquarters, bearing the despatches and explaining the plans and wishes of the Commander-in-Chief. The latter moved his headquarters from Gorni-Studen to Poradim on the 7th, and finally on the same day the Emperor of Russia and his suite also came to the village of Radenitza, from which they could drive every morning to the field. Every one knew that this was to be the great struggle, and, if successful, it would probably lead to the complete defeat of the Turks throughout the whole theatre of war. Let us therefore examine in detail the relative forces of the two combatants and the nature of the position which the Russians were planning to assault.

The troops composing the "Right Wing" of the Russian Army were as follows:

	INFANTRY.		CAVALRY.	
	Battalions.	Guns.	Squadrons.	Guns.
Roumanians, General Cernat	42	108	30	18
IX. Corps,* General Krudener	21	88	16	12
IV. Corps, General Kryloff	24	96	16	12
2nd Division,† } General Imeretinsky	12	48	—	—
3rd Rifle Brigade,	4	24	—	—
Brigade of Caucasian Cossacks	—	—	12	6
Brigade of Don Cossacks (21st and 26th Regiments)	—	—	12	6
Total	103	364	92	54

* One regiment of Krüdener's corps, No. 19, which had lost all its baggage in the fight of July 20th, was at Nikopolis refitting; and one battery of his corps was also there. A portion of his artillery had also been at Lovtcha, but it was returned before the assault of the 11th.

† Imeretinsky brought with him from Lovtcha the three batteries belonging

THIRD BATTLE AT PLEVNA

The normal strength of the infantry of a Russian army corps is 24,000 men (1000 men to a battalion), but the details for detached service, sickness, &c., keep the battalions as low as 800 men when at their fullest. These two corps, however (IV. and IX.), had done all the fighting at Nikopolis and at Plevna up to date, and had lost 13,000 men in killed and wounded.

But this loss counted some of the lightly wounded who had subsequently recovered and joined their regiments; and moreover, the losses had been partially replaced by reinforcements from the reserves in Russia. To what extent these losses had been replaced I do not know; but on the 2nd of September General Krüdener told me that his corps numbered 15,000 present for duty, and the IV. Corps 17,000. The Roumanian troops, as already stated, numbered 30,000. The 16 battalions under Prince Imeretinsky had only been engaged at Lovtcha, and their strength was fully 750 to the battalion, or 12,000 in all. This gives a total of 74,000 infantry.

In the artillery, besides the 364 field guns (of which one half were 4.2-in. 9-pdrs. and the other half 3.4-in. 4-pdrs.), there were 20 siege guns—24-pdrs., 6-in. cal.—which arrived at Poradim from Zimnitza on the 4th of September; and also the 4 Turkish siege guns (probably 12-pdrs.) taken from among those captured at Nikopolis, and which were now with Imeretinsky's troops. The number of men in the artillery was about 8000. With this heavy artillery came 3 battalions of sappers, about 2500 men.

In the cavalry the squadrons may be taken as numbering 110 men (their maximum strength is 150). This gives the total strength of the cavalry at 10,000 sabres. The 9 mounted batteries which accompanied them were served by about 1800 men.

The force brought against Plevna therefore numbered over 90,000 men, and was composed of 74,000 infantry, 10,000 cavalry, 24 siege guns, 364 field guns, and 54 horse guns.

to the brigade of the 3rd Division which remained as a garrison of that place. These are the 24 guns credited to the 3rd Rifle Brigade above.

As for the Turkish Army, the only means of arriving at a knowledge of its strength is by computing backward as follows:

Surrendered December 10th, including 2128 officers	39,000
Killed and wounded December 10th	4,000
Sick and wounded found in the town December 10th	20,000
Killed between September 1st and December 9th (estimated)	5,000
Total	68,000
From this must be subtracted the reinforcements which entered Plevna September 22nd	12,000
Strength of Osman Pasha's Army September 1st	56,000

A small number of the wounded of September 11th were transported back to Orkhanie, but the great majority of them remained at Plevna, and died there or were found in the town at the surrender. No account is here taken of the prisoners or killed and wounded at Gorni-Dubrik and Telis, since these troops (although part of the garrison of Plevna) only arrived in October. On the other hand, there were a few regiments of regular cavalry and several hundred bashi-bozouks present in September, who were sent away in the early part of October. At the surrender, 77 field guns were delivered over, and a few were afterward found buried in the ground; but the Turks were at all times deficient in their artillery, and it is not probable that Osman had over 80 pieces. This was also the estimate at the time of the battle in September.

The Turkish Army therefore numbered about 60,000 men, viz., 56,000 infantry and 2500 cavalry, and 80 guns.

Plevna itself is a little town of 6000 or 7000 inhabitants, lying in the midst of a series of hills whose crests are from 200 to 600 feet above the town. Its only military importance lies in the fact of its being the meeting point of roads.

THIRD BATTLE AT PLEVNA

from Widdin, Sophia, Shipka, Biela, Zimnitza, and Nikopolis. An army posted there was a vital menace to the safety of the Russian communications in any advance.

Osman Pasha, having arrived from Widdin too late to prevent the capture of Nikopolis, occupied Plevna and began throwing up entrenchments to strengthen his position in case of an attack from the Russians. He was attacked on the 20th of July, and having repulsed his assailants he continued to fortify his position, constructing redoubts as well as trenches. Again attacked by the Russians on the 30th of July, and again having beaten them back, he continued unremittingly the work upon his defences; not following any systematic plan for the fortification of the place against an attack from all sides (because he had not troops enough to occupy the whole extent of the dominating ridge forming the rim of the little Plevna basin, nor time enough to construct works upon so extended a front), but confining his efforts to the hills nearest the town on the north and east, since it was on these sides that the Russians threatened him with the greatest force. At the time of which we are speaking (the first week in September) these works had already reached a development of 18 redoubts, supplemented by several lines of trenches. These works may be divided into three groups:

1. The Grivitza works, consisting of two redoubts situated 2000 yards north-west of the village of Grivitza, and a line of trenches and batteries running north-west along the Grivitza ridge to the Bukova creek. Beyond these was a large entrenched camp on the heights of Opanetz, overlooking the Vid.

2. The middle group, consisting of 8 redoubts more or less perfectly connected with lines of trenches, on the knolls just east of the town of Plevna.

3. The Krishin group, consisting of the Krishin redoubt on a commanding point 3000 yards south-west of the town, a redoubt half-way between it and the town, and two redoubts connected by a strong trench just outside of the town, commanding the approach by the Lovtcha road.

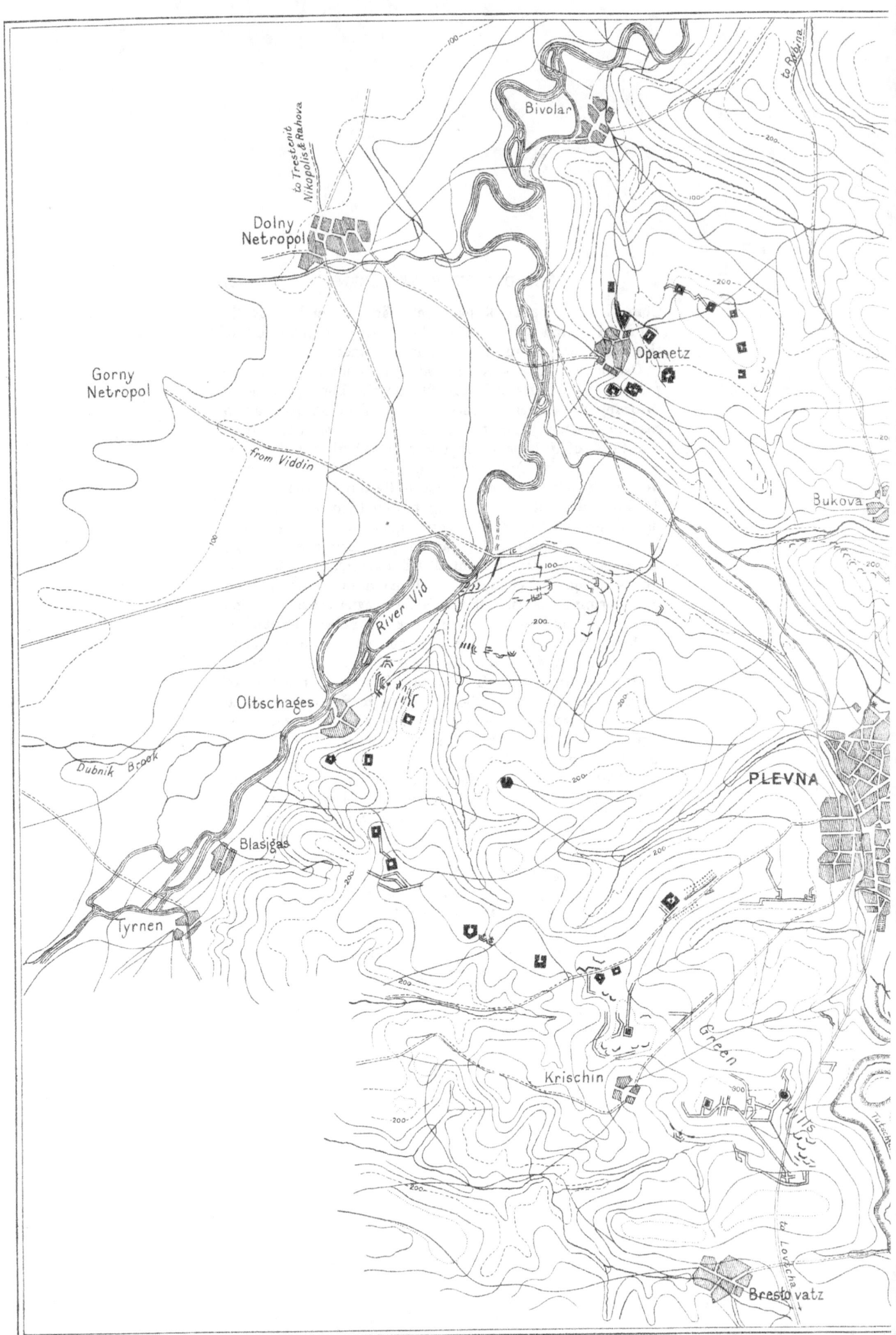

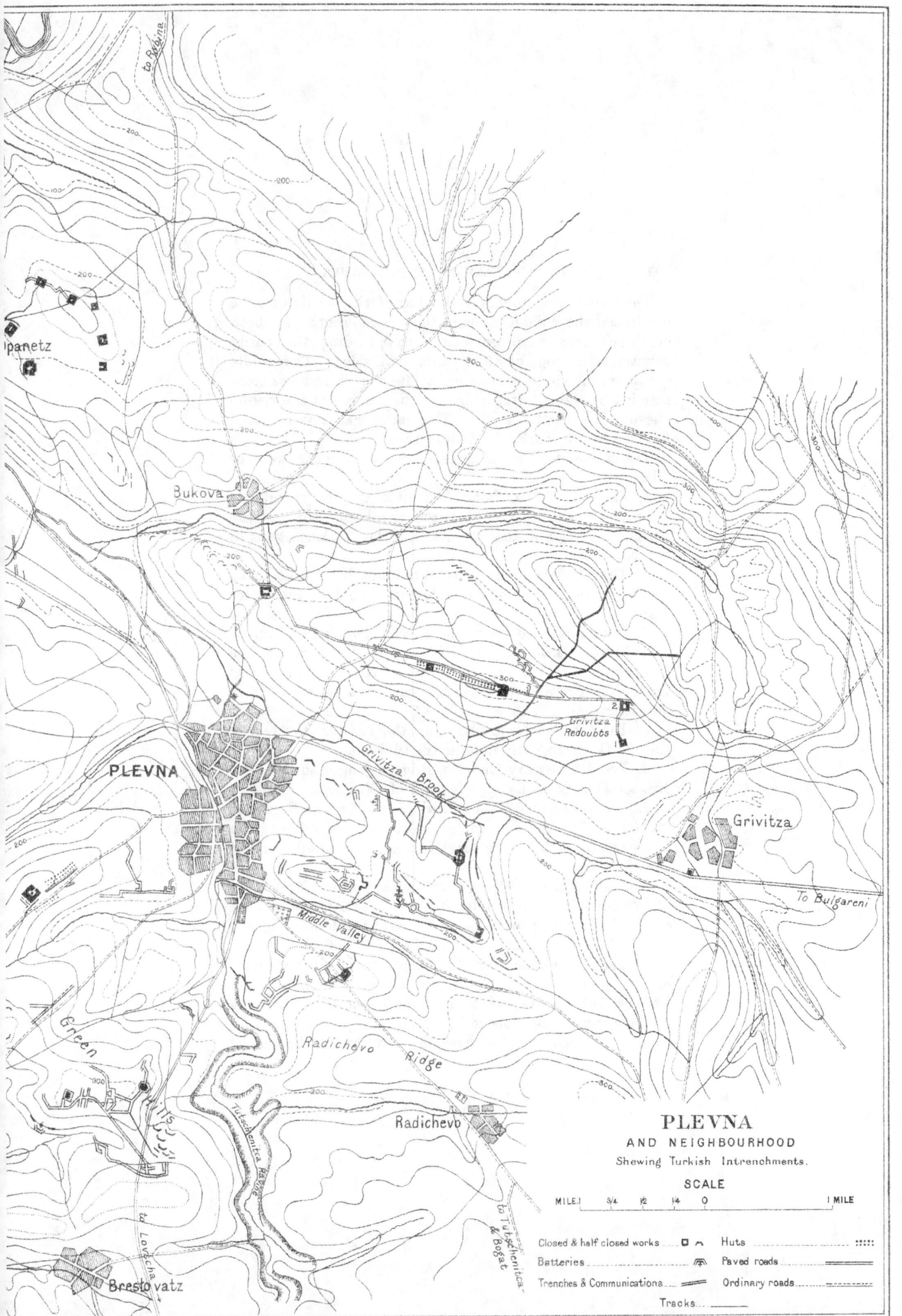

108   THE CAMPAIGN IN BULGARIA

The Grivitza redoubt was the key of the position on the north, and the Krishin redoubt that on the south; for both of these works were on points commanding the entire country for a range of 3000 yards on all sides. The middle group, on the contrary, was on a lower level, and was commanded by the Grivitza ridge on the north and the Radischevo ridge on the south. This latter had not yet been fortified by the Turks, for lack of time.

The orders for the advance of September 6th were as follows:

1. The IX. Corps, from Zgalevitza to the vicinity of Grivitza, to take position between the high road and the Radischevo heights, and to establish the 20 siege guns in two batteries.

2. The IV. Corps, from Pelishat to Radischevo, to establish its 9-pdr. batteries on the ridge in front of the latter place.

3. Imeretinsky's detachment from Bogot to Tutchenitza.

4. Roumanians—4th Division, from Verbitza to the vicinity of Grivitza on the north of the high road; 3rd Division and reserve to Verbitza; cavalry between Verbitza and Riben.

5. The 9th Cavalry Division, on the high road in rear of the IX. Corps and 4th Roumanian Division.

6. The 4th Cavalry Division, Brigade Caucasian Cossacks, Brigade Don Cossacks, on left flank of IV. Corps.

7. General reserve (2nd Brigade 30th Division, Regiment No. 20 of 5th Division, three 4-pdr. batteries, 4th and 9th Hussars, and 1 horse battery), in rear of the left flank of the IX. Corps.

8. Ammunition. Flying Park of IX. Corps at Zgalevitza, of IV. Corps between Tutchenitza and Bogot. Reserve Park of IX. Corps at Bulgareni, of IV. Corps at Leschan. Baggage of IX. Corps at Karagatch, of IV. Corps at Poradim.

9. Field Hospitals. Of IX. Corps at the "three wells" on the Zgalevitza road (2 miles in rear of batteries); of IV. Corps at Tutchenitza; of Roumanians at Verbitza. As many country carts as possible to be collected.

10. The men to take three days' rations (2 lbs. cooked

THIRD BATTLE AT PLEVNA

meat and 4 lbs. biscuit) in their haversacks; to take overcoats slung over the shoulder; to leave their knapsacks and shelter-tents in their bivouacs, under guard of small detachments formed of men fit for light duty.

The troops were all under way at dark on the evening of the 6th. The men in Krüdener's corps carried on their shoulders fascines, gabions, and hewn logs for platforms for the siege guns. Two regiments were thrown forward nearly to Grivitza, to cover the construction of the batteries; but the Turks discovered nothing, and not a shot was fired all night. The construction of the batteries was begun at 9 o'clock and finished at a few minutes past midnight, the infantry battalions working under the direction of the sappers. The first siege battery, containing 8 guns, was built at a point south-east of the Grivitza redoubt and 4300 yards from it; the second siege battery, 12 guns, was on its left and rear and 5200 yards from the redoubt. All the field artillery and the infantry of the IX. Corps were massed in the valleys near these batteries, the infantry with three regiments in the first line a little in advance of the batteries, one regiment in reserve on the right and two on the left; the remaining regiment formed part of the general reserve.

The IV. Corps also came into position during the night, placing 5 batteries (40 guns) of 9-pdrs. on the eastern part of the ridge in front of Radischevo. These batteries were due south of the Grivitza redoubt and 5100 yards from it; and they were 2700 yards from the nearest of the redoubts of the "middle group." Of the infantry of this corps, three regiments lay behind the batteries in the Radischevo valley, three regiments formed the corps reserve placed about a mile back on the Pelishat road, and two regiments were in the general reserve.

Imeretinsky on the morning of the 7th moved to the west of Tutchenitza, sending Skobeleff with a small force to reconnoitre the position at Krishin.

The Roumanians brought four 9-pdr. batteries (24 guns) into action about 9 A.M. of that day, at a point 4000 yards due east of the Grivitza redoubt. The infantry of the 4th

Roumanian Division lay behind these batteries and on their right.

September 7th.

At 6 A.M. the first shot was fired from the 8-gun siege battery. Several Turks appeared immediately on the parapet of the Grivitza redoubt, and this shot seemed to be the first knowledge they had of the arrival of the Russians; it was not answered for half-an-hour. The cannonade then became general along the whole line. About 10 A.M. Krüdener sent three 9-pdr. batteries (24 guns) to take position on the hill south of the village of Grivitza, whence they opened fire on the Grivitza redoubt at 3500 yards. The cannonade continued till after dark, the losses on the Russian side (and probably on the Turkish also) being next to nothing. It will be noticed that the Russians had 20 siege guns and 88 9-pdrs. in action—about one-fourth of their artillery—at ranges from 2700 to 5200 yards. Most of their fire was concentrated on the Grivitza redoubt, a square earthwork with parapet 18 feet thick; and the firing was reasonably accurate, a cloud of dirt being thrown up from the parapet every few minutes; yet the 8 guns of this redoubt continued to answer all day.

During the afternoon Imeretinsky moved from Tutchenitza to the vicinity of Brestovetz.

September 8th.

The cannonade continued all day.

The three batteries of the IX. Corps were reinforced by two more batteries, and all moved forward to within 2500 yards of the redoubts of the "middle group," to which they confined their attention.

A portion of the reserve batteries of the IV. Corps were brought into action farther to the left, on the Radischevo ridge, against Redoubt No. 10, at 1800 yards.

The 3rd Roumanian Division advanced to the front of Verbitza and on the right of the 4th Roumanian Division,

THIRD BATTLE AT PLEVNA

and brought a portion of its batteries into action on the north of the Grivitza redoubt at 2500 yards.

General Loshkarieff, with the 9th Cavalry Division and four Roumanian Cavalry Regiments, was sent across the Vid at Riben, and thence to Dolni-Dubnik on the Sophia high road, to cut the communications of the Turks, and in case of their retreat to fall upon them.

During the afternoon Skobeleff brought on an infantry engagement near the Lovtcha high road, as will be subsequently explained.

Toward evening the fire of the Grivitza redoubt began to grow very feeble. During the night the 8 guns of the first siege battery were moved over to the Radischevo ridge, whence they could play upon the redoubts of the middle group.

September 9th.

The cannonade continued without abatement, except from the 12-siege-gun battery, whose ammunition was nearly exhausted. The Grivitza redoubt was entirely silent. Noticing this, the Roumanians made a reconnaissance toward it, but were promptly beaten back by a murderous infantry fire. During the afternoon there was a general movement of the IV. Corps to the left, along the Radischevo ridge, as far as the Tutchenitza ravine, and the 123rd and 124th Regiments were brought from the right of the IX. Corps to the left, in order to keep up connection with the IV. Corps. The IX. Corps Artillery was advanced to within 1800 yards of the redoubts of the " middle group," and increased to 8 batteries in action.

September 10th.

The cannonade continued as usual. During these four days of incessant artillery firing the Russian losses were between 300 and 400; those of the Turks are not known. The Grivitza redoubt was silent (as to its artillery only), and was more or less knocked out of shape. Redoubt No. 1 of the central group was also considerably damaged. The rest of the Turkish works were but little injured, though from lack of ammunition their artillery ceased firing altogether.

During the afternoon it began to rain, and during the night there was a succession of violent thunderstorms, in which an immense quantity of water fell, converting the ground everywhere into a pasty black mud, and making it very difficult for the Russians to bring up their ammunition.

September 11th.

Dense fogs and a cold drizzling rain remained over from the last night's storm. The Turks attacked Skobeleff early in the morning, and there was fighting on the left flank all day. The artillery on the centre and right fired but little during the morning; but at noon, as the fog lifted a little, they opened with great fury, and kept it up until 3 P.M., when the assaults were made.

Before describing these, it is necessary to explain the course of events on the left flank, beyond the Tutchenitza ravine.

Imeretinsky on the 7th had taken position near Brestovetz, his advance guard under Skobeleff (5th and 8th Regiments, 9th and 10th Rifle Battalions, four 9-pdr. batteries, 4 siege guns, and the 21st and 26th Don Cossacks) being posted on the "Red Hill" to the right and rear of the village of Brestovetz. From here on the 8th these batteries opened fire on the Krishin redoubt at 4000 yards. The rest of the detachment with Imeretinsky was about 1½ mile in rear toward Bogot. On the afternoon of the 8th Skobeleff moved forward with the 5th Regiment supported by two battalions of the 8th, drove the Turkish picquets out of the woods on the first knoll of the "Green Hills," and then attacked the second knoll, which was occupied by some battalions of Turks. A very warm skirmish took place with these, but they soon retreated, and following them, Skobeleff crossed the high road and took the "third knoll" of the Green Hills, and was at 5 P.M. only 1500 yards south of the town of Plevna. Here, however, he came under the fire of the Krishin redoubt on his left, and the two redoubts near the town, which were quickly reinforced by Turkish reserves from Plevna. Skobeleff was driven back to the second knoll, where his own reserve (Regiment No. 8) enabled him to halt and stop the Turks. Here he remained until some time during the night, when, receiving word that the general assaults which had originally been intended for the 9th had been postponed to a later day, he withdrew to the first knoll, and there entrenced himself. His losses during the 8th were 900 men. At 5 A.M. on the 9th he was attacked in this position by the Turks, but drove them back with shrapnel; at 8 A.M. they renewed the attack with increased strength, and came within 60 yards of the trenches, but were again driven back. For the rest of the day the Turks left Skobeleff alone, and remained in their own positions on the second knoll.

On the afternoon of the 9th Imeretinsky's detachment stood as follows: In the first line, under Skobeleff, the 2nd Brigade 2nd Division, the 9th and 10th Rifle Battalions, and 2 batteries of the 3rd Division, posted from the "first knoll" of the Green Hills on the right to the ridge north of Brestovetz on their left. Behind them, on the Red Hill, were the three 9-pdr. batteries (24 guns) of the 2nd Division, which had been exchanging shots all day with the Krishin redoubt. Behind these batteries were the 1st Brigade 2nd Division, the other two Rifle Battalions, the three 4-pdr. batteries of the 2nd Division, and one 9-pdr. battery of the 3rd Division.

Up to this time Imeretinsky had had the general command of all the troops on the left flank; Skobeleff, although of the same rank as himself (Major-General in the Emperor's suite), was junior to him in date. At Lovtcha Skobeleff had an independent detachment at the time of Imeretinsky's arrival, but he was then placed under the latter's orders, and had so remained till now. Late in the night of the 9th–10th Imeretinsky received an order from General Zotof, Chief of the Staff, dividing his troops into two independent portions, assigning Skobeleff to the command of the first and himself to the second, and stating that Skobeleff would attack according to instructions which had already been given him, and that he (Imeretinsky) *was to support Skobeleff in his attack*, as well as protect the extreme left flank with his Cossacks. The effect of this was of course to give Skobeleff the entire control of the operations on the left flank, and virtually to relieve Imeretinsky from command. The order also stated that the 1st Brigade 16th Division would be sent at daylight to report to Skobeleff, taking the road from Radischevo to Brestovetz, which crosses the Tutchenitza ravine at the mill just behind the Green Hills.

At daylight on the 10th Skobeleff sent the 8th Regiment forward, and, almost without fighting, they seized the "second knoll" and immediately fortified themselves there, the men using their copper soup dishes, bayonets, and naked hands, as the supply of spades was very small. As soon as the 1st Brigade 16th Division arrived, one regiment was placed on the "second knoll" and the other on the "first knoll" in reserve. On the "second knoll," therefore, from west of the high road to the Tutchenitza Creek, there were sixteen 9-pounders in position, and the 8th and 61st Regiments on either side; in reserve, the 7th and 63rd Regiments and the 9th and 10th Rifle Battalions. Sixteen 9-pounders were sent to the east side of the Tutchenitza Creek, from which they could bring a cross-fire upon the "third knoll" at 2500 yards' range. Judging a further advance imprudent before the general attack, Skobeleff remained in this position all day.

THE ASSAULTS OF SEPTEMBER 11TH.

During the evening of September 10th orders were issued for a general assault the next day at 3 P.M. The assaults were to be directed upon three principal points, the Grivitza redoubt, redoubt No. 10 (2000 yards south-east of the town), and upon the two redoubts on the Lovtcha road close to the town. The Roumanians and part of the IX. Corps were to make the first, a part of the IV. Corps the second, and Skobeleff's detachment the third. The 31st Division (IX. Corps) was to support the line of batteries from Grivitza to Radischevo, but was not to make an attack.

THIRD BATTLE AT PLEVNA

The orders prescribed a cannonade along the whole line, to commence at daybreak and last till 8 A.M.; then a pause till 11 A.M.; then a heavy cannonade till 1 P.M.; then another pause till 2.30 P.M.; then to fire as rapidly as possible till 3 P.M., when the assaults were to begin. In the morning, however, there was such a dense fog that it was hard to tell when daylight began, and impossible to see anything to aim at, so that this elaborate artillery programme was somewhat disarranged. About 10 A.M. Skobeleff began to move his men forward to the "third knoll," since from there he could more advantageously begin the assault upon the line of redoubts in front of it; but in so doing he had some rather lively skirmishing, the noise of which came through the fog to Radischevo. At the same time the Turks in Redoubt No. 10, thinking perhaps to take advantage of the fog, advanced with the idea of driving the 63rd Regiment out of a very advantageous position which they occupied on the extreme left of the Radischevo ridge and near the Tutchenitza ravine. They were repulsed. The 63rd Regiment then, in ignorance or disregard of the general plan of assault, or perhaps from the fog and the unexpected firing on the left, thinking that the plan had been changed, or for whatever other reason, but without the order of the Division Commander, followed the retreating Turks; and as they soon became pretty hotly engaged, the 117th Regiment, which was nearest on their right, went to their aid. These two regiments pressed on in the fog and gained the line of trenches running from the redoubt to the Tutchenitza Creek. They then got a terrible fire on their right flank and front from the redoubt, and from some troops in the open to the west of it. The two regiments fell back to their positions on the Radischevo ridge. Their adventure cost them dear, for they lost one half of their men and over two-thirds of their officers, and, worse than all, it put these two regiments practically out of the fight for the rest of the day. The programme of the attack was therefore still more disconcerted.

About noon the fog began to rise, so that the redoubts were visible, and then a cannonade opened and kept up furiously till about 2 P.M., when it slackened down again.

By the lifting of the fog Skobeleff's position became very critical, for there was but little cover for his men, and they were exposed not only to the fire of the works in front, but also to that of the Krishin redoubt on his left flank. He called upon Imeretinsky for reinforcements, which were sent to him in succession until the latter had not a battalion left under his orders, and at the same time sent to Zotof for permission to attack without waiting till 3 o'clock; his position was an excellent one for beginning his assault, but not one in which he could remain still; the permission was granted, but it did not reach Skobeleff till 2.30 P.M.

About 3 o'clock the artillery recommenced a tremendous thundering on all sides (there were over 250 guns in position), and the infantry began to move forward to the assault. There was a cold drizzling rain at the time, in which the immense quantity of smoke hung low, but was occasionally blown off by the wind; objects could be fairly well seen.

Let us follow the assaults in succession:

1. GRIVITZA REDOUBT.

This was to be attacked in four columns, as follows: The 3rd Roumanian Division, which was under shelter in the ravine on the north, with its batteries on the hill behind it, 2800 yards from the redoubt, was to send one brigade to approach through a little ravine on the north-west, and the other brigade on the north-east; the 4th Roumanian Division, whose batteries had gradually crept up to about 1800 yards on the east of the redoubt, was to send one brigade along the ridge on the east and keep the other in reserve; the 1st Brigade 5th Division (Russians), which was in the valley south of Grivitza, was to advance with two 4-pdr. batteries from the south.

The Roumanians began to move forward at a few minutes past three. Column No. 1 did not get anywhere near the Grivitza redoubt; what had been thought to be a mere auxiliary line of trench was found to be a second

THIRD BATTLE AT PLEVNA

redoubt 400 yards north of the main one, and equal to it in size and construction. The approaches on the north were very steep and difficult, and when the Roumanians came within about 80 yards of it they were driven back, and retreated to a secondary ridge about 700 yards to the north, and there entrenched themselves. Column No. 2 was delayed in climbing the slope, but column No. 3, having only an open space of 1800 to 2000 yards to pass over, came against the redoubt by half-past 3 o'clock; but it was alone of all the columns, and was driven back and sought refuge in the slopes between the redoubt and the village. Column No. 2 then made its appearance from the northeast, but, advancing alone, was in turn driven back, 4 to 4.30 P.M.

Meanwhile the Russian brigade did not pass through Grivitza until 4 P.M.; it then deployed on the west of the village and advanced up the slope northward toward the redoubt, the 17th Regiment in the lead, followed by the 18th, which inclined a little to the left. The two 4-pdr. batteries were brought into action against the trenches on the west and south-west of the redoubt, which were delivering a fire on the left flank of the brigade as it advanced. These two regiments worked their way slowly up the hill, being much annoyed by the fire on the left, against which finally a part of the 18th Regiment advanced and gained possession of a portion of the trenches in that direction. Thus assisted, the leading battalion of the 17th Regiment, made a rush for the redoubt on the south, at the same time that a portion of the brigade of the 4th Roumanian Division which had been kept in reserve made a desperate attempt on the east. They were successful, and the troops entered from the two sides about the same time, the commander of the 17th Regiment, as well as that of the Roumanian brigade, being both killed within a short distance from the parapet. But the Turks kept up a terrible fire from the second redoubt, only a few hundred yards off, and from the trenches on the left; and after a half hour they assaulted the allies, and in turn drove them out. It was now growing dark, and a confused fight was kept up at short range and partly hand-to-hand until about 7.30 P.M., when the arrival of the other battalions of the 17th Regiment, as well as a small reinforcement of Roumanians, finally decided the day in favour of the allies.

Their trophies were five guns and one flag. The terreplein of the redoubt as well as its ditch had a complete pavement of dead bodies. Some idea of the closeness of this fight may be gathered from the fact that the Roumanians had more men killed and wounded. Their losses were:

	Officers.	Men.
Killed	15	1335
Wounded	41	1176
Total	56	2511

The Russian brigade lost 22 officers and 1305 men.

The total force which had been brought into action numbered about 25,000 men.

During the night the Turks made three successive sallies from the second redoubt and from the trenches, but they were each time driven back.

2. REDOUBT No. 10.

The unfortunate mis-step which had been made by the 63rd and 117th Regiments in this part of the field just before noon was barely over, and these troops, somewhat disorganised, back in their positions on the left of the Radischevo ridge, by 2 P.M. Desultory picket-firing followed. General Schnidnikoff, chief of the 30th Division, who commanded this part of the line, was anxious to carry out his part of the assault at the hour specified, 3 P.M., and at that hour his two remaining regiments, Nos. 64 and 118, were moved forward. Four batteries of the IV. Corps were posted on the left of the ridge, and were doing their utmost against the redoubt. The 64th and 118th Regiments passed on the right of these batteries down the ridge, and into a little valley where they found shelter; then turning by the left flank, they advanced westward against the redoubt. This was at 4 P.M. The fire became hotter and hotter as they neared the redoubt, but still they kept on. Just then appeared the head of a column of reinforcements for the Turks, taken either from the reserves in the town or from redoubts 7, 8, and 9; they came up the slope and deployed on the left (north-east) flank of the redoubt, and fought there in the open. The Russians, however, still moved on, and at 4.30 P.M. disappeared in the smoke overhanging the ditch, their right flank slightly refused on account of the Turkish reinforcements which had just arrived there. For about three minutes the affair hung in the balance; then the Russians began falling back somewhat hurriedly. The Turks them streamed out of the eastern angle of the redoubt, and joining their comrades, began to follow the Russians at a run; thereupon two battalions stopped, faced about and lay down at about 200 yards from the redoubt, and opened the hottest possible fire. The Turkish pursuit was at once arrested, and the Turks retreated pell-mell into their redoubt again. The Russians then continued their retreat rapidly, but without any running or disorder, although they were losing terribly under the murderous fire which the Turks kept up from the redoubt. One battalion, which formed the only reserve of these two regiments, and which had, during the half hour of their attack, been lying under cover in the little ravine 1200 yards east of the redoubt, was now brought forward; but it was too late, and one battalion was a mere drop in the bucket—it simply joined in the retreat. The two regiments reached the shelter of the little ravine at 5 P.M.

Meanwhile more or less firing had been going on between the left flank of the Russian position (63rd and 117th Regiments) and the trenches between the redoubt and the Tutchenitza creek, but no serious assault had been made there. At Schnidnikoff's request, Zotof had ordered the 123rd and 124th Regiments from their position behind the batteries on the right of the Radischevo ridge, to the extreme left of the ridge, to replace the 63rd and 117th, which had been so knocked to pieces during the morning. Of the general reserve, the 119th and 120th Regiments were ordered to replace the 123rd and 124th behind the batteries, and the 20th as reserve to Schnidnikoff's line. The 123rd and 124th Regiments did not arrive on the left till about 5 o'clock, when the attack of the 64th and 118th was already repulsed. From 5 to half-past 5 o'clock there was a somewhat oppressive silence over this part of the field; then the guns on the hill began working again, and very quickly there was also heard the musketry of the 123rd and 124th. They advanced over the same ground as the 63rd 117th in the morning; the fire was very hot for about 20 or 25 minutes, but the men could not get nearer than 150 or 200 yards from the redoubt. In the darkness which was setting in about 6 o'clock they fell back to the Radischevo ridge. The assault of Redoubt No. 10 was over—and had failed. The Russian losses were in all 110 officers and 5200 men, nearly half of which were in the two regiments (63rd and 117th) which had become engaged during the morning. The dead and a large part of the wounded were left on the field.

3. REDOUBTS ON THE LOVTCHA ROAD.

Skobeleff's position during the night of the 10th–11th was on the "second knoll" of the Green Hills, 2000 yards south of the redoubts he was to attack; in front of him was a little valley, then the "third knoll," then another little valley, then the long sloping ridge, extending from Plevna to the Krishin redoubt, on which were the redoubts. The third knoll was occupied by the Turks only with a feeble skirmish line, and at 10 A.M. Skobeleff advanced and drove them out of there in order to have this position in his own possession, from which to launch his troops to the assault during the afternoon. He occupied it without difficulty, but then he was greatly annoyed by the fire from the trenches on the slope in front of the redoubts, which, being something under 1000 yards away, brought his men in easy range. Skobeleff

THIRD BATTLE AT PLEVNA

sheltered his men as much as possible behind the crest of the hill, but still he was losing a good many men, not only in the first line, but in the reserve placed in the little valley between the two knolls. The Turkish fire meanwhile grew warmer and warmer, and about 2 P.M. a strong skirmish line began advancing from their trenches up the slopes of the hill. The 62nd Regiment was sent forward to drive back these skirmishers, which they did; there was then for nearly an hour a lull in the fight.

Skobeleff's troops stood as follows:

First line, behind the crest of the third knoll, 61st and 62nd Regiments, with the 9th and 10th Rifle Battalions in reserve; between the second and third knolls, 7th Regiment. Second line, on the fortified position of the second knoll, 5th and 8th Regiments and 24 guns.

In reserve, between first and second knolls, 6th Regiment and 11th and 12th Rifle Battalions.

At 2.30 P.M. his batteries opened fire over the heads of the advanced line of troops, and at 3 P.M. he sent these latter forward to the assault. They went down the slope of the third knoll in two lines of company columns, preceded by a strong line of skirmishers and with all the bands playing, cleared the Turks out of their rifle-pits at the foot of the slope, crossed the little stream, and began ascending the hill. Here it got very hot, and the men stopped advancing and began to lie down and open fire upon the trenches connecting the two redoubts in front of them, about 200 yards off. Seeing the line begin to waver a little, *at this instant* Skobeleff sent forward the 7th Regiment to their support, and ordered up the 6th Regiment and 11th and 12th Rifle Battalions to the reverse slope of the third knoll; meanwhile the artillery kept up an incessant fire over the heads of the men. The arrival of the 7th Regiment gave new courage to the men already so hotly engaged, and they made a renewed effort to advance up the slope, but found it impossible, and again they lay down and opened fire. But it was evident that they could not long remain in such a position, only 200 yards from the redoubts, the Turks behind trenches and the Russians in the open, and exposed not only to the infantry fire in front, but to artillery fire on both flanks—on the left from the Krishin redoubt and on the right from the redoubts of the "middle group." The critical moment had therefore arrived, and Skobeleff sent forward the rest of his troops, viz., the 6th Regiment and the two remaining rifle battalions; and he himself, leaving the second knoll, whence he had been directing the attack, rode forward rapidly, caught up the two rifle battalions, and went forward with them. He was well known to his men as being the only general officer who always rode a white horse and wore a white coat in battle, and there is no doubt that his personal presence encouraged the men; he had the good luck not to be hit, though nearly all his staff fell, and he entered (on foot, his horse being killed) the redoubt with his men. As these reinforcements came forward there was a tremendous enthusiasm and "hurrah" among the men; one more final effort was made to get up the slope; the Turks were driven out of the trenches in front of the redoubt; then for a few minutes, just as at Redoubt No. 10, the affair hung in the balance, but here it succeeded: the Turks began to weaken, a portion of the Russians entered the trenches between the two redoubts, then turned to the left, and finally at half-past 4 the middle redoubt was in the hands of the Russians. The Turks, still firing, retreated to a camp surrounded by a light trench about 600 yards in rear of the line of redoubts.

The Russians had lost 3000 men in the assault, which lasted little less than an hour.

But the fight did not now in the least abate. The middle redoubt, which the Russians had taken, as well as the eastern one, which was still in the hands of the Turks, were properly speaking not redoubts at all, since they were only built up on three sides; the front side of each was simply an increased height to the strong line of trench connecting the two and extending to the west (left) of the middle one; the other two sides were properly mere traverses to this line; and the fourth side—the rear—was wholly open and exposed to the fire from the trench of the camp only 600 yards off. The ground was hard and rocky, and there were

THIRD BATTLE AT PLEVNA

no spades at hand for digging. While the Turks therefore kept up an incessant fire from this camp and from the eastern redoubt, which was still in their possession, a force of one or two battalions sortied from the redoubt (No. 13) on the left of the Russians, and advanced to the attack of the left flank. Seeing this, Colonel Korupatkin, Chief of Staff to Skobeleff, and the only one of his staff not killed or wounded, took about 300 men and went forward to meet these Turks in the open. A desperate fight at short range took place, in which the Russians lost the greater part of this little force, but drove the Turks back to their redoubt (No. 13). Just at this time some of the artillery which remained in front of Brestovetz increased their fire upon the Krishin redoubt from the other side, and a portion of the Cossacks on the left flank dismounted and advanced on foot against the same redoubt. This created a diversion upon the Russian left flank, and relieved them for a time from further attacks in that quarter. Meanwhile a small force of a few hundred volunteers came out of the middle redoubt and make an effort to get into the eastern one, but they all or nearly all perished. Then Colonel Shestakoff, of Imeretinsky's staff, came across the valley from the third knoll to the line of redoubs, with three companies of the 6th Regiment and portions of the other regiments which had been left in reserve, and, picking up on the way the stragglers and scattered detachments in the valley, made a force of about 1000 or 1200 men, with which he made a desperate effort against the front of the eastern redoubt, at the same time that a fresh lot of volunteers sortied from the middle redoubt against its flank. The attack succeeded, and at 5.30 P.M. the eastern redoubt was also in the hands of the Russians. Soon afterward darkness set in, and the flight slackened down to desultory picket-firing, with an occasional shell from the Krishin redoubt.

Skobeleff's precarious position will be at once evident. He occupied, with the 6th, 7th, 61st, and 62nd Regiments, and the Rifle Brigade, the line of trench and redoubt just south-west of the town. In his front, at 600 yards, was the entrenched camp of the Turks; on his left flank, at 800 yards, was Redoubt No. 13; and on his left rear, at 2300 yards, was the Krishin redoubt (No. 14). On his right flank was the "middle group" of redoubts, and on his right rear was Redoubt No. 10, where the Russians had been repulsed during the afternoon. He was entered like a wedge into the midst of the Turkish lines, and on three sides of him were strong works against which either no attack had been made at all or the attack had failed. In his rear, at about 1800 yards, were still the 24 9-pdrs. supported by two battalions of the 8th and two very weak battalions of the 5th Regiment, which had lost 700 men in the affair of September 8th. The other battalion of the 8th was at Brestovetz, and that of the 5th Regiment was keeping up connection between the two portions of his command. If the Turks in the Krishin redoubt were strong enough to come down upon his rear, there was a good chance that his whole force would be lost. He sent word to Zotof explaining his position, and saying it was untenable unless he was strongly reinforced, at the same time that other reinforcements were sent against the Krishin redoubt; saying also that he would hold on as long as he could, and asking for further instructions.

Not only was his position most critical, but his men were exhausted and their ammunition was running very short. Skobeleff was indefatigable. He posted himself the battalion of the 8th Regiment between the two positions, with one company facing east across the little valley between the redoubt-line and the third knoll, another company facing west toward the Krishin redoubt, and the other three companies in the centre. Some Cossacks who arrived during the night he employed to bring up cartridges; and himself personally visited the left flank of the redoubt-line and set the men to work with their bayonets, soup-dishes, and whatever they had, in throwing up a sort of traverse or trench against the fire from the Redoubt No. 13. Twice during the night he was attacked, once from Krishin and once from the valley on the side of Plevna. The troops making the latter attack were in the darkness mistaken for Russians, supposing that they might be a portion of the IV. Corps coming to their

THIRD BATTLE AT PLEVNA

aid from that direction. The Turks thus got within 100 yards of the Russians before it was discovered; the latter fell back upon the three remaining companies of the battalion (8th Regiment), and then fired by volleys on the Turks, and thus drove them back. This was about midnight. About the same time arrived an aide-de-camp (Colonel Orloff) of the Grand Duke, who had been riding since 6 o'clock in the darkness and absence of roads (it was nearly fifteen miles round through the Russian lines from the Grand Duke's headquarters to Skobeleff's position); the critical condition of affairs was explained to him, and he returned to headquarters. A little before daybreak Skobeleff brought 4 9-pdrs. forward and established them in the middle redoubt, to open fire against No. 13.

The morning of the 12th of September dawned bright and clear, after forty hours of continuous rain and fog. At 6 o'clock the Turks opened fire with their artillery from the redoubts surrounding Skobeleff's position, and with musketry from the camp in his front; and not long after appeared a strong column of infantry from the direction of the Krishin redoubt, which advanced to within 300 yards of the Russian position before it was arrested by their fire; it then fell back to Redoubt No. 13. At 8 o'clock they made their second attack in the same direction, but with no better success. Skobeleff had meanwhile brought up 8 4-pdrs. to the third knoll, which did good service with shrapnel against the advancing Turks. At 10.30 A.M. they made a third desperate assault, still upon the left flank of the Russian position; it was repulsed, but now the men in that part of the line, worn out and discouraged with 30 hours' continuous fighting, began to drop out one by one and make their way to the rear. Seeing this, Skobeleff, who was on the third knoll, rode over and expostulated, threatened, ordered, and encouraged the men, and got them back into the redoubt again.

Meanwhile Skobeleff had received two orders from Zotof, the first about 7 A.M. and the second at 10.30 A.M. They were as follows:

1. *To* General Prince Imeretinsky: By direction of the Commander-in-Chief, I give you and General Skobeleff the order to fortify yourselves in the position which you have taken to-day, and to hold out to the last extremity. We can send you no reinforcements, for we have none.

(Signed)   Zotof, *Lieutenant-General.*

2. *To* General Skobeleff: By order of the Commander-in-Chief. If you cannot hold the positions which you have taken, then you must retreat slowly—but, *if such a thing is possible,* not before evening—to Tutchenitza, covering your retreat by the cavalry of General Leontieff. Send a copy of this order—which otherwise keep secret—to General Prince Imeretinsky. The Gravitza redoubt is in our hands, but in spite of this the attack cannot be continued; but the retreat must be slowly begun. 8.30 A.M.

(Signed)   Zotof, *Lieutenant-General.*

This latter order was brought by the same Colonel Orloff who had visited Skobeleff during the night, and thence returned to the Grand Duke and Zotof to explain the condition of things in Skobeleff's front.

Skobeleff did what he could to obey these orders—to hold on till evening; but from the very first his case was hopeless. He always kept hoping, in spite of Zotof's first order, that a portion of the IV. Corps would be sent to help him, or at least that the attack would recommence on some other part of the line, and thus relieve the pressure on him. But this did not happen. There was hardly a shot fired from any other part of the line throughout this day. Zotof and Levitzky were at the Grand Duke's headquarters all the morning, over on the hills east of Grivitza, about $6\frac{1}{2}$ miles in a straight line from Skobeleff's position, watching the fight with their glasses, but unable, of course, at that distance to make anything out of it. The distance over the route which messengers had to take through the Russian lines was about 12 miles. As to the question of reinforcements, the Roumanians and the 1st Brigade 5th Division were fully occupied in holding the Grivitza redoubt; from the Grivitza village to the Tutchenitza Creek the line was held by 5 regiments of the IX. Corps and 6 regiments of the IV.

THIRD BATTLE AT PLEVNA

Corps; and of these 11 regiments 5 had not been engaged the previous day at all, viz., the 121st, 122nd, 119th, 120th, and 20th. Whether two or three of these regiments might not safely have been sent to Skobeleff—as there was no intention of attacking in any other part of the line—is, of course, a matter about which opinions will differ. The fact was, however, that at the Russian headquarters it had been determined not to continue the attack (on the ground that their force was not strong enough), and the Chief of the Staff had *no realisation* of what a desperate position Skobeleff was in. Hence the orders cited above.

Skobeleff's position, however, was most desperate. As the morning wore on and there was no sign of a renewal of the attack on the other parts of the line, Osman began to mass a strong force in Plevna to drive Skobeleff out. Whether these troops were drawn from the reserve camp in the valley between the town and the river, or from the Bukova position, or from the middle redoubts, is not known; but it is certain that Osman reinforced the troops in front of Skobeleff to the extent of not less than 12,000 men. Part of them went over the hill and round into the Krishin redoubt, and thence against Skobeleff's left flank, and part of them came out of the town and followed up the Tutchenitza brook for about three-quarters of a mile, and then climbing up its bank endeavoured to get possession of the third knoll from the rear and thus cut off Skobeleff's retreat. This latter movement began to make itself apparent about 1 P.M., and to meet it Skobeleff brought up the two battalions of the 5th Regiment, which up till now had remained with the batteries on the second knoll. Meanwhile, of the four guns which he had placed in the middle redoubt, two had been dismounted and the other two had lost all their horses and gunners; to replace these guns, Skobeleff sent three of the eight guns which he had kept on the third knoll; they had been in the redoubt but a short time before they were dismounted; and about this time a caisson which had been brought under the shelter of the side of the redoubt for protection was nevertheless found by a shell from the Krishin redoubt, and exploded in the midst of the men, not only creating a fearful loss, but carrying dismay to those who were not hurt. Skobeleff again rushed forward in person to the redoubt, and endeavoured to reassure his men; and he was barely in time, for a few minutes later, between 2 and 2.30 P.M., the Turks from the direction of the Krishin redoubt and from No. 13, reinforced now by fresh troops, made their fourth assault. The Russians let them approach to within 400 yards, and then opened on them with well-aimed volley-firing, and with deadly effect. The Turkish line halted and sought shelter, and returned the fire; but every time they endeavoured to move forward they met with such terrible losses that they finally gave it up and returned to No. 13.

As Skobeleff was returning from the redoubt to the third knoll, he learned that the 118th Regiment was arriving; it had been sent to him as reinforcement by General Kriloff, commanding IV. Corps, *on his own responsibility*, on account of the heavy firing which he had heard so long on Skobeleff's front. The regiment numbered 1300 men. At 4.30 P.M. the Turks, greatly reinforced in numbers, began their fifth assault, from the direction of Krishin, and simultaneously from the camp. They kept advancing in spite of the murderous fire of the Russians, and as they neared the redoubt the majority of the latter, worn out with 36 hours of continuous fighting with no appreciable result, began to make off to the rear in small groups; the little band of 200 or more brave men, who remained behind under Major Gortaloff, were cut down to the last man in a fierce hand-to-hand fight.

The middle redoubt was thus lost, but still the men in the eastern redoubt and a part of the trenches between the two remained in their places and kept up the fight. To prevent their being massacred, Skobeleff hastily sent them an order to fall back to the third knoll; and in order that this might be possible, he himself took the 118th Regiment (which had recently arrived as just stated) and led them to the assault of the line between the two redoubts. Under cover of this they returned (what was left of them) to the third knoll. The retreat was then continued under the protection of the 24 guns and 2 battalions (8th Regiment) on the second knoll. Except those who fell in the last affair in front of the redoubts, nearly all the wounded were carried off; the dead were left on the field.

Skobeleff retreated to the " first knoll," and remained there all night, and all of the 13th. The Turks were too much used up to follow or attack him. At night of the 13th he returned to Bogot. His losses were 160 officers and over 8000 men. About 18,000 men had been engaged. On the 13th, 14th, and 15th the Russian batteries bombarded the town and the Turkish positions, though with what object is not quite apparent. On the evening of the 14th, just before dusk, the Turks sallied out of the second Grivitza redoubt and attacked the first, which was held by the Roumanians and part of the IX. Corps. They attacked with energy, but were repulsed. With this exception the Turks made no attempt to take the offensive. The Russians took up a defensive line from Verbitza to Radischevo, and began fortifying it. The cavalry was between each flank of this position and the Vid.

The third and great assault on Plevna was therefore over, and like the two previous ones it had resulted in a bloody and terrible repulse, the losses reaching the large total of more than 18,000 men out of 75,000 infantry present and 60,000 actually brought into action.

The Turkish losses are unknown, but they were not small. Osman stated after the surrender that he lost more men on the Lovtcha road than Skobeleff did. It is probable that the Turkish losses were in all between 12,000 and 15,000.

The Russian losses were as follows:

		KILLED.		WOUNDED.		TOTAL.	
		Officers	Men.	Officers	Men.	Officers	Men.
In the bombardment, September 7–10 .		—	—	—	—	10	300
In Skobeleff's fight of September 8th .		—	—	—	—	—	900
September 11th.	Grivitza Redoubt. { Roumanians	15	1335	41	1176	56	2511
	Grivitza Redoubt. { 1st Brigade 5th Division .	—	—	—	—	22	1305
	Redoubt No. 10. { 2nd Brigade 16th Division / 1st Brigade 30th Division / 2nd Brigade 31st Division	—	—	—	—	110	5200
Sept. 11th and 12th.	Lovtcha Road. { 1st Brigade 16th Division / 2nd Division / 3rd Rifle Brigade . / 118th Regiment .	—	—	—	—	160	7200
Sept. 14th.	Grivitza Redoubt. { Roumanians	—	—	—	—	4	500
	Grivitza Redoubt. { 1st Brigade 5th Division .	—	—	—	—	3	300
Total		75	7558	29	10658	365	18216

The telegraphic despatch of the Grand Duke, dated Poradim, September 15th, gives the Russian losses as in all 300 officers (of which 60 killed) and 12,500 men, of which about 3000 killed; the Roumanian losses at 60 officers and 3000 men. This despatch states that 239 officers and 9482 men (Russian) had passed through their hospitals. At the time this despatch was written the total losses in Skobeleff's column were not fully known at headquarters. Both Prince Imeretinsky and General Skobeleff personally stated to me a few days after the battle that their losses were over 8000 men. The 2nd Division, while waiting for its reserves to arrive from Russia, was temporarily re-organised *into one regiment* of 4 battalions, each about 1000 strong.

The figures given above for the losses at the Grivitza and Redoubt No. 10 are taken from Russian official reports. The large proportion of killed is accounted for partly by reason of the fierceness of the fighting, and partly from the fact that all the wounded left in Turkish hands in front of Redoubt No. 10 and the Lovtcha road were never afterward heard of, and must therefore be counted as dead.

THIRD BATTLE AT PLEVNA

That the repulse of the 11th of September was a great disaster for the Russian arms there is no doubt; that it was in no sense an irreparable one, the subsequent course of the campaign abundantly proves. While it is no business of foreigners to attempt to fix the personal responsibility for this failure (which also would be impossible by means of the documents which have as yet been published), yet there are certain facts which will hardly be denied by any one who was present, which largely contributed to the defeat, and which are as much matters of public discussion as the number of men engaged and the losses on either side.

1. There was a certain lack of unity in the command of the army.

The troops assembled at Plevna were under the command of Prince Charles of Roumania, as already stated; but this command was to a certain extent nominal, and the dispositions previous to the battle depended largely upon Lieutenant-General Zotof, who had commanded the troops before Prince Charles's arrival, and who was now his Chief of Staff. General Zotof was unfortunately not a general of the calibre to command 80,000 men; but even had he been a military genius of the first order, it would have been very difficult for him to gain a victory in the circumstances in which he was placed; for a few days before the movement on Plevna began, the assistant chief of the General Staff, Major-General Levitsky, arrived at Poradim to explain to General Zotof the wishes of the Commander-in-Chief. On the day that the bombardment began the Commander-in-Chief arrived in person, and with him his Chief of Staff, General Nepokoitchitsky. He of course confirmed the dispositions already taken, but from this time forward he commanded. Although he rode over the field as far as possible, and even exposed himself imprudently to the enemy's picquets, yet it was impossible for him to be properly familiar with the ground before the assaults were made; so that while he commanded he had to rely upon the information and opinions of others rather than upon his own judgment. Finally, the Emperor was present, with the Minister of War and a large suite. The Emperor came merely as a spectator, to encourage his troops by his presence and in the hope of witnessing their victory. But the Emperor of Russia is regarded by every Russian soldier, from the highest to the lowest grade, with a feeling which it is difficult to explain in other countries; *at all times* his will is law, and his wish a command, and it is not possible for him to be a mere spectator. He took no part, however, in the command, although every report and order was instantly communicated to him, until after the assaults of the 11th and 12th. On the 13th and 14th long councils were held on the field, at which the future "policy," so to speak, of operations against Plevna (i.e., the investment without further assault) was determined upon. The Emperor presided at these councils, at which *all* of the following officers took part, viz., The Grand Duke Nicholas, Commander-in-Chief; General Milutin, Minister of War; Prince Charles, Commander of the troops at Plevna; General Nepokoitchitsky, Chief of Staff of the Army; General Zotof, Chief of Staff of the troops at Plevna; General Levitsky, Assistant Chief of Staff of the Army.

The subject is a somewhat delicate one, and I have no wish to pursue it beyond a statement of the bare facts which were evident to every one present at headquarters who chose to see them; and my only object is to cite enough to show that the ancient and unquestioned maxim of war, that there should be one man in an army to command and all the others to obey, was not fully observed at Plevna.*

---

* It will always be said, in extenuation of McClellan's failure in 1862, that he was improperly interfered with by Mr. Lincoln and Mr. Stanton. On the other hand, when General Grant took command of the armies in 1864, he was never summoned to a council of war, and never asked by either the President or Mr. Stanton to explain his plan of campaign. Full confidence was placed in him and full assistance given him. This I have from General Grant himself; and he has also told me that throughout the war he never called a council of war, though he listened patiently to the volunteer advice of those whose position warranted their offering it. But before every principal movement, and before every battle, he wrote out himself the rough draft of the orders, and as soon as it was finished gave it to his chief of staff, to be copied at once and immediately sent to its various destinations.

See also Sherman's "Memoirs," vol. i., p. 344.

THIRD BATTLE AT PLEVNA

2. As a result of this division of authority, the plan of battle, such as it existed, was a general idea of attacking on all sides, rather than a carefully prepared attack upon the points of greatest importance, or where the enemy was weakest. The importance of the Grivitza redoubt, the key-point on the north, was well known from the previous struggles around it; but *even the existence of the great Krishin redoubt*, the key-point on the south, was not known till the 7th of September. During the month of August the topographers of the IX. Corps had reconnoitred the country in front of Grivitza and Radischevo, and had represented with tolerable accuracy the position of the Grivitza and Bukova lines and the middle group of redoubts upon a reconnaissance sketch, of which several lithographic copies were made. It was on this map that the dispositions for the attack were made. This map shows (in dotted lines, and as a matter of fact in wholly erroneous positions) two redoubts on the Lovtcha road just outside the town of Plevna, but otherwise, west of the Tutchenitza creek, the map is a blank; no reconnaissance had ever been made of that part of the ground, and no one of the chief officers previously named had ever been within sight of it. Their only information concerning it came from a report of Skobeleff, who had fought over this ground on the 30th of July; but at that date the Turks had no fortifications there, and the redoubts and trenches which had since been built had changed the whole condition of affairs. I give these details because they have a bearing upon the great and vital question raised by this war as to the propriety of making direct attacks upon fortified positions defended by breech-loaders; and because they seem to me to warrant the conclusion that *the Russians were defeated at Plevna, not because the position was impregnable, nor because they did not have sufficient forces, but because they were ignorant of the enemy's position, and failed to concentrate their efforts upon the decisive points.* Had they confined their assaults to the Grivitza and Krishin redoubts on the two flanks, and concentrated their forces there, leaving in the centre only the troops necessary to support their line of batteries and to make a demonstration, the

result of the 11th of September might and probably would have been far different ; and this both the Grand Duke and General Nepokoitchitsky acknowledged in conversation after the battle, when they were more familiar with the nature of the Krishin position. As it was, in their ignorance of this position, Skobeleff was sent forward almost as into a funnel, leaving commanding positions on either side of him, and attacking a position which if gained led to nothing, and which, as the sequel proved, was totally untenable. As for the attack on Redoubt No. 10, it would have been reasonable in the condition of the fortifications in July; but after the construction of the Krishin works it had no reason whatever.

It only remains to be added, concerning the general dispositions of this battle, that out of 103 battalions present only 72 were actually brought into action. The reserve division of the Roumanians (16 battalions) and the following Russian troops were not actively engaged: 1st Brigade 31st Division, 6 battalions; 2nd Brigade 30th Division, 6 battalions; 20th Regiment, 3 battalions. When Zotof wrote to Skobeleff during the night of the 11th-12th that he had no reinforcements to send him, he must have meant (being ignorant of the critical position in which Skobeleff was placed) that he did not consider it judicious to withdraw the troops above mentioned from his centre, between Grivitza and Radischevo, where these troops were placed in support of the batteries.

3. If we now come down to the tactics, the manner in which the troops were led to the different assaults, we find that at Grivitza the attack was made by four columns, from the north-west, north-east, east, and south; that these columns endeavoured to start at the same hour, 3 P.M.; that, having different distances and different nature of ground to pass over, they arrived one after another, and were all; in their first efforts, beaten in succession. Subsequently a second effort, simultaneous on two sides, was successful, after fearful losses, in gaining possession of half the position, i.e., the southern one of the two redoubts.

At Redoubt No. 10 there was also a succession of assaults

on different sides, *all* beaten in detail; in the morning an attack brought on by misapprehension, in the afternoon an attack at the specified hour (3 P.M.), and later an attack by the reinforcements when they arrived, which was after the second attack had been *wholly* repulsed.

In Skobeleff's column, on the contrary, there was none of this lack of *ensemble* and tactical confusion. He held his men well in hand, sent a portion of them forward in reasonably open order, and *at the critical moment when the line began to waver, but before the attack had failed*, sent in his reserves and went in himself with the last of them and carried the place. Once there, he held on to the last extremity, in accordance with his orders, and always in the hope that reinforcements would arrive and enable him to begin an assault against Redoubt No. 13. The reinforcements not arriving, and overwhelmed by numbers, he withdrew his force (as ordered) toward evening of the second day, under cover of artillery and of a small force of infantry which he had kept all the time in a fortified position (second knoll) in his left rear. Skobeleff's extremely reckless courage, while it compels that personal admiration which such qualities always command, is of course open to serious criticism when it is remembered that he was the commanding general on all that part of the line. On the other hand, there is no doubt that without the aid which this display of daring gave to his men the position would not have been carried or held as it was; and the legendary stories of his personal bravery which circulated among the soldiers from this day, especially among the recruits who afterward arrived, constituted a positive military factor of which good use was made at the subsequent assault of the Green Hills (November 15th-17th, 1877) and at the storm of Shenova (January 8, 1878), which compelled the surrender of the Turkish army at Shipka.

CHAPTER VI

THE INVESTMENT OF PLEVNA—BATTLE OF GORNI-DUBNIK, OCTOBER 24TH, 1877

THE INVESTMENT OF PLEVNA

IN the councils of war which were held as already stated on the 13th and 14th of September, it was decided to make no more assaults upon the works of Plevna, which had already cost the Russians well-nigh 30,000 men, but to fortify their own position on the east from Verbitza to Tutchenitza against any counter-attack, and, upon the arrival of more reinforcements, to proceed regularly to invest the place. Meanwhile the Roumanians were to run a sap forward toward the second Grivitza redoubt and try thus to gain possession of it; and the whole cavalry force was to be united on the other bank of the Vid and cut off the communications of the Turks, and if possible prevent the entry of any supplies, munitions, or reinforcements.

On the other portions of the theatre of war everything was to remain on the defensive, and if possible *in statu quo*.

On the 7th of September, General Loshkarieff, Chief of the 9th Cavalry Division, who was then on the high road east of Grivitza, between the Roumanians and the IX. Corps, received an order placing the two regular regiments of Roumanian cavalry and two of their militia (Dorobanz) regiments under his orders, making in all 32 squadrons and 3 mounted batteries, and directing him to proceed across the Vid at Riben and act upon the rear of the Turks, and in case of their retreat to pursue and harass them. On the 8th Loshkarieff crossed the river and established a picquet line on the other side, about 20 miles long, from Riben through Dolni-Etropol and Dolni-Dubnik to Gorni-Dubnik, the bulk of the Roumanian cavalry being placed behind this line at Gorni-Etropol (Widdin road), and of his own division at Dolni-Dubnik. On the 8th and 9th the Turks sortied in small numbers from Plevna and skirmished with Loshkarieff, but without any important result. On the afternoon of the 9th the scouting parties beyond Gorni-Dubnik reported a camp of 10,000 Turkish infantry a few miles west and south-west of Gorni-Dubnik. Upon this report Loshkarieff withdrew the bulk of his force to Gorni-Etropol. On the 10th Loshkarieff advanced again the four regiments of his division and took up a position near Dolni-Dubnik, facing south, and sent a few squadrons to his left across the Vid to establish communication with the cavalry of General Leontieff. On the 11th a squadron from General Leontieff's (4th) Division arrived at Dolni-Dubnik, and the communication was thus established. From the 11th to the 18th scouting parties were sent out along the Sophia road as far as Radomirtza, and also westward to and beyond the Isker; they found everywhere plundering parties of Tcherkesses and bashi-bozouks, but otherwise learned nothing. During this time the Turks made no effort to enter Plevna with supplies or reinforcements, and, as already noted, they did not retreat from that place. On the 18th Loshkarieff's division was ordered back across the Vid to take position on the Lovtcha road and form the left flank of the infantry force on that side, and all the rest of the cavalry (except some regiments of Roumanian militia on the right flank) was ordered west of the Vid; the command thus formed was entrusted to Lieutenant-General Kriloff, who had originally commanded the 4th Cavalry Division, and had temporarily replaced General Zotof in command of the IV. Corps when the latter was made Chief of Staff of the "West Army."

Kriloff's command was composed as follows:

4th Dragoons, 4th Hussars, 4th Lancers	12 squadrons,	2 batteries.
Don Cossack Brigade, Regiments 21 and 26	12 ,,	1 battery.

Caucasian Cossack Brigade, Regiments Kuban and Vladikavkas   12 squadrons, 1 battery.
Regular (Roschiori) Roumanian Brigade, Regiments 1 and 2 .   8 „   1 „
Militia (Dorobanz) Roumanian Brigade, Regiments 5 and 6   .   8 „   0 „

In all, 52 squadrons and 30 horse guns.

His instructions were to clear the country between the Vid and the Isker of bashi-bozouks, to seize all the food and forage in that region, to break up Osman's communications, to find out what force lay on the roads to Sophia, Vratza, and Widdin, and above all to prevent the entry of supplies or reinforcements into Plevna.

We thus see that on the 19th of September there was a *quasi* investment of Plevna; but as the infantry stood on but one side, leaving the other three sides to be occupied by cavalry, it was nothing more than a paper investment; and its insufficiency was rendered still more complete by the incompetency of General Kriloff as a cavalry commander.

On the 20th of September Kriloff sent a detachment of four squadrons to reconnoitre in the direction of Telis. Before reaching that village they met some regular Turkish cavalry and skirmished with them, and in so doing discovered that they were the advanced guard of a strong force of infantry; they therefore fell back to Dubnik. On the 21st Kriloff sent the Caucasian Cossacks to make a strong reconnaissance in the same direction. They found Telis occupied by 10,000 infantry, and defended by some earthworks which were partly completed. On the 22nd, early in the morning, the picquets reported a strong column of infantry moving on the road from Telis toward Dubnik and Plevna. Kriloff immediately sent word to Loshkarieff across the Vid to advance in the direction of Telis with his division and take this column in rear. Soon afterward he received word that a strong column of Turkish infantry was advancing from the direction of Plevna over the bridge and along the high road toward his rear. Thereupon Kriloff, almost without firing a shot, withdrew his force 15 miles to the north, to the village of Tristenik in the vicinity of Riben, leaving a small portion of it at the village of Etropol to skirmish with the Turks who had sortied from Plevna. During the night the Turkish convoy quietly continued its road to Plevna. By Turkish reports its strength was 20 battalions (say 12,000 men) of infantry, a regiment of cavalry, 2 batteries, and about 2000 waggon-loads of provisions and ammunition. Kriloff placidly congratulates himself in his report upon having delayed this column for two days, and states that one of the principal objects of his command was to "spare his men as much as possible, since they constituted the greater part of the cavalry strength of the West Army"!

On the 23rd and 24th of September nothing was done, and on the latter date a second small convoy slipped past the Cossacks at Etropol. On the same day Kriloff, according to his report, received an order from Prince Charles to secure the right flank of the West Army (it was not in any way threatened) by a position at Brest, away off near the Danube, " and to base himself in case of necessity upon Riben." Later in the day he received information that the Tcherkesses were recruiting men and horses and obtaining supplies in the district between the Vid and the Isker. On the 25th, therefore, Kriloff, abandoning the care of the Sophia road to the Don Cossack Brigade and the Roumanian militia, took the greater part of his force (32 squadrons and 18 guns) and went off to the west beyond the Isker, to the valley of the Skitt River, which flows into the Danube at Rahova. The bashi-bozouks disappeared before him, and then Kriloff took his cavalrymen down the valley against Rahova (a fortress similar to Nikopolis), and actually began a bombardment of the outlying redoubts with his little 4-pdr. horse-guns! This he kept up for one day (September 27th), and in so doing dismounted one gun in the Turkish works. On the 28th he turned back toward the Vid, and arrived at Tristenik on the 30th. During his absence the Don Cossacks which had been left at Etropol had captured two little convoys, one of 20 and the other of 100 waggons, loaded with flour and barley. Otherwise the Sophia road was now open, and the Turkish communications and telegraph were completely restored.

On the return march to Tristenik Kriloff had detached Colonel Levis-of-Manera, Chief of the Vladikavkas Regiment, with four squadrons of his own regiment, two of Lancers, and two of Hussars, and one battery, to follow up the valley of the Isker to Sumakova, and thence up a small stream which was crossed by the Sophia road over a bridge near Radomirtza. On the 1st of October Colonel Levis struck the road near Radomirtza, routed a party of bashi-bozouks, captured about 1,000 head of cattle and a small train wholly loaded with quinine and salt, and—at last something important—partly destroyed the bridge. Radomirtza is two days' march from Plevna, and therefore too far distant for a convoy arriving from the south to receive prompt aid from that place; the hills on the north of the little stream completely command the bridge and the road for a distance of a mile south of it. Six thousand cavalrymen and 30 guns (which was the strength of Kriloff's force), if properly handled at this point, could make a very stout defence against even a superior force of infantry. But instead of this, Kriloff sent a little detachment of eight squadrons to this place, and with the bulk of his force made a demonstration (October 1st) against the heights of Opanetz, in conjunction with one Roumanian battalion, which was operating a reconnaissance of the fortifications of Opanetz from the north. The Turks sallied out from Plevna across the bridge and attacked Kriloff; an insignificant combat took place, of which the principal result was the setting fire to the village of Etropol: and at evening the Turks retired across the Vid.

On the 2nd of October Colonel Levis's detachment at Sumakova was reinforced by the 4th Dragoons and 2 guns, making its total strength 12 squadrons and 8 guns. At the same time little detachments of one squadron each were sent scouting across the Sophia road (of which Osman was already beginning to fortify the villages of Dolni- and Gorni-Dubnik, Telis, and Radomirtza) toward the Vid, where they found portions of Loshkarieff's division—and then returned. Colonel Levis skirmished for three days with the Tcherkesses in the region of Sumakova and Radomirtza, but his detachment was too small to accomplish anything of importance; and on the 5th of October Chefket Pasha, coming from Orkhanie with 5,000 infantry and a swarm of Tcherkesses, rudely brushed Levis aside, and took his troops on to Telis and Gorni-Dubnik, and himself went to Plevna to consult with Osman. Chefket brought with him also a considerable quantity of provisions and munitions; and the Radomirtza bridge had been so slightly injured as to permit its being repaired in a day.

After his demonstration against the heights of Opanetz on the 2nd of October, Kriloff remained idle at Tristenik with the bulk of his force until the 8th, on which day he was relieved from his command by General Gourko.

While these events had been in progress considerable change had taken place in the direction of the Russian Army. When it was determined to invest and besiege Plevna, General Todleben, the famous Engineer of Sevastopol, was ordered from St. Petersburg to the army. He arrived at Gorni-Studen on the 28th of September, and on the 30th accompanied the Grand Duke and a portion of his staff to the position in front of Plevna. General Gourko, who had meanwhile arrived from Russia with his proper command, the 2nd Cavalry Division of the Guard, and was in camp near Tirnova, was also ordered to Plevna. On the 4th of October was issued an order of the day assigning Todleben as "Adjunct to the Commander of the West Army," with Imeretinsky as Chief of Staff; Zotof to resume command of the IV. Corps; Gourko to command all the cavalry on the west bank of the Vid, which was to be reinforced by his own division; Kriloff to proceed to Russia as Inspector of Cavalry Remounts. These changes took place within the next few days; the Grand Duke returned to Gorni-Studen, and General Todleben assumed the direction of the siege. At that time the Roumanian works at Kalysovat and Verbitza, and redoubt Alexander, were nearly completed; their approaches on the east of the second Grivitza redoubt were within 70 yards; the Russian batteries from Grivitza to the Tutchenitza ravine were finished and armed. The 20 siege-guns (24-pdrs.) were distributed in three batteries, one just south of the Grivitza brook and the other two on the

Radischevo ridge. From these new positions the siege-guns could reach every point in the Turkish lines along the whole length of the Grivitza ridge, and also in the "middle group." They could not reach the Turkish works, which were increasing every day, on the Krishin heights.

The rest of the batteries were armed with 9-pdrs., and in all there were about 250 guns in position. There was no firing except as the Turks were discovered enlarging their works, when the Russians opened upon them with shrapnel; they were thus forced to prosecute their work wholly at night. But little change was evident in the main works of the middle group, except that they were all being connected by trenches serving as covered ways for communication as well as for lines of defence; but along the crest of the ridge between Grivitza and Bukova the works were in course of construction in spite of all the efforts of the Russians to stop them. On the other hand, occasionally the Turks would drop a shell among the men at work on the Russian batteries; immediately more than 100 Russian guns would concentrate their fire upon the Turkish redoubt whence this shot had come, and reduce it to complete silence. The Turks, as already stated, were greatly inferior in artillery, having only about 80 pieces and no siege-guns. These pieces were moved about from one redoubt to another at night, and ventured but rarely to open fire, and always with the result just stated.

While these changes had been taking place on the Russian side, the Turks had been making efforts to reinforce Plevna and secure its communications. Chefket Pasha, who previously commanded a division in Mehemet Ali's army, had been sent to Sophia about September 12th, to take charge of these operations. The troops placed at his disposal were nearly all new recruits from Asia or reserves which had been kept at Sophia, Philippopolis and Adrianople. From Sophia to Plevna the distance is about 135 miles over the high road, which was then in excellent condition; but as 60 miles of this was over the main chain of the Balkans and up and down over its foot-hills, it was a march of ten days for troops or ox transports. Chefket established his depôt of supplies at the town of Orkhanie, at the northern entrance of the defile passing through the main range, and seven days' march from Plevna. From here he sent a force of 12,000 men, accompanying 2000 waggons loaded with provisions, which entered Plevna on the 22nd of September, as already described. After that he sent smaller convoys, of which some were captured and some succeeded in reaching Plevna. He came himself with 5000 men and a large train, whose exact numbers are not known, on the 5th of October, as we have seen, and, posting his men on the road behind Plevna, went himself to Osman's headquarters and then returned to Radomirtza and commenced fortifying points along the road in order to keep it open. A few days later he sent about 3000 more men into these works, and had besides a certain force, numbers not known, at Radomirtza and farther back on the road. In all it is probable that he sent into Plevna about 3000 waggon-loads of provisions, or, estimating the load at a ton, about 60 days' full rations for 60,000 men.

Meanwhile, on the Russian side the troops of the Guard were arriving daily, and were now (October 1st) nearly all on the south bank of the Danube. The Grenadier Corps was following closely behind them. This gave a disposable force of 70,000 infantry and the proportionate cavalry and artillery—all fresh troops; and the question arose as to what disposition to make of them. There was a certain party among the Grand Duke's advisers who warmly urged him to leave matters in their present condition at Plevna and on the Lom (the Russian fortifications in front of Plevna being now quite sufficient to withstand any effort of Osman to break through them, and the force on the Lom having already proved its capacity to repel any attacks from that quarter), to unite the newly arrived troops with those of Radetzky at Shipka, and with this column of 100,000 men to dislodge the Turks at Shipka and advance at once over the Balkans to Adrianople. On the 23rd of September an order of the day was issued directing the Cesarevitch to resume command of the Corps of the Guard (his usual command in time of peace); on the 6th of October this order was revoked, and the Cesarevitch was directed to retain command of the troops on the Lom. Between these two dates the plan of advancing had been rejected, and it had been decided to send the Guard and Grenadiers to Plevna, and to capture or destroy Osman's army as a precedent to any farther advance. Had an advance been made the Cesarevitch would have commanded it; but it was not thought becoming for the heir to the throne of Russia to serve under the orders of the Prince of Roumania, as would have been necessary had he accompanied the Guard to Plevna.

On the 19th of October the Roumanians made another effort to gain possession of the second Grivitza redoubt. Their approaches were already within less than 20 yards of the ditch of the Turkish redoubt. At noon four Roumanian battalions jumped out from their trenches and from the first redoubt, and rushed forward toward the Turkish work; they were received by the fire of about 1000 infantry posted in the work, and that of an equal or greater force which immediately came out from the Turkish trenches and covered ways in the rear of their redoubt to meet them. The Roumanians were obliged to fall back under cover. At 6 o'clock the attempt was renewed by three Roumanian battalions. This time they drove the Turks out of their places along the counterscarp of the ditch, and got possession of the ditch. The Turks then came out on the parapet of the redoubt, and opened fire at arm's length upon the Roumanians; and as the latter tried to climb up the parapet the Turks received them with the bayonet. Meanwhile the artillery and infantry fire from the Roumanian trenches in rear caused the Turks to leave the parapet and put themselves under cover; but no sooner did the Roumanians appear on the parapet again than the Turks again jumped up to meet them, and drove them back into the ditch. This was kept up for nearly an hour, until darkness had set in; then, finding it impossible to carry the place, the Roumanians returned into their own trenches. Their losses were 2 officers and 200 men killed, 20 officers and 707 men wounded; those of the Turks were probably

INVESTMENT OF PLEVNA

about equal. This was the last assault ever made upon any of the Turkish redoubts around Plevna east of the river.

On the 20th of October the Guard had all arrived at Plevna, and Todleben prepared to complete the investment. His plan, in brief, was to throw forward his two wings from the Verbitza-Radischevo fortified position, and join them together on the other side of the Vid, thus forming a complete circle. There was nothing to oppose his right wing (which in fact was, with cavalry, already at Etropol), but his left wing would have to dislodge the Turks from their fortified places along the Sophia road, of which there were four within a distance of 35 miles from Plevna, viz., Dolni-Dubnik, Gorni-Dubnik, Telis, and Radomirtza.

The Guard was designated for this purpose, and had already been massed in the villages between the Lovtcha road and the Vid, near the village of Cirakova. The 1st and 2nd Infantry Divisions and its Cavalry Divisions were placed under the orders of General Gourko, commanding all the troops on the west bank of the Vid, and were to first attack Gorni-Dubnik, and afterwards Telis and Dolni-Dubnik in succession, and then join hands with the large cavalry force, now commanded by General Arnoldi, and reinforced by seven infantry battalions from the 3rd Roumanian Division, which was at Gorni-Etropol. Meanwhile the 3rd Division of the Guard was to advance parallel to the Vid and seize the heights near Medevan, and continue advancing until they came within close range of the Turkish redoubts, which had lately been constructed all along the Krishin ridge to the bluff overhanging the river. At the same time a detachment which had just been formed under the orders of General Skobeleff, consisting of his own (16th) Division, the 1st Brigade of the 30th Division, and the 3rd Rifle Brigade, was to advance from Tutchenitza to the Lovtcha road and seize the Red Hill (where he had been September 7th) and the heights in front of Brestovetz. This detachment was then gradually to extend to the left, and the 3rd Division of the Guard to the right, until they came together. Finally, on the day fixed for this simul-

K

taneous movement (October 24th), an energetic bombardment was to be kept up by all the batteries on the east of Plevna, in order if possible to prevent the Turks from sending reinforcements from Plevna to the aid of their works on the Sophia road.

Skobeleff's detachment and the 3rd Division of the Guard occupied the position assigned to them almost without resistance; but at Gorni-Dubnik Gourko met with most stubborn opposition, as will presently be seen.

The force acting under Gourko's orders on the 23rd of October was as follows:

	Battalions.	Guns.	Squadrons.	Guns.
1st Division of the Guard	16	48	—	—
2nd Division of the Guard	16	48	—	—
Rifle Brigade of the Guard	4	—	—	—
Sapper Battalion of the Guard	1	—	—	—
2nd Cavalry Division of the Guard	—	—	24	18
Emperor's personal escort	—	—	4	—
1st Brigade 3rd Roumanian Division	7	6	—	—
4th Cavalry Division	—	—	18	12
Brigade Don Cossacks	—	—	12	6
Brigade Caucasian Cossacks	—	—	12	6
Regular Roumanian Cavalry Brigade	—	—	8	6
Militia Roumanian Cavalry Brigade	—	—	8	—
Total	44	102	86	48

Or about 35,000 infantry, 10,000 cavalry, and the usual proportion of artillery for each arm.

On the 22nd Gourko personally reconnoitred the positions at Telis and Gorni-Dubnik, and on the 23rd issued the necessary orders for his advance the next day.

The country on the west of the Vid differs completely from that on the east. As seen from the heights of Medevan, it appears to be a vast plain, but, on descending into it, is found to have long gradual slopes, rising perhaps to the height of 150 feet at the most above the level of the Vid. These slopes are cut through by occasional rivulets flowing to the Vid, and forming what are known on our Western plains as *coulées*. The villages of Telis and Dolni-Dubnik are situated about 7 miles apart, in the same *coulée* which flows north to Gorni-Etropol, and thence east, emptying into the Vid about three miles north of the Plevna bridge.

The village of Dolni-Dubnik is near the head of another similar *coulée*. The depth of these *coulées* varies from 60 to 100 feet, and their width from 200 to 1000 yards.

The high road coming from Sophia passes through the village of Telis, and then keeps a straight course to Dolni-Dubnik (and thence to the Plevna bridge), leaving Gorni-Dubnik about half a mile on its left (north).

On the plain around Dolni-Dubnik were six little redoubts, three north and three south of the village. At Telis was a large irregular line of breastwork, north-east of the village, divided in two by the road, and running down on either flank to the stream in the *coulée*. On the other (south-west) side of the village was a large redoubt.

Near Gorni-Dubnik the fortifications were weakest of all. At the point (about a mile south-west of the village) where the road crosses the *coulée* was one of those ancient tumuli so frequently found in Turkey, about 40 feet in diameter at the base and 15 feet high. The Turks had levelled off a part of the top of this mound so as to make a *cavalier* holding four guns, and they had then surrounded this with a rudely constructed redoubt upon a polygonal figure about 300 yards in diameter. The parapet of this redoubt was only 4 feet high and 6 feet thick, and the ditch had about the same proportions. In order to partly cover what would otherwise have been a dead space at the bottom of the *coulée*, there were some trenches on the slope outside of the redoubt. At the edge of the road near the redoubt was a small stone post-road station, and just opposite it, on the southern side of the road, the Turks had built a three-sided lunette of about 50 yards front. Two thousand yards farther to the south-east, their picquets had a few rifle-pits, on a little eminence covered with thick brushwood.

Gourko's plan of attack was as follows:

1. 20 battalions, 6 squadrons, and 48 guns to attack the position at Gorni-Dubnik on three sides, viz., from the north, east, and south.

2. 12 battalions, 11 squadrons, and 44 guns, to cover the attack on the side of Dolni-Dubnik.

3. 4 battalions, 17 squadrons, and 20 guns, to cover the attack on the side of Telis.

4. 7 battalions, 44 squadrons, and 34 guns, under General Arnoldi, to make a strong demonstration on the north of Dolni-Dubnik, in order to retain the garrison in that place; and at the same time a portion of these troops to operate on the west of Gorni-Dubnik, in order to cut off the retreat of the Turks, and another portion to reconnoitre in the valley of the Isker and towards Lukovitza.

1. ATTACK OF GORNI-DUBNIK

The troops designated for this purpose passed the Vid at the Cirakova ford between midnight and daylight of the 24th of October, and were divided into three columns, viz.:

On the right, under Major-General Ellis, the Rifle Brigade (4 battalions), with 3 sotnias and 16 4-pdr. guns.

In the centre, under Major-General Zeddeler, the Moscow and Grenadier Regiments, and the Sapper battalion (8 battalions), with 1 sotnia and 16 9-pdr. guns.

On the left, under Major-General Rosenbach, the Paul and Finland Regiments, 8 battalions, with 16 4-pdr. guns.

These columns took up the march soon after 6 A.M., and at 8.30 A.M. they arrived in position: the centre column on the little eminence south-east of the redoubt, the right column on the high road north-east of it, the left column on the high road on the south-west, all at a distance of about 1800 yards. They deployed their troops in two lines of company columns and a reserve, and placed their batteries in the centre of the first line and opened fire. At the same time the brigade of Caucasian Cossacks (coming from the command of General Arnoldi) arrived on the hill north-west of the redoubt, and opened fire with six horse-guns. The redoubt was therefore at 9 A.M. surrounded with 56 guns, which kept up an incessant fire upon it, inflicting considerable losses on the Turks, whose means of shelter in their hastily constructed redoubt were not very good. A little after 10 A.M. Colonel Lioubovitzky, commanding the Grenadier Regiment, led it forward to the assault. They carried the lunette on the south-east of the road, and then followed the retreating Turks and made a vigorous effort against the main work; but they were driven back by a murderous fire and took refuge behind the lunette, the post-house, and in the ditches on either side of the high road. General Zeddeler then sent the Moscow Regiment and the two batteries to their support; the regiment found shelter in the ditches of the road on the right of the Grenadiers. The batteries advanced to within 900 yards of the redoubt, but at this distance their horses and gunners were picked off by the Turks with such accuracy that they were obliged to return to their first position. General Zeddeler, Colonel Lioubovitsky, and Colonel Scalon (chief of staff of the division) were all wounded about this time; the troops remained in the ditches of the road, which was nearly parallel to one side of the redoubt and but 60 to 80 yards from it, and from there kept up a fire with the Turks.

Meanwhile the column of the right, upon arriving on the high road, had come under the fire of the artillery in the works near Dolni-Dubnik. Leaving one battalion to face these works, the other three had turned to the left and advanced to some small mounds about 1900 yards from the redoubt, and had here opened fire with their artillery. When the Grenadier Regiment assaulted the redoubt from the east, their men remained so close to the redoubt that at that distance it was impossible to tell exactly where they were, and therefore the batteries were advanced to 900 yards and there commenced their fire, but were soon obliged to retire to a greater distance. The place of the battalion which had been left facing Dolni-Dubnik was now taken by the 1st Brigade 1st Division, which arrived on the high road, and the other regiment (Izmailof) of this column, which was to protect the right flank, was sent to the support of the batteries, while the whole of the Rifle Brigade descended into the *coulée* near the village, and crept along its slopes until they came under the fire of the trenches on the hillside, north-west of the redoubt.

The column of the left had arrived about the same time as the others (8.30 to 9 A.M.) on the high road between Gorni-Dubnik and Telis, and then, turning by the right flank, had advanced and opened fire with its batteries. When they saw the Grenadier Regiment advancing to the assault, they also formed on both sides of the high road, crossed the *coulée*, and began climbing the hill against the redoubt. But the fire was terribly hot, and they could not stand it; they fell back, the Finland Regiment to the dead angle at the bottom of the *coulée*, and the Paul Regiment behind a bend in the *coulée* on the left flank and in rear of the Grenadiers. General Rosenbach, commanding the column, and Colonel Rounoff, commanding the Paul Regiment, were both wounded in this assault.

At noon, therefore, the condition of things was as follows: The Russians had made an assault on the north, east, and south-west, and had been repulsed; the Paul and Finland regiments were in the ravine south-west of the work; the Grenadier and Moscow regiments in the ditches of the high road a few rods from the redoubt, on the south-east; the Izmailof Regiment between the high road and the village of Gorni-Dubnik, on the north-east; and the Rifle Brigade in the ravine, north and north-west of the redoubt; the artillery in nearly the same positions as during the morning, but its action much hindered by the fear of hitting their own troops, who were so close to the redoubt. The troops rested in these positions with desultory firing for the next three hours. At 2 P.M. Gourko, who had been during the morning with the column on the right, came in person to the little hill where were the batteries of the column of the centre, and here he received word that the four battalions (Jäger Regiment) sent against Telis had met with a terrible repulse, and had fallen back, leaving the road from Telis partly open to an attack by Turkish reinforcements coming from that direction. It was evidently necessary to strike hard and quickly, else his position became a very critical one. Gourko therefore determined to attack from all sides

BATTLE OF GORNI-DUBNIK

at 3 P.M. For the result I will give his own words, translated literally from his report:

"I gave in person the necessary orders to General Brock, who had taken command of the First Brigade Second Division of the Guard, and I sent a written order to General Ellis.

"In order that the attack might be simultaneously made by all the troops, I decided that, when all the orders had been given, I would have three volleys fired by the batteries on the left; that three volleys should then be fired in succession by those on the centre and on the right; and that after the last volley fired by these latter all the troops should rush forward to the assault. I calculated that a simultaneous attack made on all points and at very short distances (100 to 400 paces) would be crowned with success.

"After having given these orders, I went to the column on the left and examined the position of all the troops; I then returned to the battery, where I gave in person the necessary orders to General Count Shouvaloff, commanding the Second Division of the Guard. But before Count Shouvaloff had had time to transmit his orders to the troops, three volleys were fired in succession by the batteries of the column on the right, and this column rushed forward to the assault. The signal agreed upon was thus not observed, and my calculations for a simultaneous attack were baffled.

"It was with a sinking heart (*le cœur défaillant*) that I followed what was about to take place; for in place of a simultaneous assault on all points, there were going to be isolated assaults one after another, of which the success was more than doubtful. To remedy matters as far as possible, and to sustain the column on the right, which had already begun the assault, I sent orderly officers in all directions to give the troops the order not to wait any longer for the signal, but to support the attack of the column on the right. As was to be expected, a series of attacks one after another took place. Received by an extremely murderous fire, no one body of troops could reach the great redoubt. But, with the exception of the Finland Regiment, no one of them fell back; moving forward, they lay down behind shelter of one sort or another, and a few arrived within 40 paces of the redoubt. As for the Finland Regiment, not finding any shelter in front of it, it was obliged to fall back, and establish itself again on the slope of the ridge in the dead space. In this assault Major-General Lavroff, commanding the Finland Regiment, who was marching at the head of his regiment with heroic intrepidity, fell, mortally wounded.

"After this series of assaults, which were over by 4 o'clock in the afternoon, all the batteries ceased firing, for the troops were so close to the redoubt that their fire reached our own troops.

"As for withdrawing the troops in order to continue to cannonade the redoubt, it was absolutely impossible to do it, on account of the losses which they would unquestionably have suffered in this movement, and especially on account of the bad impression which this movement in retreat would have produced upon the morale of the troops. I decided then to leave the troops in the positions which they occupied, and to make a new assault at nightfall. After having given the necessary orders, I returned to the eminence opposite the village of Gorni-Dubnik to there await the twilight.

"There was observable a terrible silence, a silence of death. When darkness came, several bodies of troops crept closer to the redoubt. Two battalions of the Izmailoff Regiment, Major-General Ellis II., of the suite of H.M. the Emperor, commanding the regiment, at the head, advanced thus by crawling for about 150 paces, and thus came within 50 paces of the redoubt. Simultaneously the troops rushed forward, and almost from all sides they penetrated into the redoubt. The immense flame of a fire which burst forth in the centre of the enemy's work lit up the whole neighbourhood, and announced the fall of the redoubt which the Turks had so long and so stubbornly defended."

The Russian trophies were 1 Pasha, 53 officers, and 2235 men (not wounded) prisoners, 1 standard, 4 guns, and a large number of small arms and ammunition. The Turkish losses were about 1500 men. Those of the Russians were as follows: 2 brigade commanders and the chief and 3 officers of the Division Staff, wounded; 2 regiment commanders

BATTLE OF GORNI-DUBNIK

and 1 battalion commander killed; 1 regiment commander and 3 colonels wounded; and the following:

	KILLED.			WOUNDED.		
	Field Officers.	Company Officers.	Men.	Field Officers.	Company Officers.	Men.
Staff	—	—	—	1	4	1
Emperor's escort.	—	—	1	1	1	4
Izmailoff Regiment	—	1	57	—	6	219
Moscow Regiment	—	3	95	1	12	421
Grenadier Regiment	—	3	310	4	22	594
Paul Regiment .	—	6	164	2	11	500
Finland Regiment	1	2	106	4	10	328
Rifle Brigade .	—	1	66	1	12	214
Sapper Battalion	—	—	5	1	—	58
Artillery . . .	—	1	7	2	1	49
Total . .	1	17	811	17	79	2384

Total, 116 officers and 3195 men.

2. ATTACK OF TELIS

The column whose mission was to protect the Russian left flank against any attack from the direction of Telis, and if possible to gain possession of that place, was composed of the Jäger Regiment (4 battalions), the 1st and 2nd Cavalry Brigades, 1 sotnia of the 4th Don Cossacks, and 20 guns. It crossed the river also at the Cirakova ford during the night, and at 6.15 A.M. took up its march towards Telis, leaving the greater part of the cavalry to cover its left flank. The infantry arrived on the high road in front of the Telis redoubt about 9 A.M., and its artillery (12 pieces) opened fire upon the Turkish work at 1200 yards. At 10 A.M. the Jäger Regiment, formed in two lines, moved forward and drove the Turks out of some small rifle-pits which they had in front of the main work. But these shallow trenches being wholly open in the rear, i.e., toward the redoubt, and only about 200 yards from it, when the Russians had gained possession of them it was not possible to remain there under the fire of the Turks; it was necessary to retreat or assault the main work. They chose the latter, and rushed at it with great bravery, but without success. They found a little shelter in the irregularities of the ground about 100 paces in front of the parapet, and were lying there keeping up a hot fire with the Turks, when word was received from the cavalry off on the left that considerable Turkish reinforcements were approaching Telis from the south. As his force was evidently unequal to the task of gaining the redoubt, the Colonel of the Jäger Regiment then sounded the retreat, and the regiment fell back about a mile and a half in the direction of Cirakova. The Turks, however, did not make an effort to follow them or to go past them to the relief of Gorni-Dubnik.

In this short affair the Jäger Regiment lost 26 officers and 907 men.

The result of the 24th October was therefore the capture of the position of Gorni-Dubnik, by which Gourko got a firm footing in the centre of the Turkish line of fortifications along the Sophia road. He immediately set to work to fortify his position, facing both ways on the road. The 1st Division was placed in position in front of Dolni-Dubnik, the Rifle Brigade on its left joining hands with the 1st Brigade 3rd Roumanian Division, which was on the north and west of that place; the 2nd Division was placed in the works at Gorni-Dubnik, with one brigade in advance towards Telis, and the 1st Brigade 3rd Division was brought from the vicinity of Medevan toward Telis on the east. The Cavalry Division was sent in observation on the left (heights of Rahita), threatening the communications of the Turks by the high road, while the Caucasian Brigade of Cossacks demonstrated from the west against the Turkish works on that side of Telis. On the 28th of October these troops were simply advanced to within 1500 yards of the Turkish fortifications at Telis, and from there opened fire with 72 guns, firing principally shrapnel. This concentrated artillery fire was kept up from 11 A.M. to 2 P.M., when Gourko sent one of his prisoners with a note summoning the Pasha to surrender, and threatening to attack on all sides if his answer was not received in half-an-hour. The Pasha (Izmail Hakki) surrendered, with 100 officers, 3000 men, 4 guns. and an enormous quantity of small-arms ammunition destined for Plevna.

As soon as this surrender took place, the cavalry of the Guard and the Cossacks joined hands on the south of the village, and attacked a large band of Tcherkesses supported by infantry who were posted about half-way between Telis and Radomirtza. They drove back the Tcherkesses, but were naturally brought to a halt by the infantry, and after a loss of about 50 men they fell back a short distance toward Telis, establishing a picquet-line in observation of the Turks. During the night the latter fell back upon Radomirtza, and, assembling his force there, Chefket Pasha abandoned all his fortifications and took up his retreat to the positions about Pravetz in the foot-hills of the Balkans.

Meanwhile, on the other side of his position—*i.e.*, toward Dolni-Dubnik—Gourko had posted the 1st Division across the high road, and on its right a portion of the 9th Cavalry Division, keeping up communication with the 2nd Brigade 3rd Division (Guard), on the heights in front of Medevan, on the east bank of the Vid; on its left was the Rifle Brigade, then the Roumanian Brigade, and then a large force of cavalry near Etropol. The two divisions of the Grenadier Corps which were *en route* to Bulgaria had meanwhile partly arrived, and the first of them had been directed to the army of the Cesarevitch beyond Biela; but they were recalled by forced marches to Plevna, and, passing around the right flank of the Roumanians, were to cross the river at Riben. Gourko only awaited the arrival of these troops to fill up the space on the north, and then he intended to repeat at Dolni-Dubnik the measures which had gained Telis—*i.e.*, surround it on three sides with a large force of artillery, supported by infantry four times as numerous as the defenders, then open a concentrated fire with shrapnel, and finally, if the Turks refused to surrender, make a simultaneous assault from all sides. The leading troops of the Grenadiers (2nd Brigade 3rd Division Grenadiers) arrived at Etropol late in the afternoon of October 31st. Gourko then wrote out his orders for the attack, fixing it at the 2nd of November. But the next morning at daylight the Rifle Brigade noticed a lack of defenders in the Turkish work near it, and immediately sent a party of volunteers to reconnoitre, who found the redoubt empty. The Turks had in fact abandoned all their positions at Dolni-Dubnik, and during the night had retreated into Plevna; and as the day became more clear the last of the column could be distinguished just crossing the Plevna bridge. The troops immediately moved forward and took up a position just outside the range of the Turkish guns on the heights north of Medevan. The investment of Plevna was complete.

CHAPTER VII

EVENTS ON OTHER PORTIONS OF THE THEATRE OF WAR FROM SEPTEMBER TO DECEMBER, 1877—SHIPKA—THE LOM—THE LOWER DANUBE—GOURKO'S ADVANCE TO ORKHANIE.

It is now necessary to refer briefly to the course of events at the other points of the theatre of war.

SHIPKA PASS

In a previous chapter we have seen that Suleiman Pasha made a succession of fierce, mad assaults upon the Russians at Shipka from the 21st to the 26th of August, and that, having caused great losses on both sides, but having gained no ground whatever, he was forced to desist and to reorganise his force and call for more reinforcements. The Russians on their side did what they could to repair losses and prepare for a new struggle; they strengthened their own position by fortification, dug trenches and covered ways along that part of the road commanded by the Turkish fire from the Bald Mountain, and brought a few mortars into position; but as they received no reinforcements (all those which arrived in Bulgaria at this time being directed toward Plevna for the great purpose of capturing or defeating Osman's army), they had no troops available for undertaking any operations to dislodge the Turks from their commanding positions; and therefore they (the Russians) remained on the same ground, viz., the three hills on the high road at the summit of the pass. Their daily losses were from 5 to 10 men. On the 13th of September the Turks increased their fire both in infantry and artillery, and the latter included four large mortars concealed in the woods in front of Mount St. Nicholas, which did great damage to the Russians, whose losses increased to about 40 men per day. At the same time some demonstrations were made on either flank by Tcherkesses, resulting in some skirmishes which accomplished nothing.

This cannonade continued for four days, and then, at 3 A.M. on the 17th of September, Zuleiman sent forward his infantry to the assault on all sides, directing as previously his strongest efforts against Mount St. Nicholas. Here the Turks, under cover of the darkness, climbed up to within about 100 yards of the batteries and trenches on the summit, drove the Russians out of the advanced trenches, and established their own position by means of the gabions and fascines which they had brought with them. At daylight a fierce fight opened for the possession of this hill, and lasted till noon. Radetzky hastened thither in person, taking with him the 56th Regiment to reinforce the 53rd, which held this portion of the line. The Turks made several desperate efforts to drive the Russians from the top of the hill, but without success; and the Russians in turn were unable to drive the Turks back beyond the trenches they had taken and constructed before daylight. The struggle went on all the morning, and the bayonet was very freely used on both sides. A part of the 35th and 55th Regiments was brought up to the hill during the morning, and finally about noon portions of the 53rd and 56th rushed forward upon the Turks, and succeeded in driving them out. This assault cost the Russians dear, but nevertheless it accomplished the defeat of the Turks.

Upon the Russian right flank (northern hill) the Turks had begun their attack also at daylight; the Russians allowed them to approach within fifty yards, and then opened on them with volley-firing, under which the Turkish lines withered, and the men fell back. Twice more they tried it, and with the same result. At 9 o'clock they withdrew altogether in this quarter.

The loss of the Russians on this day was 31 officers and something over 1000 men. That of the Turks was naturally much larger, and was estimated by General Radetzky in his report at not less than 3000 men. The south side of Mount St. Nicholas was a mass of corpses. Suleiman, having gained nothing by this assault, resumed the ordinary mortar and sharpshooter practice, which continued for ten days; when he was nominated to the command of the Army in the Quadrilateral, and succeeded at Shipka by Reouf Pasha.

Reouf found it necessary to reorganise the army which Suleiman had turned over to him. Soon afterward bad weather arrived, and, in this high altitude, a considerable quantity of snow. This impeded operations during the month of October, and in November Gourko began advancing toward Sophia, which caused a portion of Reouf's troops to be moved in that direction. Reouf soon afterward was recalled to Constantinople and made Minister of War, and was succeeded by Vessil Pasha, whose force was then increased by troops brought from the Quadrilateral,

But, although desultory firing was kept up during all these months, the Turks undertook no serious assault after the 17th of September; and, on the other hand, the Russians never loosened their grip upon the position which they had captured on the 19th of July. In the first week of January, as will be subsequently explained, they turned the pass on both flanks and captured Vessil Pasha and his army *in toto*.

OPERATIONS ON THE LOM

We have already followed in a previous chapter the advance of Mehemet Ali against the detachment of the Cesarevitch during the months of August and September, his successes in the battles of Karahassankoi and Katzelevo, his defeat at Cerkovna, and his subsequent retreat to the line of the White Lom, where on the 2nd of October he was replaced by Suleiman.

The detachment of the Cesarevitch at this time counted, as before, the XII. and XIII. Corps; and the 26th Division on their right, keeping up communication with the XI. Corps on the west of Tirnova; but the dispersion of his force, which had so largely contributed to the necessity for his retreat before the force of Mehemet Ali in September, was now avoided, and his troops were well in hand, in fortified positions between the Danube near Metchka and the mouth of the Banitchka Lom—a distance of only about 18 miles. The country on his right, being most difficult of approach, was occupied only by detachments of the 26th Division in observation. The defence of the road from Osman-Bazar to Tirnova was entrusted to the XI. Corps under General Dellinghausen, who had replaced Prince Shakofskoi, the latter being broken down by sickness.

Although Suleiman took command of the Army in the Quadrilateral in the first week in October, it was not until the 26th of November that he undertook any serious operations. He first assembled a large force at the village of Kadikoi, eight miles south of Rustchuk, and apparently threatened the Cesarevitch's left flank, and at the same time began building a bridge from Silistria toward the Roumanian bank of the Danube. Against this the Russians simply diverted the 24th Division, which was *en route* through Bucharest. This demonstration against Roumania was made in conjunction with an intended descent of some Hungarians from the Carpathians upon the line of the Russian communications; but this latter proved wholly abortive, and, the 24th Division being more than ample for the defence of the passage of the river at Silistria, the Turkish bridge was taken up and the whole movement amounted to nothing. Suleiman then moved the bulk of his force to Razgrad, and began reconnoitring in front of that place, at the same time that bands of Tcherkesses and some infantry made demonstrations on the road from Osman-Bazar to Elena. Still, nothing serious was attempted. The troops of the Cesarevitch were kept constantly on the alert and made frequent reconnaissances in order to keep themselves informed of Suleiman's movements. The result was a constant series of skirmishes. Finally, in the latter part of November (Gourko's troops being already in the foot-hills of the Balkans on the Sophia road), Suleiman rapidly assembled a large force near Rustchuk, and on the 19th drove the Russians, with a loss of about 200 men, from their advanced position near Pirgos to their principal position near Metchka; but in the afternoon of the same day the Russians reinforced the point attacked, and drove the Turks out of Pirgos and back across the Lom. On the 26th Suleiman renewed his attack in greater force upon the position of the XII. Corps at Metchka and Tristenik. A very considerable affair took place, in which the whole of the XII. Corps was engaged; the Turks attacked with great energy, but were wholly unsuccessful, and in their retreat were followed by the XII. Corps and driven across the Lom. The Russian official report states that the Turks lost 1200 men, and that their own losses were 28 officers and 738 men.

On the same day demonstrations were made by the Turks in front of Katzelevo, as well as on the roads leading from Osman-Bazar.

On the 4th of December a large force (reported at 30,000 men), which had advanced by the road leading from Osman-Bazar through Elena to Tirnova, fell upon the two regiments of the 9th Division (VIII. Corps) occupying a fortified position in the ravine of Mahren, two miles east of Elena. The attack was made at daylight, and the Russian commander, Prince Mirsky, seems to have been taken somewhat by surprise; his position was surrounded on three sides, and his troops were driven back to Elena with a loss of 50 officers and 1800 men, as well as 11 guns, 4 of which had been dismounted and the other 7 had all their horses killed. This affair was also remarkable as being almost the only one in the whole course of the campaign in which the Turks took any prisoners. They here captured about 500 men, who were taken to Constantinople and well cared for.

The Russians fell back in disorder to their fortifications at Elena, and hastily brought up part of the XI. Corps from the vicinity of Tirnova to their aid. The Turks did not follow up their success, and on the 6th, the Russian reinforcements having arrived, Prince Mirsky advanced to his old positions, and the

Turks retreated, after some skirmishing, in the direction of Osman-Bazar.

At last, after this long series of indecisive combats, skirmishes, and demonstrations upon both flanks of a line 75 miles long, Suleiman made an attack in force with about 35,000 men (60 battalions) upon the left flank of the Cesarevitch's detachment, *i.e.*, at Metchka and Tristenik, near the Danube. This was on the 12th of December, Plevna having fallen two days before.

At this time the position of the XII. Corps, forming the left of the Cesarevitch's detachment, was as follows: at Metchka, near the Danube, 1st Brigade 12th Division; at Tristenik, 4 miles south-east of Metchka, 2nd Brigade 12th Division—both in positions well fortified; in reserve to this line, the 2nd Brigade 33rd Division. The 129th Regiment of the same division was at Damogila, and the 130th at Tabashka, in observation of the Lom. On their right was the XIII. Corps, of which the 2nd Brigade 35th Division was nearest (and was brought into action on the 12th of December). The 12th Cavalry Division was on the right and left of Tristenik, and furnished the cavalry picquets on a line from the Danube to the Lom, about four miles in front of the infantry position. The total strength of these troops was therefore 30 battalions, about 25,000 men, with 16 squadrons and 120 guns. The XII. Corps was commanded by the Grand Duke Vladimir, second son of the Emperor.

The two villages of Tristenik and Metchka lie each in a deep ravine, flowing to the Danube, and the branches of these ravines make the country in front of Tristenik very broken and difficult for manœuvres. On the other side of the high road are shorter but equally deep ravines flowing into the Lom, whose banks are precipitous, and the bed of its stream fully 350 feet below the level of the plateau between it and the Danube. The position of the Russians was a very favourable one, completely commanding, over an open plateau, the approaches from Rustchuk, either by the high road which passes near Tristenik, or by the river road near Metchka. Behind their left flank, at the island of Batin, the Russians had a pontoon bridge (built in the month of October) over the Danube, and on the Roumanian shore, near Giurgevo, were several siege batteries.

On the afternoon of the 10th of December the Turks drove in the Russian picquets, and appeared in considerable force in front of the Russian positions. The troops of the latter were on the alert, but the Turks retired at sunset without making an attack. The next day the Russians made preparations for an expected attack, and brought the 129th Regiment to Tristenik, replacing it at Damogila by the 2nd Brigade 35th Division, and also moved the 130th Regiment a short distance down the Lom. On the morning of the 12th, the Russian batteries at Parapan (5 miles southwest of Giurgevo) signalled that the Turks were moving out of Rustchuk, and at the same time another force of them was discovered by the picquets crossing the Lom just below Kadikoi. Each column contained about 30 battalions and 25 guns. That from Rustchuk immediately advanced along the river road, and at 9 A.M. opened the battle by an attack upon the Russian position at Metchka. Soon afterward the other column came into position on its left (south-east) against the interval between the works at Metchka and those at Tristenik. A strong line of skirmishers extended on its left all the way to the Lom.

The 2nd Brigade 33rd Division was immediately moved forward to occupy the small trenches in this interval; but no other change was made in the position of the troops until the Turks should have developed their plan of attack. The Turks made several unsuccessful assaults upon the Russian redoubt at Metchka, and by noon it was evident that their plan was to throw their whole weight upon the left flank of the Russian position, gain possession of the works at Metchka, and then advance against the Batin bridge; the left flank of the Turks, between the high road and the Lom, seemed to be very weak. As the most efficacious way of meeting this attack, the Russian commander determined to throw forward his right flank against this weak line and thus threaten the Turkish left and rear, and at the same time to attack in force with his centre; and also to execute this movement before the enemy should have had time to concentrate too strong a force against Metchka. The 2nd Brigade 12th Cavalry Division was therefore moved forward in the space between the high road and the Lom, and, dismounting a part of its force, gained possession of the plateau about four miles in front of Tristenik; the 2nd Brigade 35th Division and the 47th Regiment at the same time followed on its left along the high road, and coming on the plateau, supported the cavalry, who were just beginning to be forced back. These three regiments then established themselves on this plateau, and, bringing five batteries into action, opened a terrible fire with shrapnel upon the flank of the Turkish reserves, which were still massed in the ravines. At the same time the 2nd Brigade 33rd Division began to advance through the interval between Metchka and Tristenik. The result of this double attack was not long in doubt; by 2 o'clock the Turks were in full retreat, and then the troops in the works at Metchka in their turn began to advance. The result was a complete rout of the Turks at every point, and a somewhat precipitate retreat to Rustchuk and across the Lom at Krasnoe. They were followed by the Russian cavalry until darkness set in. Their losses were nearly 3000 (as estimated in the Russian official report), among which were 800 dead left on the field. The Russian losses were 24 officers and 775 men. The Turkish losses were caused in large part by the shrapnel of the Russian artillery.

For more than five months the detachment of the Cesarevitch—which, even counting the 26th Division, had never numbered over 55,000 infantry—had guarded the left flank of the Russian Army and secured its communications against any attack coming from the direction of the Turkish fortresses. During the latter part of August and the 1st of September, having stretched itself out over a line more than 60 miles in length, and having its right flank within a few miles of Razgrad, it was attacked by Mehemet Ali, who had at his disposal a force of more than 65,000 infantry. It was thus driven back and driven together, but it checked Mehemet Ali's advance by the defeat it inflicted upon him at Cerkovna (September 21st); immediately after which

Mehemet Ali returned to his old positions. It then took up a more compact position in front of Rustchuk, and here awaited the further attacks of the Turks. Suleiman, having at his disposal about the same force as Mehemet Ali, and having very thoroughly reconnoitred the whole Russian position, endeavoured on the 26th of November to break through the left flank of it near the Danube. Failing in this, he ordered the attack upon Elena (in which Prince Mirsky's detachment of the VIII. Corps was so badly cut up), with the apparent object of diverting a portion of the Russian troops from the vicinity of the Danube to the neighbourhood of Tirnova; and a week later Suleiman again attacked (December 12th), this time with the bulk of his force, in the vicinity of the Danube. But his troops were tactically badly handled, and before they were all engaged the Russians took advantage of this and fell upon his exposed flank at the same time that they engaged him in front. Suleiman was badly defeated and driven back across the Lom. Plevna had already fallen, and Gourko was threatening the Balkan defences near Sophia. Placing a portion of his troops within the fortifications of Rustchuk and Shumla, Suleiman hastened to the south of the Balkans with the remainder.

Thus ended all operations on the Lom. The achievements of the Cesarevitch's detachment have been somewhat obscured by the more bloody engagements around Plevna, and the subsequent brilliant advance over the Balkans; but it must not be forgotten that throughout the campaign it fulfilled to the letter, and without drawing reinforcements from the other parts of the army, the task which was assigned to it, viz., to assure the safety of the left flank of the Army and to mask the Quadrilateral of Turkish fortresses.

OPERATIONS IN THE DOBRUDJA AND ON THE LOWER DANUBE

General Zimmermann, as we have already seen, had crossed the Danube at Galatz on the 22nd of June and gained a footing on the south bank of the river, the Turks retreating up the Dobrudja. As soon as the water fell low enough to use his bridge at Braila, Zimmermann crossed the rest of his force at that point and advanced slowly up the Dobrudja. His force consisted of the XIV. Corps, with the 1st Don Cossack Division and part of the 7th Regular Cavalry Division. A portion of the infantry of the VII. Corps took up the line of observation on the Lower Danube below Galatz.

Zimmermann reached the line of Trajan's Wall and occupied it without opposition on the 18th of July. His own communications were maintained by the river, which was in possession of the Russians as far as Silistria, and also by the Dobrudja and the Braila bridge. His instructions were to hold the line of Trajan's Wall from Kustendje on the coast to Tchernavoda on the Danube, against any advance by the Turks, and to observe the Black Sea coast and prevent any landing there. He had about 22,000 infantry; at least half this force would necessarily have to be left to occupy the points above named, leaving him only little over 10,000 men for any offensive movements. The latter were therefore out of the question, as the Turks had about 25,000 men in his front, 10,000 at Bazardjik, and 15,000 at Silistria, besides small forces at Mangalia and Kavarna on the coast. The infantry of Zimmermann's corps therefore remained on the line of Trajan's Wall until after the passage of the Balkans in the following January; his cavalry were occupied with skirmishes and reconnaissances in their front, by which they kept themselves informed of the position of the Turks —who on their part undertook no serious offensive movements. Zimmermann's rôle was purely defensive, and he accomplished the task assigned to him, viz., to cover the Russian line of communications in Roumania from any attacks from the direction of the Dobrudja.

In short, the detachment of the Cesarevitch on one side and that of Zimmermann on the other, with the aid of the Danube on the third, completely masked the fortifications of the Quadrilateral.

On the Lower Danube nothing of consequence took place until the first week in October. The Turkish fleet of three ironclads and as many wooden ships of war remained all the time in the harbour of Sulina, and attempted nothing. On the 8th of October a combined force under Lieutenant-General Verevkine, consisting of one regiment of the VII. Corps on the land, and six small gunboats and six torpedo boats on the river, advanced toward Sulina. At 12 miles from the port they halted and placed a line of torpedoes across the Sulina arm; the Turks kept up a heavy fire from their gunboats, but did not succeed in interrupting the Russian works. During the night the Russians advanced a short distance and placed a second line of torpedoes.

On the morning of the 9th, Commander Dikoff advanced in a gunboat of light draught toward the port of Sulina; the Turkish wooden ship Kartal came out and engaged him. Both of these crafts, having a light draught, passed over the line of torpedoes as Commander Dikoff retreated; but about 9 A.M. a large ship also came out to the attack, struck one of the torpedoes in the first line, and instantly sank with nearly all her crew. The ship was a three-masted, sea-going, broadside ironclad, carrying 5 guns and a crew of about 225 men.

After this affair the Russians erected batteries on the shore, and by means of them and their little flotilla defended their lines of torpedoes. The two Turkish ironclads remained at Sulina. They exchanged shots occasionally with the Russian batteries, but nothing of importance occurred until the following month of January.

GOURKO'S ADVANCE TO ORKHANIE

With the arrival of the two divisions of Grenadiers at Plevna a few days after Gourko had completed the investment on the west side, the total force of Russians and Roumanians blockading that place amounted to 191 battalions, 120 squadrons, and 650 guns, or about 160,000 men. This was much more than was absolutely necessary for the investment. At the same time it was known that Mehemet Ali Pasha had been sent to Sophia to relieve

Chefket Pasha, and if possible to organise a force sufficient to march to the relief of Plevna and raise the siege. As the most efficacious means of preventing this lay in an offensive movement against Mehemet Ali, and as the troops could be spared, a detachment of about 36,000 men (1st and 2nd Infantry Divisions, Rifle Brigade, and 2nd Cavalry Division of the Guard, and the Brigade of Caucasian Cossacks) was formed under the orders of General Gourko and sent south along the Sophia road toward the Balkans.

About the same time, or in fact a little before, the 3rd Division of the Line, which was posted at Lovtcha, had pushed forward toward the Balkans and occupied the town of Trojan, and then, moving west over the foot-hills, had captured, after a small fight on the 31st of October, the town of Tetevan. The smallness of this force prevented its penetrating farther, and it was to operate in the district west of Tetevan, *i.e.*, in the neighbourhood of the high road to Sophia, that Gourko was sent forward.

Gourko began his march southward on November 15th, the infantry of his command and 20 squadrons of cavalry following the high road to Sophia, and 20 squadrons of cavalry on his right following up the valley of the Isker and thence over the foot-hills of the Balkans to Vratza—the principal town on the direct road from Sophia to Widdin —which they captured after a skirmish on the 9th of November.

The Cossacks had already occupied Yablonitza on the 5th, and the infantry of Gourko's column arrived there on the 18th, and was joined by the 2nd Brigade 3rd Division (Regiments No. 11 and 12), coming from Lovtcha and Tetevan. The next two days were occupied in reconnaissances, in addition to those which had already been made by the cavalry. From these it was learned that all the roads leading over the Balkans in this vicinity were fortified and occupied by the Turks. The first of these positions was on the high road near the village of Pravetz. Here the road, after leaving the village of Osikova, climbs over a high spur of mountain, and then suddenly descends into a narrow gorge through which flows a little stream called the Pravetz into the Isker River. The heights on either side of this gorge were fortified with batteries and trenches, so situated as to command the gorge and to enfilade the road along the portion of it which crossed the spur. On the eastern slope of this spur, and about five miles from Pravetz, was another defile, through which flowed a considerable stream known as the Little Isker, at the head of which lies the town of Etropol. Along the banks of this stream is a road to Etropol, and beyond (south) of that town there is a trail leading over the mountains. To defend this trail the Turks had several small works just in front of the town of Etropol.

After passing through the Pravetz gorge the high road comes into a little valley and makes a sharp turn to the west, and follows this direction for about eight miles, when it reaches the town of Orkhanie, and then turning sharp to the south-east follows another narrow defile to the crest of the Balkans at Araba-Konak, and over them into the plain of Sophia. At Orkhanie, the entrance of this defile, was a very extensive series of fortifications. On the left of this town and five miles from it were some fortifications covering a trail which led over the mountains past the village of Lutikova. The position of Pravetz, with Etropol on its right flank, was the first line of Turkish defence; that of Orkhanie, with Lutikova on its left flank, their second line; and Araba-Konak (the crest of the Balkans) their third line. The high road was in good order, although its grades were often as steep as one in ten; the other roads were of the most primitive nature. In all their positions the Turks had about 25,000 men, of whom the greater part were at Orkhanie.

Gourko's plan of operations against this whole series of positions was to make a strong attack upon the Pravetz position, at the same time that demonstrations were made against the two flanks—*i.e.*, Lutikova and Etropol—in order to prevent the Turks from reinforcing Pravetz. The demonstration against Etropol was to be made in considerable force, and might be converted into a serious attack at the discretion of the officer commanding the column. The tactical dispositions for the attack of the Pravetz position were to demonstrate against its front, which was nearly inaccessible, and turn its left flank from the north. In pursuance of this plan, Gourko's field orders, dated Yablonitza, November 21st, prescribed the following movements for the next day:

1. Regiment No. 12, with 8 4-pdrs., and 3 sotnias, to follow the road leading from Tetevan to Etropol, and arrive in front of the latter place and open fire by 10 A.M.

2. Preobrazhensky Regiment, with 2 9-pdrs. and 2 mountain guns, and 3 sotnias, to follow the road through the gorge of the Little Isker toward Etropol.

3. Grenadier Regiment (of the Guard), 1 battalion of 11th Regiment, 12 field-guns, the 4th Dragoons, and 12 horse-guns, to be on the Tetevan-Etropol road in reserve to the first two columns.

The above troops (12 battalions, 28 guns, and 10 squadrons) to be under command of Major-General Dandeville, who was to confine his movement to a strong demonstration against Etropol, unless the enemy showed signs of weakness; in which case, according to his own discretion, he was to convert it into a serious and energetic attack.

4. Moscow Regiment, 2nd and 3rd Rifle Battalions, 3 sotnias, and 14 guns, under command of Major-General Ellis, to follow the high road and attack the front of the Pravetz position.

5. Simeonof Regiment, 1st and 4th Rifle Battalions, 3 sotnias of Cossacks, and 1 squadron of Hussars, and 8 guns, under Major-General Rauch, to follow the small road through Vedrara, Kalugerova, and Lakovitza, and attack the Pravetz position on its left flank, and if possible from its rear.

6. Izmailoff Regiment, 2 battalions of 11th Regiment, 2 squadrons of Hussars, and 8 guns, to remain as reserve to columns 4 and 6, and take position on the high road near Osikova.

The troops of Nos. 4, 5, and 6 (17 battalions, 9 squadrons, and 30 guns) to be under command of Lieutenant-General Count Shouvaloff.

7. Jäger, Paul, and Finland Regiments, 2 squadrons and 72 guns, to form a general reserve for the whole force, and be posted on the high road at the intersection of the road to Etropol.

8. Two Regiments of Cavalry to leave Vratza at such time as to arrive in front of Lutikova and open fire upon it with artillery by 10 A.M.

The movement took place very much as ordered, barring a delay due to the impassability of the mountain paths which Rauch's column had to follow. These troops started on the evening of the 21st, and marched the greater part of that night and the next two days, but did not arrive in range of the Turks until the afternoon of the 23rd. Meanwhile the troops of General Ellis had advanced along the high road, driven the Turkish advanced posts out of their trenches on the mountain sides east of the Pravetz defile, and dragged some artillery into position on the eastern side of this defile in range of the Turkish position, and opened fire with them across the deep gorge. Three battalions of the Moscow Regiment had also been sent down the mountain into the valley on the left near the village of Pravetz (their places being filled by the Izmailoff and 11th Regiments from the reserve), thus threatening the right flank of the Turks. Nothing decisive took place, however, until Rauch's column, climbing an extremely steep mountain, appeared on the very back of the Turkish position, about 4 P.M. November 23rd. The Turks then made but a slight resistance, and hastily retreated down the other side of the mountain in the direction of Orkhanie. Their retreat was effected under cover of a dense fog which settled in the valleys, and by the darkness of night which soon set in.

The two detachments of the Etropol column arrived in front of the Turkish position near that town on the 22nd, and an effort was made to seize the redoubts on either flank of the Turkish line by a *coup-de-main*, but it was unsuccessful at both points. The Russians then concentrated their labours upon dragging artillery on to the high ridges flanking the Turkish line, which ridges the Turks had failed to occupy.

During the 23rd and the following night they then succeeded in quite reaching around both flanks of the Turks. The latter were greatly outnumbered, and when the Russians opened a vigorous fire about 3 P.M. November 24th, they abandoned all their works and made a hasty retreat through the town of Etropol. There they divided, one portion following a trail leading over the mountains to Slatitza, and the other portion following a trail up to Mount Shandarnik, which formed the right flank of the Turkish position across the Araba-Konak Pass. The latter abandoned 3 Krupp guns, 2 caissons, and over 300 carts loaded with ammunition.

The cavalry column, which, forming part of the general movement, was to threaten the Turkish position at Lutikova and Novatchin, met with misfortune. In the mountain-roads in that region, it got into a *cul-de-sac*, and came near being cut off. It was obliged to retreat, losing two guns, one of which was thrown down a precipice to prevent its falling into the hands of the enemy. In this unfortunate affair 10 officers and 69 men were killed and wounded. The detachment, however, may be said to have accomplished its object, since it diverted the attention of the Turks and caused them to send a considerable force toward Novatchin, and not toward Pravetz, the real point of attack.

As soon as the Pravetz position had been carried, General Rauch crossed over (November 25th) by a mountain-road into the Etropol valley, taking with him the Simeonoff Regiment; this united the whole of the 1st Division of the Guard and the two regiments (Nos. 11 and 12) of the 3rd Division of the Line in the Etropol valley, leaving the 2nd Division of the Guard and the Rifle Brigade in the Orkhanie-Pravetz valley. The advance guard of the latter, under General Ellis, composed of the Moscow and Finland Regiments and the Rifle Brigade, advanced about six miles west from Pravetz, and brought their artillery into position in front of two large redoubts which guarded the high road a few miles east of the town of Orkhanie. During the night of the 26th the Turks evacuated these two redoubts, as well as their position at Novatchin and the town of

Orkhanie, and fell back to their works near the village of Vratches, which guarded the entrance to the long defile of the Araba-Konak Pass. These works were very extensive and admirably constructed; rising above one another in tiers on the mountain-side, they completely commanded every point of the plan in front of the mouth of the defile. They might fairly be considered as *impregnable* to a front assault. Ellis's troops therefore simply halted in observation in front of them.

But meanwhile a portion of the troops in the Etropol valley, viz., the Ismailoff Regiment of the Guard and the 12th Regiment of the Line, under command of General Dandeville, had been climbing the mountain range which formed the eastern side of the Araba-Konak defile, and on the afternoon of November 28th they drove the Turkish outposts away from a mountain called Greote, in front of Shandarnik. A portion of the 12th Regiment even followed the retreating Turks into the Shandarnik redoubt, but there the Turks rallied in superior numbers and drove them out again. Nevertheless, Dandeville maintained his position on the Greote mountain. The western slope of this mountain is a ridge which has a gently sloping crest for a few miles, when it is abruptly terminated by a steep descent terminating in the high road at the bottom of the gorge. By simply moving to the western end of this ridge—as he would have done the next day—Dandeville could post his men on inaccessible heights completely enfilading the high road for a distance of nearly two miles. In short, the Vratches position at the northern entrance of the defile was completely turned, and during the night of the 28th the Turks evacuated it and retreated to the redoubts of Shandarnik. Their retreat was so hasty that, for the lack of transportation, they abandoned 3,000,000 rounds of small-arms ammunition, several thousand rounds of artillery ammunition, a complete pontoon train of 25 iron boats, about 2,000,000 rations in flour, rice, and hard bread, several thousand bushels of oats, and a large quantity of clothing. In fact, the bulk of the stock of the depot which had been formed at Orkhanie, to be sent to Plevna with the "Relief Army," fell into the hands of the Russians; and very welcome it was in view of the bad weather which had just set in, the length of Gourko's line of communication (130 miles from the Danube at Sistova), and the bad condition of the roads.

Gourko's losses at Pravetz, Etropol, Shandarnik, and Novatchin were in all less than 500 men. There was not much hard fighting, but an almost unprecedented amount of hard marching, climbing, and dragging of guns by hand. Several of the men had died from sheer exhaustion in hauling the guns up the mountains. Gourko's force was not so very much superior to that of the enemy, the numbers being about 35,000 and 25,000; but by his manœuvres of demonstrating against the front of impregnable positions and turning their flanks, he succeeded in eight days in dislodging the Turks from all their fortified points in the foot-hills, and forcing them back—with the loss of immense quantities of supplies—to their main position on the crest of the Balkans.

All hopes of relieving the beleaguered army of Plevna vanished from this time. For Mehemet Ali it was no longer a question of marching to the aid of Osman, but of defending the line of the Balkans.

Gourko immediately sent the Grenadier Regiment (of the 1st Division of the Guard) to observe the enemy's position at Slatitza, and disposed the rest of his troops in front of the Shandarnik position. General Rauch, with the Preobrazhensky and Simeonoff Regiments, and the 11th in reserve, took position opposite the right flank (east) of the high Shandarnik redoubt; but being nearly 1500 feet lower than it, his artillery could accomplish but little. General Dandeville, with the Izmailoff, Finland, and 12th Regiments, occupied the ridge extending from Mount Greote west to the high road; while General Ellis, with the Moscow Regiment and the Rifle Brigade, took up a position on a height on the west of the road, and was here somewhat fiercely attacked (December 1st) by the Turks, but held his ground, after a loss of 150 men.

The Turks therefore were on the Shandarnik ridge, *i.e.*,

the main crest of the Balkans, with six redoubts, containing 15 guns, forming a fortified position about 7000 yards in length on both sides of the high road. Gourko's troops were on the Greote ridge, nearly parallel to the other, and about 4000 yards from it, and on a height on the other (western) side of the Araba-Konak gorge. Mount Greote is at an altitude of over 4,000 feet above the sea (and the ridge but little less), while the Araba-Konak and Etropol valleys are at an altitude of from 1500 to 1800 feet. There were no roads worthy the name leading up the mountain, but nevertheless Gourko's men, assisted by a levy of 200 or 300 Bulgarians, succeeded in the course of four days in hauling up, by drag-ropes, 60 guns (of which half were 9-pdrs.), and placing them in position on these heights. Gourko was therefore greatly superior to the Turks in artillery, but its use was much hindered by the dense fogs and clouds which hung over the ravines separating the two lines; and moreover, it is impossible to destroy earth-works at 4000 yards, or to render them uninhabitable, by shrapnel. The works were considered too strong for an open assault, and with the force *then* at Gourko's disposal it was deemed imprudent to advance over the Balkans by a turning movement (such as was subsequently executed) and increase the length of his line of communication, which was already very great. Gourko therefore remained simply in observation, keeping up a desultory artillery fire, until the fall of Plevna should give him more troops. The main object of his advance, viz., to prevent the possibility of a relief army coming to break the investment of Plevna, had been most completely accomplished.

Meanwhile the Roumanians had brought a portion of their reserve force, which had been in observation along the course of the Upper Danube throughout the campaign, across the river above Nikopolis, and advancing along the south bank, had attacked the Turkish fortifications at Rahova and carried them by assault on the 19th of November. They then advanced to the next fortified point on the river, viz., the town of Lom-Palanka, which the Turks abandoned after sustaining a bombardment for six days.

The large fortress of Widdin is only two days' march from Lom-Palanka, but it was much too strong to be taken by this small force of Roumanians. The latter confined their attention to occupying these points on the Danube, the whole course of which from Lom-Palanka to Rustchuk, a distance of 160 miles, was now in the hands of the Russians and Roumanians; and the entire country between the Danube and the Balkans over this width of 160 miles was cleared of bashi-bozouks and Tcherkesses, as well as of the small Turkish garrisons.

We have now followed the course of events on the other points of the theatre of war up to the 10th of December, on which date Osman made his desperate effort to break through the circle of Russian investment, and in so doing lost his whole army. It is now necessary for us to return once more to Plevna.

CHAPTER VIII

THE FALL OF PLEVNA.

AFTER a close investment of Plevna had been effected by the operations of General Gourko on the west bank of the Vid, beginning at Gorni-Dubnik, October 24th, but little had taken place beyond strengthening the lines of works on either side. On the 8th of November Skobeleff's troops, having gradually worked their way with trenches up the slope of the first knoll of the Green Hills (1000 yards north-east of the village of Brestovetz), made an assault during the night, and drove the Turks out of their trenches on top of the knoll. On the 10th, 11th, 15th, and 19th of November, the Turks made obstinate and determined attacks upon Skobeleff's new position, but in every case they were driven back. This new position of Skobeleff shortened the line of investment by about a mile, and gave the Russians possession of a commanding point from which to observe the Turkish movements. The Roumanians meanwhile kept extending the right flank of their works in front of Bukova; and on the night of the 11th-12th of November they advanced along the valley of the Vid from Riben, seized the heights in front of Bivolar, and began erecting works there facing those of the Turks on the heights of Opanetz.

With these exceptions there was no fighting along the lines—except desultory artillery and picquet firing—until the 10th of December. But on both sides the work of fortification continued unabated up to the last minute.

On the 13th of November the Grand Duke sent a flag of truce to Osman Pasha with a letter summoning him to surrender in order to prevent the further effusion of blood, as it must be evident to him that his surrender was only a question of time, since he was completely surrounded with superior forces. Osman replied that he recognised the humane motives of the Grand Duke, but that as a soldier the Grand Duke would readily understand that his military honour forbade him to surrender his army until all his means of defence were exhausted—which was not the case at present.

A few days later arrived the news of the brilliant assault of Kars, which fired the imaginations of that same portion of the Grand Duke's staff which had advised a march over the Balkans, without taking Plevna, upon the arrival of the Guard. They now began counselling him to make an assault upon Osman's works; they cited the brilliant example of Kars, they referred to the sufferings of the men in the cold, and rain, and mud of the trenches (the weather had recently become very bad), and argued that if the siege were to last two months longer, more men would be lost by sickness and exposure than in an assault, which, from the positions now occupied by the Russians and their previous experience, could be successfully made. But against any such proposition Todleben protested with the whole weight of his influence, arguing that, although the date of Osman's surrender could not be predicted, owing to lack of positive detailed information concerning the amount of his provisions, yet his ultimate surrender was *a certainty*, and against such a certainty it was most unwise to risk an uncertainty of a most hazardous nature, such as an open assault. Moreover, Todleben reasoned, though you may only lose 10,000 men *hors de combat* in an open assault, you demoralise 50,000, and a considerable time must elapse before they can be reorganised for any ulterior operations; whereas, by pursuing the investment patiently till the end, the troops will then be in good condition for anything. Todleben's advice prevailed, and the assaults were not made.

Meanwhile, Osman's provisions had reached their last limit; one-third of his army lay sick and wounded without proper medical attendance; alternating rain and snow for the last six weeks had rendered his trenches almost uninhabitable; and desertions were increasing every day. He determined to make an effort to break through the Russian lines on the west of the Vid, either with the hope of reaching Widdin, or of reaching Sophia (since he knew nothing of Gourko's operations), or, as is most probable, since neither of these plans had any chance of success, simply from a preference to surrender his army in the midst of battle rather than without having made any effort to break through the Russian lines. During the night of the 9th-10th of December he abandoned the Krishin and Second Grivitza redoubts and Redoubt No. 10, left about 6000 men in the redoubts of Opanetz and Blasivatz, built two pontoon bridges alongside of the high-road bridge over the Vid, assembled a train of about 1000 ox-carts near these bridges loaded with ammunition and baggage and the effects of the Turkish inhabitants of the town, distributed what rations of bread and rice he had (about six days' supply) to his army, and then, with about 40,000 men, made a most impetuous attack upon the position held by the Grenadier Corps on the Widdin road. Although he carried the first line of Russian works, his army was by noon completely defeated and himself wounded. He surrendered at discretion.

It is perhaps best to describe this affair by giving a literal translation of the whole of General Todleben's report, addressed, under date of January 9th, 1878, to the Grand Duke Nicholas, Commander-in-Chief, as follows:

"The army of Osman Pasha occupied under the walls of Plevna an entrenched camp very easy to defend, and presenting several lines of formidable positions, which the enemy, during our long sojourn in front of Plevna since the end of July, had rendered still stronger by making good use of all the advantages of the ground, and in adapting his sapping operations skilfully to them. The strength of resistance of these works became all the greater, thanks to the violent fire of quick-loading guns and to the mass of cartridges which the enemy had at his disposal, which enabled him to cover the ground in front of his works as far as a distance of two versts* with a hail of lead. Besides this, the positions of the enemy, by their width and depth, enabled him to keep

* A mile and one-third.

his reserves out of range of our artillery. Finally, all the ravines came together near the town itself, which allowed the Turkish reserves, in case of an attack on our part, to come immediately to the threatened point. These conditions, so disadvantageous for us, explain in great part the insuccess of the assault on the 11th and 12th of September against the positions of Plevna, and the decision taken, in order not to shed blood uselessly, to attempt no more to gain possession of them by open assault, but to await the arrival of reinforcements and proceed to the investment of the Turkish army.

"This investment of the intrenched camp of Plevna became complete with the arrival of the Guard, and the capture of Gorni-Dubnik on the Sophia high road, on the 24th of October, by the troops of this corps. From that date the communications of Osman Pasha were definitely cut, and his army had no longer but to choose between an effort to break through the line of investment or to lay down its arms when all its provisions should be exhausted.

"The length of stay of the Turkish Army at Plevna after its investment depended directly, of course, upon the quantity of provisions which it had at its disposal. It was difficult to state exactly the quantity of provisions which Osman had, but we could conclude, from the information that we had, that the provisions of the army of Plevna could not allow it to subsist more than about two months at the very utmost. From the moment that, in order to reduce Plevna and its army, we had chosen the method of investment, it only remained to follow strictly this line of action, without making any attempts at assault, which could lead to no definite result, and would only have increased the number of our losses; it was necessary simply to endeavour to make the circle of investment as close as possible, and to take all the necessary measures to prevent the enemy from being able to force it at any point. These measures consisted in strengthening the lines of investment by digging lines of rifle-pits and trenches, in erecting batteries, and in establishing lunettes and redoubts upon the most important points. It was above all necessary to concentrate the fire of our artillery upon the enemy's fortifications, and to carry forward our trenches and ditches to a point near enough to those of the enemy to remove as far as possible from our batteries the fire of the enemy's musketry. It was, moreover, necessary to build good roads connecting our own positions, and to provide them with sign-posts to facilitate the movements of the troops. It was necessary to construct bridges, establish telegraphic communication around the whole line of investment, and finally to take all the necessary measures to receive the enemy, in case of a sortie, with the greatest possible number of troops concentrated immediately upon the spot that ho should choose as a point of attack.

"With this view the positions established around Plevna, and having an extent of 70 versts" (46 miles), "were divided into six sectors,* the defence of which was confided to a number of troops corresponding to the relative extent and importance of each of them. Moreover each Chief of

---

* "*First Sector*, between Bivolar and the Grivitza redoubt; the Roumanian troops, under the orders of General Cernat, Commandant of the Roumanian Corps.

"*Second Sector*, from the Grivitza to the Galitz redoubt; the 31st Infantry Division with its artillery, and the 2nd Brigade 5th Infantry Division with four batteries, under the orders of Lieutenant-General Baron Krüdener, Commandant of the IX. Corps.

"*Third Sector*, from the Galitz redoubt to the Tutchenitza ravine; 2nd Infantry Division with the 30th Artillery Brigade and the 12th Rifle Battalion, under the orders of Lieutenant-General Zotof, Commandant of the IV. Corps.

"*Fourth Sector*, between the Tutchenitza ravine and the Kartushaven ravine; 16th Infantry Division with its artillery, 30th Infantry Division with the 2nd Artillery Brigade, 9th, 10th, and 11th Rifle Battalions, and 9th Regiment of Cossacks, under the orders of Lieutenant-General Skobeleff, Commandant of the 16th Infantry Division.

"*Fifth Sector*, between the Kartushaven ravine and the right bank of the Vid at the village of Tyrnen; 3rd Infantry Division of the Guard with its artillery, two squadrons of the Guard, and the 10th Don Cossack battery, under the orders of Lieutenant-General Kataley, Commandant of the 3rd Infantry Division of the Guard.

"*Sixth Sector*, along the left bank of the Vid, including the positions of Bivolar on the right bank of that river; the Grenadier Corps, the 1st Brigade 5th Infantry Division with two batteries, the 2nd Roumanian Division with its artillery, the 9th Dragoons of Kazan, the 9th Lancers of Bug, the 9th Hussars of Kieff, the 4th Cossacks of the Don, the 7th Horse battery, the 2nd Don Cossack battery, and a regiment of Kalarash" (Roumanian Militia Cavalry), "under the orders of Lieutenant-General Ganetzky, Commandant of the Grenadiers Corps"

Sector received an approximate summary of the sorties which Osman Pasha might make, and a plan of the concentration of troops which he would have to make upon such or such a point threatened. Finally, a few days before the attempted sortie of Osman Pasha, I had had some manœuvres executed under my own eyes, in the sectors of Generals Ganetzky and Kataley, in order to calculate the exact time necessary for the concentration of the troops in case of an energetic attack on the part of the invested army.

"The eve of the 10th of December found us in the situation which I have just described.

" We could conclude, from all the reports received by the Staff from all the sectors of investment, throughout the whole day of the 9th of December, that Osman Pasha was taking energetic measures to move out his army by seeking to break through our line of investment. Deserters informed us that rations of biscuits and foot-coverings had been distributed to the troops, and their arms had been inspected. A great deal of moving about was noticed near the town on the Sophia high road, and a great concentration of troops and carts was seen in the camps. The Turks were beginning to construct a bridge over the Vid under the protection of the fortified works of Opanetz. All these indications tended to prove that the enemy was preparing to move out, and that his principal effort would probably be directed against the sector of General Ganetzky.

" In consequence, after having made a report of all these facts to the Commandant of the Army of Investment, His Highness the Prince of Roumania, I gave the following orders by authority of His Highness :

" 1. One brigade of the 16th Infantry Division, with three batteries, and a brigade of the 3rd Infantry Division of the Guard, will; under the command of Lieutenant-General Skobeleff, proceed, at daylight on the 10th of December, to the left bank of the Vid, and take post as follows : the brigade of the 16th Division, with three batteries, near Dulni-Dubnik, to be ready to support the troops of General Ganetsky; the brigade of the 3rd Division of the Guard, until further orders, behind the two redoubts nearest the Vid

THE FALL OF PLEVNA

and on the left bank, in order to be able to support in case of need the troops of General Ganetzky or those of General Kataley.

" 2. The other brigade of the 16th Infantry Division, with three batteries, will remain at its post, but will hold itself in readiness to march.

" 3. The three battalions of the 3rd Rifle Brigade, which used to form part of the garrison of the 4th Sector, will proceed early on the 10th to the village of Grivitza to reinforce the garrison of the 2nd Sector, commanded by Lieutenant-General Baron Krüdener.

" 4. The advanced position on the Plevna-Lovtcha high road, between the Mirkovitch redoubt and the Tutchenitza ravine, will be occupied by one brigade of the 30th Infantry Division. Its other brigade will remain in the camp on the Red Hill, and hold itself in readiness to march. The command of the troops of the 4th Sector is confided to General Schnidnikoff.

" 5. Four Roumanian battalions, with three batteries, will be directed, at daylight of the 10th, from Verbitza toward Demirkioi. Four Roumanian battalions and two batteries will be in readiness to march on Verbitza.

" This disposition of the troops, reinforcing the corps of Lieutenant-General Ganetzky, allowed reinforcements to be sent at the same time to the other sectors of investment in case of an attack of the Turks in another direction with the object of diverting our attention from the real point of attack.

" During the night of the 9th-10th a deserter informed the commandant of the corps on the Plevna-Lovtcha road that the Krishin redoubt had been evacuated by the Turks. General Skobeleff immediately sent a detachment of volunteers to satisfy themselves of the truth of this news. The volunteers found the redoubt deserted, and in consequence of this discovery the Great and the Little Krishin redoubts, as well as the trenches on the Green Hills, were occupied by the troops of the 30th Infantry Division.

" At the same time that I received the news of the occupation of the Krishin redoubts by our troops, I was informed, about 9 A.M., that the Turks had abandoned Redoubt No. 10, and that the redoubt in front of that of Grivitza had been occupied by the Roumanian troops. In presence of these facts I gave orders for all the troops on the right bank of the Vid to move forward. As for the brigade of the 16th Infantry Division, with three batteries, and the 9th, 10th, and 11th Rifle battalions which had not yet reached the village of Grivitza, I sent them to the left bank of the Vid to be placed at the disposition of General Skobeleff, for the purpose of reinforcing the troops of General Ganetzky.

"At noon the Emperor arrived at the Imperial redoubt, between the village of Radischevo and the Tutchenitza ravine, whence His Majesty could observe the forward movement of our troops, as well as the cannonade on the left bank of the Vid.

"At daylight the struggle began between the army of Osman Pasha and the troops of General Ganetzky.

"During the night of the 9th-10th of December, the detail of troops for duty in the positions occupied by the Grenadiers had been made in the 2nd Division of Grenadiers by the 5th Regiment of Grenadiers of Kieff; in the 3rd Division, by the 9th Grenadiers of Siberia. These troops occupied the trenches of the line of defence. Their nearest supports were the 6th Grenadiers of Taurida and the 10th Grenadiers of Little Russia. All the 9-pdr. guns of the two artillery brigades were in position in the first lines of defence, and the 4-pdrs. in the second line at Gorni-Etropol and Dolni-Dubnik. The trenches and lunette on the north of Gorni-Etropol, as well as the village itself, were occupied by the 17th Regiment of Archangel of the 1st Brigade 5th Infantry Division, and by two Roumanian batteries; the 18th Regiment of Vologda, of the same division, served as reserve to the two batteries.

"During the night the cavalry patrols had already reported that a great concentration of Turkish troops was taking place along the Vid. The attack of the Turks began to show itself about half-past seven in the morning. Our outposts having fallen back before them, Major-General

THE FALL OF PLEVNA

Daniloff, of the suite of the Emperor and Commandant of the 3rd Division of Grenadiers, ordered the 2nd Battery of the 3rd Artillery Brigade of Grenadiers, which occupied the fixed Battery No. 3, to open fire, and the 10th Regiment of Grenadiers of Little Russia to march in the direction of Kopany-Moguila. At the same time the 2nd Brigade, with its 4-pdr. batteries, had been ordered up from Gorni-Etropol.

"While these orders were being executed, it began to be clear enough to see the Turkish troops which had been concentrated in front of us during the night, and which were followed by a long line of carts of every description. The Turks, having opened fire with their guns established on the heights near the bridge and along the Vid beyond the bridge, rapidly deployed their forces, taking advantage for this purpose of the fog which covered the plain on both sides of the river, and of a long undulation in the ground which exists in front of the bridge, and which afforded shelter for the numerous troops which had been brought there during the night.

"The attack of the enemy, directed against the trenches of the 3rd Division of Grenadiers, was made with extraordinary impetuosity; thick lines of skirmishers marched in front, followed by battalions deployed in line, behind which came the reserves. The artillery followed the skirmishers, advancing rapidly, only stopping to fire a shell, and hastening to rejoin the skirmishers.

"In spite of the rapidity of the fire of our 9-pdrs., and in spite of the musketry fire of the infantry posted in our intrenchments, the Turks crossed in less than three quarters of an hour the distance which separated them from our position and reached our line of defence, which was occupied near battery No. 3 by a part of the troops of the 3rd Division of Grenadiers. The enemy penetrating into the intervals between the trenches, after having killed all those who defended them, found there only a few survivors, who, too weak for resistance, began to fall back. When the trenches of work No. 3 had been occupied by the enemy, and the greater part of the gunners of the 2nd Battery had been killed or cut down, our artillerymen only succeeded in withdrawing from the work two guns, carrying off the breech-blocks of the six other pieces.

"Thus at 8.30 A.M., the troops which occupied the centre of the position, viz., the 2nd battalion and the 2nd and 3rd Rifle companies of the 9th Grenadiers of Siberia, having lost a great number of men and many officers, began to fall back on Kopany-Maguila and on the lunette to the left. The 3rd Battery of the 3rd Artillery Brigade of Grenadiers, which occupied work No. 4, held its ground for a little while longer, firing shrapnel upon the Turks, but, seeing itself threatened with being turned on the right, abandoned its position, succeeding moreover in carrying off only six guns, the horses of the other two having been killed.

"The 10th Regiment of Grenadiers of Little Russia, having arrived on the field of battle while the Siberian Regiment was struggling with the enemy, formed in companies and advanced through the interval between lunette No. 4 and Kopany-Moguila. Having rallied the Siberian Regiment, the Little Russians stopped the progress of the enemy, suffering great losses in so doing; in less than a few minutes three chiefs of battalions and half the chiefs of companies were out of the fight.

"The desperate attack of the enemy became more and more threatening. The 1st Brigade of the 3rd Division of Grenadiers was exhausted by the efforts it was making to defend the lunettes; eight of our guns were in the hands of the enemy, and the 2nd Brigade of the 3rd Division of Grenadiers had not yet arrived to the support of the first.

"It arrived about 10 A.M., and at the same moment word was received that the 8th Grenadiers of Moscow and the 7th Grenadiers of Samogitia, of the 2nd Division of Grenadiers, were approaching the positions defended by the 3rd Division. The arrival of these reinforcements assured us a favourable issue of the struggle, and made it impossible for the enemy to succeed in his attempt to break through. A resounding hurrah which broke forth about 10.30 A.M., informed us that the 2nd Brigade of the 3rd Division of Grenadiers had just attacked our trenches, which were held by the Turks. Having dislodged the enemy from the two lunettes, the Grenadiers of Astrakhan and Phanagoria, supported by those of Siberia and Little Russia, continued to advance rapidly, and, without paying attention to the losses which the deadly fire of the Turks inflicted upon them, dislodged them from the trenches with the bayonet. Those of our guns which had remained in the hands of the enemy were retaken, and the Grenadiers of Astrakhan gained possession of seven guns and one flag in open fight.

"Two battalions of the 18th Regiment of Vologda, which had some time before approached the lunette to the left and the trenches of the position of the Grenadiers, operated against the flank of the Turks with the aid of a Roumanian battery.

"At the time of the attack of the 2d Brigade of the 3d Division of Grenadiers, the 7th Regiment of Grenadiers of Samogitia, under the orders of Lieutenant-General Svetchin, commandant of the 2d Division of Grenadiers, came forward through the interval between Gorni and Dolni-Etrepol. Attacking the enemy with the bayonet, the Grenadiers of Samogitia drove the Turks out of their trenches without firing a single shot, and, having put them to flight, gained possession of three guns.

"After having re-occupied their advanced lines, our troops halted for a while. It was about noon when the Turks began slowly to retreat toward the Vid, all the time keeping up a strong fire against us. The guns taken from the Turks, not having been rendered unserviceable by their gunners, were turned against them and served by the soldiers of the infantry. At the same time all the batteries of the 3d Artillery Brigade of Grenadiers, having been moved forward and brought into action on the same line as our infantry, opened a terrible fire against the enemy and covered him with shrapnel, which gave the retreat of the Turks the character of a general helter-skelter. They came together in disorganised groups near the bridge over the Vid, pell-mell with the carts which were on the edge of the high road in great numbers.

"In presence of this complete disorganisation of his army, and of the enormous losses which it had sustained, Osman

Pasha could no longer think of renewing his attempt to break through our lines, especially since the troops of the other sectors of investment had moved forward; and the speedy arrival of the 16th Infantry Division and the 3rd Infantry Division of the Guard guaranteed the complete defeat of the enemy.

"Our troops soon moved forward to the attack along the whole line. General Daniloff's Division took the lead, supported on his left flank from the direction of Gorni-Etropol, by the 1st Brigade of the 5th Infantry Division, and on his right flank by the 2nd Brigade of the 2nd Division of Grenadiers. The 1st Brigade of the 2nd Division of Grenadiers, moving out from its trenches, undertook to turn the left flank of the Turks. Moreover, the 2nd Battalion of the 5th Grenadiers of Kieff and one battalion of the 6th Grenadiers of Taurida were directed toward the Vid, which they crossed by fording, in order to occupy the heights on the right bank. The Grenadiers, having crossed the river with the water up to their waists, scaled the heights of Blasivatz and rushed upon the Turkish redoubt which crowned them, and whose garrison surrendered without striking a blow.

"The brigade of the 3rd Division of the Guard and of the 16th Infantry Division of the Line, sent, in accordance with the orders I had given the night before, to serve as supports to the corps of General Ganetzky, took no part in the battle. It appears from the report of Lieutenant-General Kataley, that at 7 A.M. on the 10th of December he had sent across to the left bank of the Vid, passing over a pontoon bridge, six battalions of the 3rd Infantry Division of the Guard, under the orders of Major-General Kourloff. At 10 A.M., this detachment, at the request of General Ganetzky, moved toward Dolni-Dubnik, where it received orders to move forward by the Sophia high road to press the left flank of the enemy. While the detachment was executing this movement, it was joined by Lieutenant-General Skobeleff, who took command of it, ordered General Kourloff to halt his troops, to deploy them in reserve order, and to await the arrival of the brigade of the 16th Infantry

THE FALL OF PLEVNA

Division. Having remained on the spot for two hours, and having received no further orders from General Skobeleff, General Kourloff again moved his detachment forward by the Sophia high road, and arrived at the stone bridge over the Vid only when the battle was over.

"While the 2nd and 3rd Divisions of Grenadiers were heroically repelling the attack of the whole Turkish Army the other troops of the army of investment—under the orders of Lieutenant-Generals Zotof, Baron Krüdener, and Kataley, of Major-General Schnidnikoff, and of General Cernat, who commanded the Roumanian Corps—were advancing against the Turkish fortifications on the east and south fronts. The greater part of these works had already been evacuated, and the troops occupied the town of Plevna in presence of Your Imperial Highness. After having entered the place, the troops, with Your Imperial Highness at the head, received orders to continue to advance in the direction of the Vid upon the rear of the enemy, and they concentrated little by little on the heights to the west of Plevna near the Sophia high road.

"The Roumanian troops, with whom H.H. Prince Charles had been since the morning, met some resistance at the redoubts of Opanetz, which the enemy still occupied. After a struggle of short duration, the garrison of these works laid down their arms, and the Roumanians gained possession of 3 guns and 2000 prisoners.

"General Kataley, having remained on the right bank of the Vid with the rest of the 3rd Infantry Division of the Guard, perceived the retreat of the Turks in the direction of the river, and resolved to gain possession of the redoubt fronting the Volhynia hill, in order to cut off every route of retreat for the enemy upon his fortified camp. At 11.30 A.M., the Red redoubt was occupied without striking a blow, and soon afterward that of Fort Mahomet surrendered in its turn, after a short resistance. About 1 P.M., the Black redoubt and the Sugar-Loaf redoubt were also taken after a short musketry fire. In these redoubts * the soldiers of the

* The redoubts here referred to are those lying along the ridge from Krishin to Blasivatz.

Guard took prisoners, 1 Pasha, 120 officers, and 3734 soldiers, and gained possession of four guns. They had on their side 3 men killed, and 15 wounded.

"Hemmed in by superior forces, the Turks could no longer continue the struggle; consequently they sent forward a flag of truce, and the chief of staff of the Turkish Army, who proceeded to General Ganetzky, announced to him that Osman Pasha was wounded, and that he desired to know the conditions of surrender. General Ganetzky demanded the unconditional surrender of the whole army. Osman Pasha consented thereto, and General Ganetzky proceeded in person to his brave wounded adversary.

"There were surrendered on the memorable 10th of December, 10 Pashas, 130 field-officers, 2000 company-officers, 40,000 foot-soldiers and gunners, and 1200 horsemen. We took 77 guns, and immense quantities of ammunition, especially of small-arms cartridges. The enemy lost during the battle about 6000 men.

"On our side, the 2d and 3d Divisions of Grenadiers sustained the following losses: Killed, 2 field-officers, 7 company-officers, and 409 soldiers; wounded, 1 General, 3 field-officers, 47 company-officers, and 1263 soldiers.

"The 1st Brigade of the 5th Infantry Division had 1 field-officer and 47 soldiers wounded.

"Thus the system adopted under the walls of Plevna, and consisting in observing a complete investment without having recourse to open assault—a sanguinary and risky enterprise —brought about the end which was had in view. The result of this system was the capture of an army of 40,000 men, the best one of the enemy, and the possession of an important strategic point, which closes the principal roads of Western Bulgaria. And during the period of the investment our troops were not only protected, but were able to replace their losses, and now, strong as they are and with the spirit which animates them, they are ready to accomplish new exploits for the glory of our arms.

"In conclusion, I feel it my duty to bring to the notice of your Imperial Highness the services of the chief of staff of the Army of Investment, Prince Imeretinsky, who has been for me a coadjutor whom it would be difficult to replace, throughout the whole period of time which was crowned by the brilliant success of the 10th of December; the former commandants of the sectors of investment, viz., Lieutenant-General Ganetzky, to whom, with the Corps of Grenadiers, belongs the honour of the last day of the investment of Plevna; Lieutenant-Generals Zotof, Baron Krüdener, Kataley, and Skobeleff; General Cernat, commandant of the Roumanian Corps; Major-General Moller, commanding the artillery line of battle; and Major-General Reitlinger, performing the duties of Chief of Engineers of the Army of Investment.

"Having been a witness for two months of the conduct of the troops assembled under the walls of Plevna, of their firmness, their bravery, their self-denial in enduring fatigues and privations, I certify to Your Imperial Highness, with a sentiment of profound respect for these troops, that the conduct of every man of the Army of Investment, from the general to the private soldier, has been above all praise.

(Signed) *Aide-de-Camp General* TODLEBEN.

"*9th January*, 1878."

The Turkish defence of Plevna is the one thing which relieves their whole campaign from a charge of complete incompetency. Much high-sounding praise has been lavished upon it in English publications, and perhaps even more by the Russians themselves, who speak of it as the most brilliant defence of the century after Sevastopol. It is well to examine this subject with some care.

It will be remembered that Osman Pasha, commanding an army at Widdin (which had very thoroughly beaten the Servians in the late autumn of 1876), was ordered about the time that the Russians crossed the Danube (June 27, 1877) to march rapidly eastward to the defence of Bulgaria. Further than this the exact nature of his orders has never been made public. It has been supposed that he was ordered to occupy Nikopolis and the line of the Danube in that vicinity. But he approached Nikopolis too late; it had already fallen (July 16th). Osman therefore kept his army at Plevna, a central point 20 miles from Nikopolis and the junction of several roads, probably waiting for further instructions and developments; but he immediately set his men to work, according to the excellent Turkish habit of fortifying every place where they remain forty-eight hours, to construct some trenches and redoubts on the east and north of the town. Hardly were these begun when the Russian brigade under Schilder-Schuldner came stumbling along without reconnoitring the ground in front of them, and attacked Osman's whole army. The latter not only defeated them, but well-nigh annihilated one of the regiments. This was on July 20th. Osman did not need to wait for any further developments; his course was now perfectly plain. He saw (and herein lies the genius of his whole defence) that so long as he could maintain himself with a large force at Plevna close to the flank of the Russians, he *completely paralysed their further advance;* and in order to maintain himself there, he renewed work with the utmost energy upon his fortifications.

While, therefore, the Russians had elaborately planned to mask the fortresses on their left flank during their advance, here was another set of fortifications springing up in the night on their right flank. They hastily concentrated a force (but a totally insufficient one) to dislodge Osman, and again attacked him, July 30th, only to be again repulsed with fearful losses, this time nearly 8000 men. Osman did not follow up the Russians after their retreat, but devoted his whole energy to elaborating his works of defence. But as the Russians delayed renewing the attack, being obliged to wait for new reinforcements, Osman at last deviated from the controlling idea of his whole defence, viz., to always await an attack. On the 31st of August he assumed the offensive in connection with the advance of Mehemet Ali on the Lom and Suleiman's attack at Shipka. But Osman's attack on Zgalevitza came utterly to naught, and resulted in nothing but the loss of some 2000 or 3000 of his men. On the 11th of September the Russians, assisted by the Roumanians, again renewed the assault, and again (barring the capture of one of the Grivitza redoubts) they were

THE FALL OF PLEVNA

everywhere beaten, and now with the appalling loss of 18,000 men.

Osman, while still keeping his men hard at work ever extending and strengthening his lines, now began to be anxious about his communications with Sophia, since he was wholly dependent on them for his supplies, and they were greatly threatened and slightly interrupted by bodies of Russian cavalry. Chefket Pasha finally (September 22nd) brought him some reinforcements and numerous supplies, and Osman immediately ordered the fortification of several points on the Sophia road in order to keep it open. But on the 24th of October the Russian Guard, which had just arrived, broke this line of defence completely to pieces, and a few days later Osman found himself tightly and closely invested. The Russians made no more assaults, and finally, when his provisions reached their last ebb, Osman found himself obliged to quietly surrender or to try to cut his way out. Unlike Bazaine, he chose the latter, and made a gallant effort, but it only resulted in defeat and the capture of his whole army.

Certainly that must be called a brilliant defence which arrested the Russian advance, and completely paralysed their whole plan of campaign and all their movements for five months; which caused them to call forth vast reinforcements from Russia, and, pending their arrival, to supplicate the aid of a petty principality; which killed and wounded and spread disease among nearly 40,000 of his enemies, and caused the affairs of a mighty empire to be directed during half a year from miserable huts in obscure villages of a foreign land.

Yet Osman seems to have failed to comprehend the limitations of his system, and, by overstraining it, broke it, and thereby lost his whole army. Up till the middle of October there seems to be hardly anything in the conduct of his defence (excepting always the foolish attack on Zgalevitza) which is open to criticism. But at that time he knew very well, by the English newspapers, that the whole of the Russian Guard and one or two fresh divisions of the Line had arrived in Bulgaria; he knew that there was a movement of some kind going on in the vicinity of the Vid on his right flank, and had he reconnoitered there he would have found about 35,000 men concentrated for the passage of the river. Although he may not have been familiar with the way in which Pemberton invited capture by shutting himself up in Vicksburg, and Lee postponed it for a whole year by not letting himself be shut up in Richmond, yet it can be taken for granted that he knew something of the history of the siege of Metz, and of the inevitable result which must happen to any army which allows itself to be closely invested in an intrenched camp by a superior force. Therefore Osman should have abandoned Plevna and retreated to Radomirtza, instead of allowing the Guard to cross the Vid and attack Gorni-Dubnik. Radomirtza was only two long days' march (about 45 miles) from Plevna; it was a position of far greater natural strength than Plevna itself, and already its fortifications were further advanced than those at Plevna on the 30th of July. He could well have afforded to risk holding them against open assaults, and if obliged to give them up by a movement of the Russians to surround him, he could again retreat towards the Balkans; everywhere there were good positions for defence, and at every step he came nearer his proper base and increased his strength by taking in small detachments, If he finally had to retreat behind the line of the Balkans, *he still had his army intact.* He could not, of course, have changed the final result of the war, but he could have deferred it, as Lee deferred the fate of the Confederacy; and he might possibly have saved his country from such an annihilating defeat as it finally received after the loss of his army.

But Osman had no such thoughts in his mind, and his own explanation of his ideas is very interesting. While a prisoner at the Grand Duke's headquarters a few days after his capture, he was called upon by General Todleben, and a long conversation ensued upon the events of the siege. Todleben asked Osman precisely this question, why he did not retreat to Radomirtza in October, when the Guard was concentrating on his right flank and threatening him with investment. Osman replied that he had then no thought of retreating—

THE FALL OF PLEVNA

1. Because he felt sure—at that date and up to the very day of his sortie—that the Russians, and especially the Roumanians near Grivitza, would renew their assaults, and he felt equally sure that he would be able to defeat them with great loss. He longed for these assaults from day to day.

2. Because at that time he had just received a fresh lot of provisions and reinforcements. He could not think of retreating under those circumstances.

There was a third reason which he did not mention in this conversation, but which is abundantly attested from other sources, and which was more imperative than the two just given, viz., that the War Council at the Seraskierate in Constantinople had telegraphed him positive and explicit orders not to retreat under any circumstances.

In this conversation Osman also said that the system of entrenched camps with modern breech-loaders is admirable so long as the enemy has not troops enough to surround them; but it is their fate to be invested, and then they are doomed.

If we compare the two parts of this conversation, we can only reconcile them by supposing Osman to have a contempt for his enemy's tactics, which, as the result proved, was by no means warranted.

There have been in the last twenty-five years six other sieges of a character similar to that of Plevna, viz., Sevastopol, Kars, Vicksburg, Richmond, Metz, and Paris. Of these, Kars, Paris, and Metz were fortified places of the first order, consisting of a strong enceinte in masonry and detached forts, supplemented slightly by earthworks built at the last moment. The other four, Sevastopol, Richmond, Vicksburg, and Plevna, were simply places which had been hastily fortified by a series of earthworks, redoubts, batteries, and trenches, constructed only just before the arrival of the enemy, and continually extended and strengthened during the progress of the siege. At Vicksburg and at Plevna the defenders allowed the enemy to attack their rear and closely invest them. Both fell when their provisions were exhausted. At Sevastopol and Richmond, on the contrary, the defenders constantly and incessantly extended their flanks and pre-

THE CAMPAIGN IN BULGARIA

vented the enemy from surrounding them. The one place was finally evacuated by its garrison after a portion of the works had been carried in assault. At the other the defensive line became finally so extended that it was too long to be held by the force of the defenders; they were obliged to leave their fortifications in an effort to retreat, and were then almost instantly overwhelmed and destroyed.

The following comparative tabular statement of some of the principal features of these great sieges may be interesting.

NOTES TO TABLE (p. 197)

1. SEVASTOPOL.

1. The trenches were opened October 9, 1854, and the place was evacuated on the night of September 8, 1855.

2. The allied trenches at the time of evacuation measured over 52 miles in length, and those of the Russians about 15, but the allied line along the first parallel, from the Tchernaya to Quarantine Bay, was only 7 miles, and that of the Russians, from Careening Creek to Fort Alexander, 5 miles.

3. Rousset, "Guerre de Crimée" (Vol. II., p. 412), gives the allied force on September 8, 1855, as follows:

French	126,000
English	47,000
Turks	40,000
Sardinians	16,000
Total	229,000

and the Russians in the Crimea at 150,000, of which 115,000 were near Sevastopol.

He also (p. 463, Vol. II.) gives the total losses of the Crimean War, exclusive of the typhoid fever cases after November, 1855, as follows:

French	60,000, of which 10,240 killed in battle.	
English	22,000 " 2,800 " "	
Sardinians	2,200	
Turks	35,000 (?)	
Total	119,200	
Russians	110,000	

Marshal Niel gives the total losses of the French during the siege at 44,497 killed, wounded, and missing, of which 7627 were killed. The English reports do not give the total losses, but Sir H. Jones (p. 600) gives the killed and mortally wounded at 4774. In the same proportion their total losses would be about 27,000. The English returns show about 12,000 constantly sick during the winter, and the sick among the allies at the evacuation may be estimated at 20,000. The total losses of the allies will then be as follows:

THE FALL OF PLEVNA

	DURATION OF SIEGE	LENGTH OF OPPOSING LINES.	STRENGTH OF OPPOSING FORCES AT SURRENDER.				LOSSES IN ASSAULTS, BOMBARDMENTS, AND SICKNESS.		EXPENDITURE OF AMMUNITION.			
			ASSAILANTS.		DEFENDERS.				ASSAILANTS. ROUNDS.		DEFENDERS. ROUNDS.	
	Days.	Miles.	Infantry.	Guns.	Infantry.	Guns.	Assailants.	Defenders.	Artillery.	Infantry.	Artillery.	Infantry.
SEVASTOPOL, Oct. 9, 1854, to Sept. 9, 1855	334	7 — 5	229,000	827	115,000	900	98,000	114,000	1,350,000	50,000,000	(?) 1,000,000	(?) 25,000,000
KARS, June 16 to Nov. 28, 1855	165	49 — 13	30,000	—	26,000	—	12,000	10,000	—	—	—	—
VICKSBURG, May 1 to July 4, 1863	65	12 — 8	71,000	248	32,000	172	9,000	17,000	—	—	—	—
RICHMOND, May 4, 1864, to April 9, 1865	340	53 — 51	121,000	408	60,000	273	87,000	60,000	—	—	—	—
METZ, Aug. 16 to Oct. 27, 1870	72	25 — 15	197,000	658	173,000	694	47,000	38,000	—	—	—	—
PARIS, Sept. 20, 1870, to March 1, 1871	133	52 — 34	200,000	788	400,000	744	15,000	25,000	—	—	—	—
PLEVNA, July 20 to Dec. 10, 1877	143	46 — 24	110,000	500	40,000	77	40,000	30,000	200,000	10,000,000	30,000	15,000,000

THE CAMPAIGN IN BULGARIA

French	44,500 ⎫
English	27,000 ⎬ Killed and wounded.
Turks and Italians	6,500 ⎭
Sick	20,000
	98,000

The Russian losses during the siege, as given in Todleben's "Defence of Sevastopol," are as follows:

Killed	15,553
Wounded	71,312
Missing	2,277
Total	89,142

To which 25,000 may safely be added for sickness, making a grand total of about 114,000.

4. On September 8, 1855, the French batteries numbered 620 guns in position (Marshal Niel's report), and the English 207 (Sir Henry Dacres's report, p. 638).

Marshal Niel gives the total amount of French artillery brought to the Crimea as 1676 guns of all calibres. Sir Henry Dacres's report (p. 209) gives the total number of English guns in use during the siege as 401. Major Delafield, however ("Art of War in Europe," p. 55), states that the English brought 911 guns to the Crimea. He also states (p. 56) that the total amount of artillery and ordnance brought to Sevastopol was 2587 guns of all calibres, 2,381,042 shot and shells, and 11,484,804 pounds of powder. Marshall Niel's report states that the French expenditure of artillery ammunition was about 1,100,000 rounds. Sir Henry Dacres (p. 205) gives that of the English as 252,872 rounds. Marshal Niel gives the amount of small-arms ammunition supplied to the French troops at 70,000,000 rounds, but does not state the expenditure. Estimating it at 40,000,000, and that of the English at 10,000,000, we have 50,000,000 for the total.

2. KARS.

After the repulse of the Russians in their assault on the west of Kars in September, Mouravieff assembled his infantry on the Erzeroum road, 7 miles south of Kars, and the rest of the long line of investment was kept up by large bodies of cavalry.

The losses are only approximate.

3. VICKSBURG.

The effective strength of General Grant's command on June 30, 1863, is shown in the following table, compiled in the Adjutant-General's office from the field returns of that date:

DESIGNATION.	INFANTRY.		CAVALRY.		ARTILLERY.		AGGREGATE.
	Officers.	Men.	Officers.	Men.	Officers.	Men.	
9th Corps	374	6,632	—	—	9	309	7,324
13th Corps	748	11,500	28	554	34	941	13,805
15th Corps	793	12,444	32	451	23	668	14,411
16th Corps	836	14,318	68	936	21	777	16,956
17th Corps	741	11,846	7	127	35	1052	13,808
Herron's Division	240	4,286	—	—	11	298	4,837
Total	3732	61,028	135	2068	133	4045	71,141

The other figures are taken from Badeau's "Life of Grant" (Chapters VII. and VIII.), which is unquestionably the best authority on the subject in print. Owing to the difficulty of separating the losses during the campaign from those during the siege proper, the figures given apply to the whole campaign from the crossing of the river to the surrender. The investment proper began on the 22nd of May and lasted 35 days, during which the losses were between 4000 and 5000 on each side. The losses of the defenders include 7000 prisoners captured in the various affairs previous to the investment.

4. RICHMOND.

The whole campaign of General Grant from the Wilderness to Appomatox is included in the "siege" of Richmond, in order to make the comparison uniform with the other sieges, which include all the battles immediately preceding the investments. The siege of Petersburg proper lasted 290 days, from June 15, 1864, when Grant crossed the James, to April 2, 1865, when he began his retreat after the battle of Five Forks.

The length of the lines is measured on the engineer map: Lee's lines from the James River above the Iron Works, around Richmond and Petersburg to the end of his line on the White Oak road; Grant's lines from the Topolopotomy across the Peninsula, past Bermuda Hundred, and around Petersburg to his extreme left in front of the White Oak road.

The strength of the armies is taken from the field returns in the archives of the Adjutant-General's office of the War Department. These show that on the 31st of March, 1865, Grant's effective force present for duty numbered 5288 officers and 115,759 men. Lee's return of February 28, 1865, the last one in the archives, shows his effective force present for duty to be 3519 officers and 55,575 men.

Grant's losses are computed as follows:

May 4 to June 10 1864 (Mead's report)	54,500
May 4 to June 10, 1864, 9th Corps	5,000
June 10, 1864, to March 31, 1865, including the attack on the Petersburg mine, on the Weldon road, and other battles and skirmishes	20,000
April 1 to April 9, 1865	8,000
Total	87,500

Lee's losses have never been compiled, and it is doubtful if the returns which have been preserved afford data for an accurate compilation. His return of January 31, 1864, gives 74 officers and 1374 men prisoners in the hands of the enemy; his return of February 28, 1865, gives 1797 officers and 26,614 men similarly accounted for. This makes his loss in prisoners alone 26,963. His losses in killed and wounded in the same period may be stated, at the least estimate, as fully one-third of those of Grant; this would give 27,000. Between Five Forks and the Appomatox he lost about 6000. The total of his losses was therefore about 60,000.

5. METZ.

The figures are taken from the "German Staff History of the Franco-German War" (French translation, 2nd part, pp. 257-297). At the time of the surrender there were 40,000 sick in the German hospitals, mostly light cases of fever arising from exposure in the wet. The French prisoners included 20,000 sick. These are not included in losses on either side in the above table. Only 5500 of the above losses of the Germans were during the siege proper. The rest were incurred in the bloody battles at Mars-la-Tour and Gravelotte in August, by which Bazaine's army was shut up in Metz.

The French had 876 guns on the walls of the place; these are not counted in the above table, which gives only the field-guns and mitrailleuses.

6. PARIS.

The figures are taken from the "German Staff History." Of the 400,000 men forming the garrison of Paris, only 100,000 (XIII. and XIV. Corps) were regular soldiers; the rest were National Guard, Mobile Guard, and sailors.

The field artillery of the French numbered 744 pieces (124 batteries), but there were in addition 1389 guns of various calibres in the outer forts and 805 on the walls of the enceinte.

The principal losses were incurred in the completion of the investment, September 17th and 19th (French, 5000, Germans, 4200), and in the French sorties of November 29th to December 3rd (French, 12,000, Germans, 6500).

The Germans made no attempts to assault the place, but from the beginning endeavoured to starve it out by a close blockade. Their inferiority in numbers was compensated by an admirable system of field works, constructed with great rapidity and with most numerous accessories, such as abattis, inundations, &c., &c., and by the superior quality of their troops.

7. PLEVNA.

The authority for the number of troops, losses, &c., is found in the preceding pages. The expenditure of ammunition is an estimate based upon my own notes made from time to time during the siege. It is probably accurate within 20 to 30 per cent. The official figures have not yet been made public.

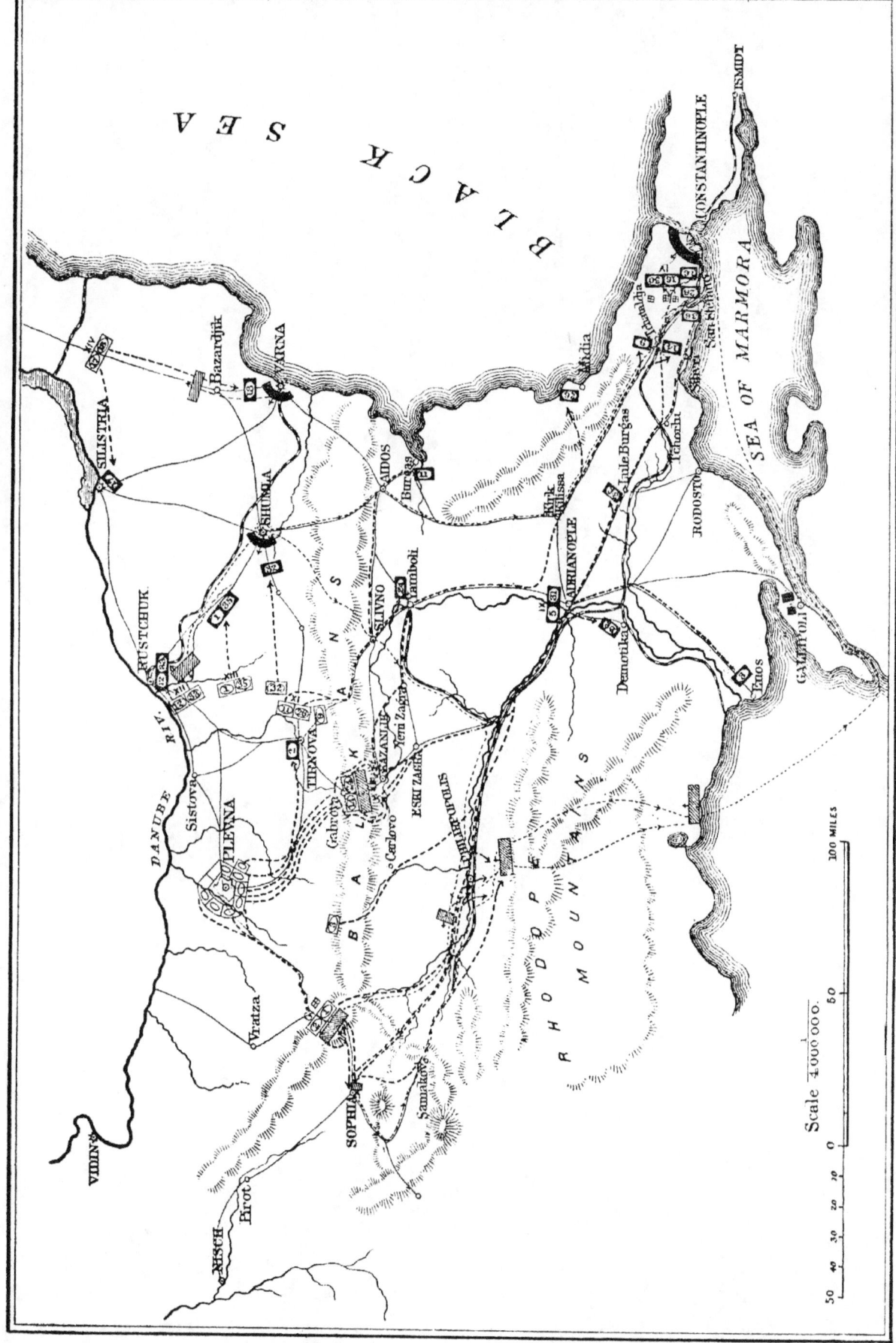

CHAPTER IX

THE PASSAGE OF THE BALKANS NEAR SOPHIA, BY GOURKO'S COLUMN

ALTHOUGH the fall of Plevna was unquestionably a great disaster for the Turks, since it lost them the best of their armies and possibly the best of their generals, yet it is by no means true, as has been generally assumed, that it rendered the Turks incapable of further resistance to the Russian advance. The Turkish cause was as yet far from being hopeless. They had still 100,000 men in the region of the Quadrilateral, 30,000 at Shipka, 20,000 in the vicinity of Sophia and the Araba-Konak Pass, 15,000 at Constantinople, and a certain unknown quantity of reserves in Asia. Of small arms and ammunition they had abundance, although now, as at all times during the campaign, they were short of artillery; they were in a rich country, and the valley of the Maritza was teeming with provisions in spite of all the drains which the war had made upon it. The Turks had, it is true, an enemy in front of them of double their own numbers, and confident of victory; but, on the other hand, that enemy had a line of communications 500 miles long from the Pruth to the Balkans, and this line absolutely cut in two now by the Danube, the ice of which had carried away all the bridges, and in front of him a rugged chain of mountains. It was the middle of December; considerable snow had already fallen, and more was to be expected; the winter climate of Bulgaria is one in which a temperature of 10° Fahr. is frequently encountered; there were but two good roads (Sistova-Shipka and Plevna-Sophia) available for the Russians, and all the rest were now mere quagmires. These various natural difficulties were almost sufficient to neutralise the difference of force, had only the Turks had a leader, a man of the calibre of Amurath I., Mohammed the Conqueror, or Suleiman the Magnificent. But, unfortunately for them, such a man they had not, as they have not had since the 16th century. Their Commander-in-Chief was now that Suleiman who had knocked out the brains of some 15,000 men against the rocks at Shipka during the months of August and September, and who had lately achieved almost equally bad results on the Lom. He was hastily summoned to Constantinople, where he arrived on the 19th of December, and was intrusted by the Sultan with the chief command in Roumelia, and especially the defence of the line of the Balkans. Of the Turkish Army on the Lom, a portion was placed in the fortresses with outposts at Razgrad and Osman-Bazar, and the rest was rapidly withdrawn by Aidos and Slivno to the south side of the Balkans. Work upon the extensive fortifications of Adrianople was pushed forward with great activity, and efforts were made to organise the recruits who were arriving in considerable numbers from Asia.

It is generally conceded that a long line of defence, such as a chain of mountains or a large river, can not successfully be defended by posting isolated bodies of troops, even large in numbers, at various points along it, since the enemy by demonstrating at several places and concentrating his forces on one point, will overwhelm the defenders at that point before the others can come to his relief. All military writers are agreed that the proper means of defence of such a line is to post small bodies in observation at the various points of passage, and keep the main body of the defenders at some central point in rear, from which, as soon as the enemy's *real* attack is made clear, a force can bear down upon him and strike him before his troops have all crossed the mountains or river. Such a point in this case was Adrianople, in itself a naturally strong position, and now defended by numerous half-finished earthworks, and from which high roads lead to Sophia, Shipka, Slivno, and Aidos, and railroads to within three days' march of Sophia, two days' of Shipka, and one day's of Slivno. But instead of

PASSAGE OF THE BALKANS NEAR SOPHIA

posting the bulk of his troops there, Suleiman tried to do that very thing which all history condemns, viz., to defend the line of mountains by means of isolated detachments. Leaving only a very small force—less than 10,000 men—at Adrianople, he increased the Shipka garrison to 40,000, and that around Sophia also to 40,000, and divided the latter into two parts, 25,000 at the Araba-Konak pass and 15,000 at Sophia. With about 20,000 more he was moving to the relief of Sophia when he met the troops from Araba-Konak in full retreat near Philippopolis, where the united force was overwhelmed and driven across the Rhodope mountains to the Ægean.

The mountain chain which separates the Sophia valley from that of the river Maritza is as high and difficult as the main chain of the Balkans; the broad valley of the Maritza is in fact completely shut in by mountains. Could the Turks have had a general capable of assembling the whole of their available force (about 150,000 men) in this valley, and using its interior lines of communication to strike against first one and then the other of the invading columns—which were widely separated—as Napoleon did in 1814, and then as a last resort have fallen back upon the strong fortifications of Adrianople and made a new Plevna of it, the war could at least have been prolonged till the next summer, and Turkey as a military power would not have collapsed in 1878. But such rapid movements require a good force of regular cavalry to keep the commander well informed of the enemy's movements; and in this, as well as in generals and various other military essentials, the Turks were sadly deficient.

Let us now turn to the Russian side. The fall of Plevna set free 110,000 men. The 25,000 Roumanians forming part of this force were to remain near the Danube; but, on the other hand, Servia declared war against the Turks immediately after the fall of Plevna, and brought about an equal number of troops into the field. But without taking any account of their small allies, the Russians had $8\frac{1}{2}$ divisions —viz., the IV., IX., and Grenadier Corps, 3rd Division of the Guard, 2nd Division of the Line, and 3rd Rifle Brigade—

immediately available for further operations. What should be the plan of operations?

General Todleben, supposing, as was natural, that the Turks would concentrate near Adrianople, and that even after passing the Balkans the Russians would arrive before Adrianople in the dead of winter with a chain of mountains at their back and a line of supplies impossible to maintain, advised the prudent military course, viz., to put the troops in winter quarters on the main roads at the foot of the Balkans on the north, and to concentrate a large force around Rustchuk and proceed to its regular investment and siege. During the winter this place could be reduced, and then in the spring, the troops having refitted and having a railroad at their back, the army could advance over the Balkans and crush all resistance between it and Constantinople.

But some time before the fall of Plevna the Grand Duke Nicholas had made up his mind, although the idea met with the hearty approval of none of his generals except Gourko and Skobeleff, to cross the Balkans during the winter in spite of all the difficulties of ground, of season, of bad roads, and of insufficient supplies. In this war, as in all others, purely military reasons had to be subordinate to the higher political considerations; and there were the strongest political reasons for an immediate advance, since by postponing active operations until the spring the Turks would have time to re-organise and strengthen their armies, and—more important than all—the war would drift into the hands of diplomacy with all its attendant complications, including the probability of England becoming an active ally of the Turks, in case a peace was not made. At all hazards, the Grand Duke determined to strike before the Turks had had time to recuperate.

Immediately after the fall of Plevna, therefore, he issued orders sending the IX. Corps and the 3rd Division of the Guard to Orkhanie, the IV. Corps and the 3rd Rifle Brigade to Shipka, the 2nd Division *via* Lovtcha and Tirnova to Rustchuk, and the Grenadier Corps in reserve behind Shipka. This gave Gourko 84 battalions, say 65,000 men, of infantry. Radetzky at Shipka 74 battalions or 56,000 men, and the Cesarevitch 72 battalions or 55,000 men, besides the cavalry

PASSAGE OF THE BALKANS NEAR SOPHIA

and artillery with each force. The 3rd Division was to advance from Lovtcha over the Trojan pass in connection with Gourko's advance; and in addition there was the XI. Corps in front of Tirnova, available as reserve, and the XIV. Corps under Zimmermann on the line of Trajan's Wall in the Dobrudja.

Gourko's task was to defeat the army in his front at the Araba-Konak Pass, capture Sophia, and then advance by the old Roman road leading from Sophia past Philippopolis to Adrianople; Radetzky was to defeat the Turks at Shipka, advance over that pass, and join hands with Gourko in front of Adrianople; while the Cesarevitch, commanding all the troops left on the north of the Balkans, was to protect the communications from any attack from the direction of the Quadrilateral and prosecute the siege of Rustchuk, with the assistance of Todleben as his Chief Engineer. The distribubution of the troops at the beginning of the winter campaign is shown in the table on the following page.

GOURKO'S PASSAGE OF THE BALKANS

Plevna fell on the 10th of December, and the troops destined to reinforce General Gourko's detachment began their march as follows: the 3rd Division of the Guard on the 14th, and the IX. Corps on the 16th. Up to this date the weather had been rainy with occasional snows, and the roads were in a very bad condition; but on the 18th the veritable winter set in with no little severity. It began with a snow-storm, which continued with but little interruption for five days; and on the night of the 19-20th the temperature fell to 3° Fahr. The roads became then an alternation of smooth ice and frozen masses of mud ten inches in diameter, and hard enough to resist even the artillery wheels. None of the horses were sharp-shod, and the little Steppe horses of the intendance waggons were not shod at all. The result was that at every hill the waggons had all to be hauled and pushed up by hand.

It was under these difficulties that the reinforcements

DISTRIBUTION OF THE RUSSIAN ARMY IN BULGARIA, DECEMBER 25, 1877.

COMMANDERS.	Gourko.			Radetzky.			The Cesarevitch.			{Zimmermann, Fanetzky, Dellinghausen, Kartzoff.			Semeka.¶		
ARMY CORPS	Guard.	IX.	3*	VIII.	IV.	24	XII.	XIII.	32 2	XIV. Grenadier. XI.	2 11 3§		VII.	X.	
INFANTRY DIVISIONS	1	5		9	16		12	1		17			15	13	
	2	31		14	30		38	35		18	3 26		36	34	
RIFLE BRIGADES	1			Bulgarian 3			—			—			—		
				Legion 4											
CAVALRY DIVISIONS	2	{Cauc. Cos. Don. Cos.} 4		1			12	{Don Cos.† 8}		Cos. No. 1 11 9 7‡ 13 Don Cos.‖			7‡	10	
Total	Men. 84½ battalions = 65,000 54 squadrons = 6,000 256 foot-guns = 8,000 24 horse-guns = 1,000 80,000			Men. 74 battalions = 56,000 18 squadrons = 2,000 240 foot-guns = 7,500 12 horse-guns = 500 66,000			Men. 72 battalions = 54,500 60 squadrons = 6,500 288 foot-guns = 9,000 86 horse-guns = 1,500 71,500			Men. 76½ battalions = 58,000 92 squadrons = 10,000 320 foot-guns = 10,000 60 horse-guns = 2,500 80,000			Men. 48 battalions = 40,000 28 squadrons = 8,000 192 foot-guns = 6,000 18 horse-guns = 1,900 50,900		

* Regiments Nos. 11 and 12, and 1½ battalion of No. 10.

† This division, consisting of Don Cossack Regiments Nos. 31, 36, 37, and 30, was in the middle of January sent over the Balkans by Shipka Pass, under command of Lieutenant-General Skobeleff I., and joined General Gourko's command at Philippopolis.

‡ One brigade only.

§ One regiment (No. 9) and half of another (No. 10), in all 4½ battalions.

‖ One brigade, Regiments Nos. 24 and 30.

¶ The troops under command of this officer constituted the "Coast Army," the greater part of which was stationed at Odessa, with detachments in the Crimea and on the Lower Danube.

PASSAGE OF THE BALKANS NEAR SOPHIA

made their march from Plevna to Orkhanie (75 miles), arriving at the latter place between the 20th and 23rd of December.

The force at Gourko's disposal, given in a detail in the previous tabular statement, was then about 65,000 infantry, 6000 cavalry, and 280 guns of all kinds.

The Turkish force opposed to him consisted in all of about 35,000 infantry, about 2000 regular cavalry, large numbers of bashi-bozouks, and about 40 guns. It was thus distributed: 25,000 men and 15 guns on the Shandarnik and Araba-Konak positions (see pp. 173-175), where the high road crossed the mountains; 5000 men and 4 guns at Lutikova; the same at Slatitza; and 10,000 men and 1500 guns at Sophia.

Gourko's plan of operations—taking advantage of his superiority in numbers—was to leave a curtain of troops in front of each of these positions, and to send a strong column over the mountains to turn the left flank of the main Turkish position across the high road. Smaller columns were to pass on either flank and protect the main column from attacks from Sophia, Lutikova, or Slatitza. For this purpose he divided his force of $81\frac{1}{2}$ battalions (3 battalions being at Vratza) into 9 detachments, and assigned 130 foot- and 20 horse-guns to them, leaving the rest of his artillery in reserve. The men were ordered to take rations of hard bread in haversacks, and beef and mutton on the hoof to last from the 25th to the 30th inclusive. The detachments were as follows:

1. Lieutenant-General Schilder-Schuldner, with 9 battalions with 32 foot-guns, and seven squadrons with 6 horse-guns, on the Lutikova road.

2. Count Schouvaloff, with 12 battalions and 24 foot-guns, on the mountain heights west of the high road.

3. Prince Oldenburg, with 8 battalions and 28 guns, east of the high road.

4. Major-General Brock, with $5\frac{1}{2}$ battalions, 2 guns, and 2 sotnias, in front of Slatitza.

These four detachments, something less than half the total force, were placed under the orders of General Krüdener, and were to remain in position, observe the Turks, bombard their positions, and pursue them in case of retreat.

The main turning column was composed of three detachments following each other over the sappers' road, viz.:

5. The advance guard, Major-General Rauch, consisting of 13 battalions with 16 foot-guns, and 11 sotnias with 4 horse-guns, which was to leave Vratches at 5 A.M. December 25th, pass over the mountains, and halt at Curiak until 4 A.M. December 26th, when it was to debouch at Eleznitza and take position on the high road at Malinne.

6. The "First Echelon," 8 battalions with 16 guns, and 5 squadrons, which was to follow the Advance Guard and take position December 26th on its left at Razdanie.

7. The "Second Echelon," 10 battalions and 8 guns, to follow the First, and take position December 26th at Stolnik as reserve to the detachment in front of it. These two "Echelons" constituted the Third Division of the Guard under the command of Lieutenant-General Kataley.

To protect the right flank:

8. Lieutenant-General Wilhelminoff, with 6 battalions, 16 squadrons, 8 foot-guns, and 8 horse guns, was to cross by an old trail over the Umargas Mountain, and debouch at Zilava on the 26th, whence he was immediately to take a defensive position against any troops coming either from Sophia or from the Lutikova road; or in case the Advance Guard was checked at Eleznitza (where the Turks had one or two battalions), then to attack the Turks there in rear.

Finally:

9. Major-General Dandeville, with 9 battalions with 8 guns, and 6 squadrons with 6 horse-guns, was to make his way from Etropol over the mountain named Baba, demonstrate on the right and rear of the Turkish position, and debouch into the plain of Kamarlee on the 26th.

Once debouched into the plains of Sophia and Kamarlee, the cavalry of the various detachments was to push forward to the Philippopolis and other roads, cut the telegraph, and reconnoitre.

The Order of the Day of December 23rd, of which the above is the substance, therefore contemplated that the principal column, 31 battalions, 16 squadrons, and 44 guns in all, should in 36 hours march 32 miles, passing over a mountain crest 1800 feet above the valleys on either side; and these dispositions were made upon the report of the chief of the Sapper Battalion that the road was practicable for artillery, which opinion was shared by the commanding general, who had passed over it in person. This opinion was somewhat sanguine, as the best parts of the road had a slope of one in six, and the worst as steep as one in three, with curves with a radius of 10 yards; and the whole was covered with half-frozen snow or frosted earth.

In the result the horses proved to be totally useless, and were unharnessed; the pieces and caissons were then unlimbered, and the ammunition unloaded and carried by hand; drag-ropes were attached to each limber and each gun; from 100 to 150 men hauled on the ropes and pushed at the wheels and boxes. The first gun reached the summit on the morning of December 26th, and the last on the 30th.

In order to descend the southern slope (where the snow melted each afternoon and froze into smooth ice each night), two drag-ropes were fastened to each side of the carriage and one to the trail; with one rope on each side, a turn was then taken around a stump or bush, the other two ropes were then slacked up, and the piece was let slide the length of the first two ropes; then the operation was repeated. Some effort was made to guide by the trail-rope, but it amounted to little; for on the steep icy slope the men could not stand on their feet without the aid of a stick or a bush. Occasionally the piece got loose, but was brought to a standstill by a stump. There was but one serious accident, caused by the parting of a cable, in which one man was killed and three were seriously injured. Not a carriage was lost or damaged.

The patience and good humour of the men—hauling at the guns twelve hours of the day, sleeping on the snow without tent or blanket, and subsisting on two-thirds of a ration of black hard biscuit and meat, which latter was not always on hand—were extraordinary. The sappers' road descended into a valley whose head was not far from the left of the Turkish position at Araba-Konak; thence it followed this valley in a westerly direction to Curiak, where it turned south for two miles, and then, again turning west, passed Potop and arrived at Eleznitza, debouching thence to the south into the plain of Sophia. The greater part of the road between the summit and the Curiak valley was in sight of the Turks along the Shandarnik position; they also had one or two battalions posted at Potop and Eleznitza, with their outposts on a mountain overlooking Curiak and Potop at the bend of the valley.

The Preobrazhensky Regiment, the 1st Regiment of the First Division of the Guard, had the advance, and passed over to Curiak during the night of the 24th. On the night of the 25th the Caucasian Cossacks passed over, and on the morning of the 27th the Kozloff Regiment (No. 123) of Rauch's column, with 4 guns. One battalion of this regiment was left in the valley above the point where the sappers' road entered it, and the other two passed through Curiak and over the mountain between it and Potop, at which latter place there was a slight skirmish with the Turks, who retreated into the plain of Sophia.

On the same day, about noon, the Preobrazhensky Regiment took possession of the mountain in front of Curiak, where the Turkish outposts had been, and then, advancing during the night, occupied and fortified a position on the left (east) of the village of Nyagesovo, facing the Turkish position at Taskosen. The Caucasian Cossacks descended into the valley of Taskosen, cut the telegraph to Sophia, and captured a provision train of over 200 wagons *en route* from Sophia to Araba-Konak. The next two days, the 28th and 29th, were occupied in hauling at the guns. Meanwhile the column on the right, General Wilhelminoff, had found its route totally impracticable, and after two days of futile effort had discovered another, by which the guns were brought to Curiak, with labour equal to or greater than that of the main column. The column on the left, General Dandeville, succeeded in getting over the summit of the mountains, but in its descent was overwhelmed by a terrible storm, causing the snow to pile up in great drifts and bury a considerable part of the artillery. All progress was impossible, and after great suffering, this column returned to Etropol, December 29th, having lost 53 men frozen to death and 810 permanently disabled by freezing.

But the main turning column met with better success, and on the 30th all the guns were in the Curiak valley, the pieces assembled and harnessed. On the same day the Turks abandoned their position on the Lutikova road, leaving 4 guns, and escaped to Sophia, with a few losses in their rear guard, which was overtaken by the Caucasian Cossacks. The dispositions were then taken for attack on the 31st.

The plain of Sophia is a shelving oval about 25 by 10 miles in extent, entirely surrounded by mountains from 1500 to 2500 feet higher than its own level. Sophia lies in the south-western corner. As the Plevna high road, after leaving Sophia, approaches the eastern side of this plain, it meets and passes a spur of the Little Balkans projecting to the north through the villages of Malinne and Razdanie to Nyagesovo. Beyond this spur is a little prairie three miles in diameter, the eastern boundary of which is formed by a spur of the Balkans projecting to the south; over this the road passes near the village of Taskosen, and descends into a second prairie about five miles in diameter—the Kamarlee plain. Here were the principal camps of the Turkish reserves, their stores, munitions, etc. On the north was their position at Araba-Konak, the main range rising abruptly from the plain; on the south-east was the road to Slatitza, and to Petricevo and Ichtimann on the Philippopolis high road.

At Malinne and Razdanie the Turks had nothing but an outpost, which disappeared on the appearance of the Preobrazhensky Regiment. At Taskosen, however, they seemed prepared to make a defence. They had there ten battalions (about 5000 men), occupying intrenchments on either side of the high road back of the village; and on the mountain north of it were three successive lines of earthworks with 4 guns. To take this position the following dispositions were made:

1. General Rauch, with 10 battalions and 8 guns, to demonstrate against its front and turn the mountain with his left.

2. Major-General Kourloff, with 10 battalions and 8 guns to make a détour to the right through Cekansevo, and take the mountain behind Taskosen; and two brigades of cavalry to go still farther to the right and descend into Kamarlee plain.

The reserve, 12 battalions and 20 guns, under General Kataley, was on the high road about two miles in rear of Rauch.

A small column of three battalions, under Colonel Vasmund, kept up the connection between Rauch and Shouvaloff through the village of Dauskioi.

On the same date, the 30th, General Wilhelminof, with 5 battalions and 8 guns, debouched through Eleznitza to Jana, and the next day took position a few miles in advance in observation of Sophia; and the Caucasian Cossacks were placed under his orders.

The columns were under way before daylight on the 31st, and took the routes above indicated. Rauch's 8 guns got in position at 9 A.M., about 1800 yards from the Turkish batteries, and an artillery duel opened with shrapnel, at the same time that the Preobrazhensky Regiment and two battalions of the Rifle Brigade began working their way through the deep snow round the mountain to his left.

Kourloff's column on the right met with a warm reception on leaving the village of Cekansevo, and lost over 200 men (including General Mirkovitch, commanding the Volhynia Regiment) in their skirmish line at a distance of *fully 2000 yards* from the Turkish position. They were obliged to advance very slowly, the men running forward a few yards and then lying down in the snow, as they were entirely exposed in the open plain to the fire of the Turks concealed behind rocks on the mountain. About two o'clock their skirmish line got within 500 yards of the Turks, and then the latter fled.

The advance guard of the cavalry column on approaching the Kamarlee plain encountered some infantry intrenchments, and was driven back by their fire; and the cavalry did nothing all day.

The Preobrazhensky Regiment and the Rifle Brigade

PASSAGE OF THE BALKANS NEAR SOPHIA

meantime kept crawling round the left of the mountain out of fire, and approached the Turkish battery from its right rear (north) about 3 P.M. Under cover of heavy clouds which settled on the mountain about this time, the Turks retired their guns to the high road and then abandoned the whole position. They took up, however, a second position of great natural strength, on a mountain crossing the high road about a mile in rear. It was now about 4 o'clock, darkness was setting in, and the men were exhausted with the fatigues of the day. They were therefore ordered to bivouac on the heights in rear of Taskosen.

During the night the outposts were somewhat carelessly kept, the men having well-nigh reached the limits of endurance with the terribly fatiguing work of the past seven days; moreover, a dense fog prevailed.

On the next morning, January 1st, the Turks could not be found. The columns began advancing between 8 and 9 A.M., Rauch by the high road, and Kataley with the 3rd Division of the Guard in two columns over the mountain on his right.

As Gourko reached the Kamarlee plain with the advance about 10 o'clock, he saw a column of about 10,000 men, the rear of the Turks, climbing the mountain behind Dolni-Kamarlee on the road to Petricevo. At the same time a reconnoitring party of cavalry advanced over the high road at Araba-Konak, and met the advance of Krüdener's corps coming from the north. The fortifications at Araba-Konak were all abandoned, and the passage of the Balkans was complete.

Kataley's column came up with the Turks at Dolni-Kamarlee about noon, but the rear guard of 200 or 300 men made a stubborn defence from behind the fences and houses of the village, and the main force secured its retreat.

In the Kamarlee plain the Turks abandoned their hospitals, with about 1000 sick and wounded under care of the English Surgeons of the Red Cross and Red Crescent Societies, about 600 tents, over five million rounds of small-arms cartridges, and a considerable quantity of hard biscuit. On Shandarnik they abandoned ten guns, unable to withdraw them under the shrapnel fire of Prince Oldenburg's batteries.

The same day, January 1st, the Turks in Sophia made a sortie with about 5000 men against the column of General Wilhelminoff. The latter disposed his force of 3500 men along the crest of a low bluff rising from the plain in front of the village of Gorni-Bugaroff, and while the Turks were approaching they constructed hastily a line of little trenches, each large enough for eight or ten men. With wonderful firmness the Russians let the Turks approach within about 100 paces, and then opened fire with well-aimed volleys, succeeded by a hand-to-hand attack with the bayonet. The Turks were completely staggered by the fierceness and suddenness of this attack, and after a few moments lost all cohesion and began to retreat in confusion to Sophia, leaving 800 dead on the field, but carrying off the 1600 wounded to Sophia. The Russians lost 6 officers and 243 men. The smallness of Wilhelminoff's force prevented his following up their retreat.

On the evening of January 1st the following dispositions were ordered: Rauch, with 16 battalions and 26 guns, to leave Taskosen at 2 A.M. and advance by the high road toward Sophia. Kateley, with the 3rd Division of the Guard, 16 battalions and 16 guns, to continue the pursuit of the Turks, joining at Bunova the detachment of General Dandeville, which had succeeded on a second attempt in passing the mountains in that vicinity. The detachments of Shouvaloff and Oldenburg, to withdraw the guns from the mountain positions opposite Shandarnik, and then descend into the plain and bivouac near Malinne. The detachment of Schilder-Schuldner to pass into the plain of Kamarlee and bivouac there. Two brigades of the Guard Cavalry to move to Petricevo in order to take the Turks in flank, and the 3rd Brigade to take position on the Philippopolis high road five miles east of Sophia.

While the movements already described had been in progress, 70,000 pounds of hard bread had been packed across the mountain by the sappers' road on the horses of the artillery left in reserve. This, with the biscuits left by the

PASSAGE OF THE BALKANS NEAR SOPHIA

Turks, furnished the bread ration to the 4th of January inclusive, when the waggons began arriving by the high road.

Rauch moved forward as ordered, and on the afternoon of the 2nd, after a march of 25 miles, came to the Isker bridge, five miles east of Sophia. Here the Turks had posted three battalions of infantry and a regiment of cavalry, which made a defence for about an hour, setting fire to the village of Razdimme and attempting to burn the bridge; but before they could get the fire well under way the Preobrazhensky Regiment crossed the Isker on the ice about a mile to the left, and threatened their rear, whereupon they retreated to the town.

The next day a reconnaisance was made of the Turkish positions, showing that they had five large strong redoubts commanding the approaches by the various roads, and several lines of trenches and batteries recently constructed, a garrison of about 12,000 men, and 15 to 20 guns (estimated). The 8 battalions of Prince Oldenburg and 16 guns were brought up from Malinne, and all the dispositions were made to attack on the 5th. Wilhelminoff, with 8 battalions and 12 guns, was to demonstrate on the north, while Rauch, with 20 battalions and 42 guns, was to make the main attack along the Plevna high road. With the previous experience of the campaign, the result of this assault would have been at least doubtful, and if successful it would have cost over 5000 men and largely demoralised the whole force. Fortunately, the necessity for it was avoided, as the Turks evacuated the place during the night of the 3rd, retreating in the direction of Dubnitza, and abandoning as usual all their tents, an immense quantity of ammunition, and about 1600 sick and wounded. Here, in addition, they left about 8,000,000 complete rations of flour, hard bread, rice, sugar, coffee, salt, etc., besides oats and barley in great quantities. With this and the abundance of hay, sheep, and cattle in the Sophia Valley, the force under General Gourko's orders was provisioned for over a month.

Gourko's total losses in action during the eleven days of his movement between Orkhanie and Sophia were 32 officers (including 3 generals) and 1003 men.

The occupation of Sophia completed a military enterprise of no ordinary character, viz., the passage of a high mountain range in the middle of winter. The attacking force was numerically superior to the defenders in about the proportion of three to two; the latter were dispersed at several points, and nearly all their troops occupied positions on the mountain crests, with only a small reserve (at Sophia) in rear. Occupying the attention of each one of these detachments in front, the Russian commander threw a strong column over the mountains between the main mountain position (Araba-Konak) and the reserves (Sophia), and, completely turning the former, caused the hasty retreat of its defenders. Against the road by which they escaped a second turning column had been sent; but, overwhelmed with a snow-storm in the mountains, it had been obliged to turn back, and thus the Turkish force escaped capture or complete destruction.

The success of such a movement depends very largely upon the secrecy and celerity with which it is accomplished. Secrecy had in this case been very well observed, since the Turks had no knowledge of the construction of the sappers' road by which the main turning column passed; and its value was augmented by the confident belief of the Turkish commanders that to pass such a range of mountains covered with deep snow at this season of the year, by any but the main road, was *totally impossible*. As for celerity, there was not so much success; for the sappers' road proved so difficult for the passage of cannon that the arrival of the troops in the valleys of the southern slope, which had been fixed in Gourko's orders for the 26th, did not take place until the 30th. For four days—days of no little anxiety—the movement hung fire, half the guns on one side and half on the other side of the mountains, the troops more or less dispersed, and a retreat in case of attack being impossible. There was, moreover, a lateral valley of the mountains, which, passing out of range of Shouvaloff's right flank, led directly against the road which the main column was descending. Here was a fine opportunity for the Turks to strike the left flank of Gourko's column as it was descending the mountain, and before the men were well assembled. But the Turks did not take advantage of this opportunity, and what would have happened had they done so it is idle to speculate.

Having compelled the retreat of the Turks from Araba-Konak, Gourko sent one division of infantry and two brigades of cavalry to their pursuit; and without giving his troops any repose, he turned the rest of his force toward Sophia; which the Turks evacuated just as Gourko was preparing to assault it. In the other column the cavalry found such difficulty in traversing the mountains that all their efforts to head off the retreating Turks and strike their flank came to naught; the cavalry arrived too late each time. The infantry followed directly on the heels of the Turks, but in the narrow mountain passes the latter managed to cover their retreat by small bodies of men posted on the heights overlooking the road. They thus from time to time delayed the Russian advance long enough to gain time for their own retreat. In one of these skirmishes, the commander of the division, General Kataley, and one of his brigade commanders, who were riding imprudently in front of the column, were killed.

The Russian troops entered Sophia on the 4th o January, and were granted the few days' rest which was absolutely indispensable to them before undertaking a farther advance. The Turks had abandoned about 8,000,000 rations* of flour, rice, barley, salt, sugar, coffee, and a small quantity of hard bread and salt beef. They also left all their tents, over 4,000,000 rounds of cartridges, and a large quantity of forage. Sixteen hundred sick remained in the hospitals under care of the surgeons of the various English aid societies. There had been between 7000 and 9000 sick and wounded in the hospitals before the Turks abandoned the town, but all those who were capable of walking or crawling, as well as the Turkish population of the town, had been ordered to leave, and had fled in the direction of Dubnitza.

* Of flour alone there was more than 30,000 tons, according to Gourko's report.

But although a great quantity of supplies had fallen into the hands of the Russians, there was very little hard bread among them; and this article was indispensable to Gourko's farther advance. A supply train loaded with it was brought over the Araba-Konak Pass, from the Russian supplies at Orkhanie. As soon as it arrived Gourko distributed six days' rations of it to his men, as well as beef and mutton on the hoof. He then issued orders for his advance toward Philippopolis, which began on the 9th of January.

CHAPTER X

GOURKO'S ADVANCE TO PHILIPPOPOLIS, AND THE BATTLES NEAR THAT POINT, JANUARY 15–17, 1878

BEFORE describing Gourko's advance from Sophia to Philippopolis it is necessary to refer briefly to the topographical features of the intervening country. The plain of Sophia, although south of the main Balkan range, is yet properly a part of the basin of the Danube, for all its drainage is collected into the Isker, which cuts its way through the Balkans in a deep gorge due north of Sophia. The Isker rises near the town of Samakoff, about thirty miles south of Sophia, in a cluster of peaks known as Mount Rilo, which attain an altitude of over 8000 feet above sea level. From these peaks two ranges of mountains radiate to the north-east and north-west, joining the main Balkans, and along these two ranges is the water-shed between the basin of the Danube and that of the Ægean Sea. A third range, known as the Rhodope Mountains, shoots off to the south of east from Mount Rilo, and between it and the Balkans lies the broad valley of the Maritza, the plains of ancient Thrace, beyond the eastern side of which lies Adrianople. The old Roman high road, built by Trajan, passes through Sophia and over the water-shed on its east, winding through a deep gorge which still bears the name of Trajan's Gate; descending into the plain of the Maritza above Tatar-Bazardjik, it follows the course of that river for 150 miles to Adrianople.

Having crossed the Balkans to Sophia, Gourko's problem was of course to advance along the direction of this road. By his movement on Taskosen he had separated the Turkish force into two detachments, but they both made good their retreat—that which had defended the Araba-Konak Pass by crossing the divide to the town of Petricevo, which is situated on the Topolnica river, an affluent of the Maritza, and that which had been at Sophia by making a wide détour to the south-west through the town of Radomir and thence east to Samakoff. The eastern detachment numbered about 20,000 men, and the western about 15,000; and they were reinforced by 20,000 men withdrawn from the Quadrilateral and forwarded by rail.

With them arrived Suleiman Pasha, who personally took command about the 5th of January. This force was then distributed along the roads leading over the water-shed, the bulk of the newly arrived troops behind Ichtiman at Trajan's Gate, the detachment of Shakir Pasha on the right at Otlukioi and Petricevo, and the garrison of Sophia at Samakoff on the left. The distance between his extreme right and left flanks was nearly forty miles, but the communications were good by means of intersecting valleys. This position at the entrance of the defile of Trajan's Gate was one of great natural strength, but it could easily have been turned by either flank by means of the valleys winding in the rear of it. Such was Gourko's plan of operations, and for this purpose he divided his force into four detachments, exclusive of a portion of the 3rd Division of the Line, which was sent along the base of the Balkans to Karlovo, there to join the rest of the division, which meanwhile was passing the Balkans through the Trajan Pass.

The four detachments were ordered as follows:

On the right, Lieutenant-General Wilhelminoff, with 8 battalions of the IX. Corps, 12 sotnias of Cossacks, and 12 guns, was to leave Sophia January 7th by the direct Samakoff road, and endeavour, 1, to cut off the retreat of that Turkish detachment which was retreating by way of Radomir (in which he was not successful), and 2, to advance through Banja against the left flank and rear of the position at Trajan's Gate.

In the centre, Lieutenant-General Count Shouvaloff, with 30 battalions, 12 squadrons, and 76 guns, all of the Guard, was to advance along the main high-road, and, arrived at

Ichtiman, to act against the front of the position at Trajan's Gate.

On the left, Lieutenant-General Baron Krüdener, with the rest of the Guard, and a portion of his own (IX.) corps, in all 24 battalions, 16 squadrons, and 58 guns, was to advance by Petricevo to Otlukioi, whence a good road descends to Tatar-Bazardjik. He was to threaten the Turkish right, and in case of their retreat to endeavour to intercept them.

Finally, the fourth column, a small detachment of 6 battalions and 8 guns under Lieutenant-General Schilder-Schuldner, was to follow the valley of the Topolnica, keep up communications between Shouvaloff and Krüdener, and endeavour to get in rear of the Turkish right. A detachment of 8 battalions, 8 squadrons, and 14 guns was left at Sophia to protect the rear of the advancing columns and guard the stores captured at that place.

The various columns arrived in front of the Turkish positions previously described on the morning of January 11th. Then followed a curious misunderstanding, each of the Turkish detachments sending a *Parlementaire* through the pickets to say that orders had been received from the Minister of War at Constantinople to cease hostilities, as an armistice had been granted by the Russians. Telegrams soon arrived from the Grand Duke, however, saying that proposals for an armistice were expected, but had *not* been received, and that active operations must not in the least be retarded. This misunderstanding on the part of the Turks resulted in delaying the column of Wilhelminoff for twenty-four hours, but otherwise had no effect.

On the 11th Wilhelminoff attacked Samakoff, and gained possession of it after a fight in which he lost 150 men.

On the 10th the Turks received news of the capture of Shipka Pass and the whole army stationed there. This of course rendered a prompt retreat of Suleiman's army imperatively necessary, and on the morning of the 11th his troops evacuated their whole line of defence along the mountains of which Trajan's Gate was the centre. Their right flank and a portion of their centre united at Tatar-

Bazardjik, and at once continued their retreat to Philippopolis.

With the Turkish left flank, however, which had been at Samakoff, the Russians at once began a race, in the hope that Shouvaloff's column, advancing by the high road through Ichtiman, might first reach the Maritza valley and thus cut off this detachment. But the Turks reached the valley before the Russians, the latter being delayed by their artillery, which again had to be hauled up and down the icy slopes of the road by hand. As the advance guard of Count Shouvaloff debouched from the mountains on the main road at the village of Vetrenova on the afternoon of January 12th, the rear of the Turkish column was in sight a few miles in advance on a parallel road—that from Samakoff to Tatar-Bazardjik. The leading regiment was sent across to that road, but only overtook the baggage—300 ox-carts—which it captured. The next morning, January 13th, it followed on the heels of the Turks, but about five miles behind them, while twelve other battalions of Shouvaloff's column advanced along the main road to about three miles from Tatar-Bazardjik. Here they found a portion of the central column, about 8000 men, under Fuad Pasha, occupying a strong position behind the Topolnica River, and prepared to defend it in order to gain time for the other Turkish column to enter by the Samakoff road. The Russians were not strong enough as yet to warrant an attack, and therefore nothing was done beyond skirmishing with the outposts. During the afternoon the advance of Krüdener's column was seen debouching from the mountains off on the left; and preparations were made to surround and attack the Turks the next day, provided they remained at Tatar-Bazardjik. But, as was expected, they abandoned their positions during the night, and the pursuit therefore was recommenced early the next morning, January 14th.

Fuad Pasha conducted the retreat of 20,000 men now united under his orders as a rear guard with no little skill. Instead of marching along the main high road, where he could have been overtaken and detained by the cavalry long enough for the infantry to come up and overwhelm him, he

BATTLE OF PHILIPPOPOLIS

at once crossed the Maritza, destroying the bridges, and followed the line of railroad with his infantry and the country roads with his artillery, and covered his rear with about 1500 cavalry, who did excellent service. The Russians were on the march before daylight of January 14th, Shouvaloff on the high road, Krüdener on a converging road on his left, Wilhelminoff and Schilder-Schuldner on the flanks somewhat in rear. About 5 P.M., after a march of 30 miles without halt, Shouvaloff's advance guard got abreast of the rear of the Turks, about three miles off, on the railroad near the little village of Adakioi. Here his troops forded the Maritza, a stream 200 yards wide and 3 feet deep, and filled with floating ice, and passed through the village. But the Turks, on the run, had got about a mile ahead, and Shouvaloff, having only 8 battalions at hand, was obliged to be prudent, especially as it was already nearly dark. The same night the bulk of the cavalry (28 squadrons) bivouacked between the Karlovo high road and the Maritza, about four miles from Philippopolis; Krüdener bivouacked at Celapitza on the right flank of the cavalry, with Schilder-Schuldner behind him on the same road; and Wilhelminoff was on the railroad about 12 miles in the rear.

The next morning, January 15th, Shouvaloff had 12 battalions in hand and 20 battalions marching toward him by the high road. He moved out of the village (Adakioi) at daylight, and at once found the Turks, who, overcome with fatigue, had been unable to continue their retreat during the night. They were posted in a good position behind a small but deep rivulet, the ice of which was not passable for artillery, extending from the village of Karatair on their left over a little hill behind Kadikioi toward the village of Airanly, their right resting on the swamps of extensive ice-fields.

Shouvaloff at once deployed his troops and opened fire upon the Turks, and sent word to General Gourko, whose headquarters were on the other side of the Maritza nearly opposite Airanly, that he had a force of about 15,000 men in his front posted in a good position, that he thought he could, if ordered to do so, carry the position in his front, but with considerable loss; and asking for instructions. Gourko sent him back word about 10 A.M., not to attack the Turks, but to keep up a sufficient fire to hold them in place while he sent the rest of the troops around their right flank to cut them off from Philippopolis.

For this purpose Gourko ordered:

1. Krüdener's column, with the 3rd Division of the Guard in the lead, to move forward at once to Philippopolis, nine miles in advance (or on the left as the line of battle stood).

2. The Finland Regiment, followed by Schilder-Schuldner's Brigade (17th and 18th Regiments), to cross the Maritza at the village of Airanly, drive the Turks out of that village, and move around the Turkish right flank.

3. The Preobrazhensky and Simeonoff Regiments to demonstrate against the centre of the Turkish position at Kadikioi.

4. The Grenadier, Paul, and Moscow Regiments and the Rifle Brigade to keep up the fire against the left flank of the Turks, and if possible retain them in place.

5. The column of General Wilhelminoff to move along the railroad and come up on the right of Shouvaloff.

As the Russian cavalry approached the Maritza on the east of Philippopolis early in the morning, the Turks saw that it would be useless to attempt to continue the retreat in that direction, and they were therefore forced to accept battle in the position where they then were, and thus cover their retreat over the Rhodope Mountains to the south.

Sulieman's whole force numbered 100 battalions, or between 50,000 and 60,000 men: but he personally escaped this morning with some 10,000 or 15,000 by Stanimaka and the road leading thence south-east over the mountains; but the rest of his force was cut off by the Russians before reaching Stanimaka, and thereafter formed the right flank of the force under Fuad Pasha, whose troops, with this addition, numbered in all about 35,000 men.

Meanwhile Shouvaloff kept up a sharp fire with the Turks in front of him throughout the day. His right flank, however, was somewhat in the air, but gave him no great anxiety, as the column of Wilhelminoff was expected to arrive every minute along the railroad and join him; but about 4 P.M., Wilhelminoff not having yet arrived, and a considerable force of Turkish cavalry having appeared between Karatair and Karadermen, Shouvaloff, not wishing to leave his flank unprotected during the night, resolved to attack the Turkish left at the village of Karatair and drive them out of that position. This attack was executed by the Paul Regiment, which crossed the stream in front of that village by fording, and after a short fight gained possession of the village. Darkness soon afterward set in, and soon arrived Wilhelminoff's column.

On the other flank the Finland Regiment was ferried over the Maritza on cavalry horses about 2 P.M., and drove the Turks out of the village of Airanly. But the column of Schilder-Schuldner did not come up till about 5 P.M.; it was then ferried over in the same manner at a ford about a mile east of the point where the Finland Regiment had crossed. It was unable to advance around the Turkish flank, however, for the country in front of it was a mass of impassable ricefields. The only fighting of the day was in Shouvaloff's column, whose losses were in all about 300 men.

The 3rd Division of the Guard, forming part of Krüdener's column, had meanwhile approached Philippopolis early in the afternoon, and had entered that part of the town on the north of the river; but they found the bridge wholly destroyed, the opposite bank occupied by infantry, and the river not fordable. Beyond preparing some bridge material, they were unable to accomplish anything on that day.

A portion of the cavalry had moved around the town of Philippopolis and reached the Maritza at a point five miles east of the town, but had not crossed.

The force against which Shouvaloff fought during the 15th of January was only the rear guard of the Turkish army, about 15,000 to 20,000 men, under Fuad Pasha. The rest of Suleiman's army, about 35,000 to 40,000 men, with Suleiman himself, had already reached Philippopolis about the 12th or 13th. On the 14th, seeing the Russian cavalry already moving around the south of the town, Suleiman saw that it would be impossible to continue his retreat to Adrianople by the high road, and he determined to try to escape by the roads on the south of the main road. For this purpose he sent a portion of his troops to the village of Markova (four miles south of Philippopolis) and with the rest he took the road leading to Stanimaka, and thence over the mountains either to Adrianople or due south to some port on the Ægean. This movement he began on the 15th, while the fight was going on around Kadikioi.

During the night of the 15th and 16th Fuad abandoned his position of the previous day, and passing through the gap between Schilder-Schuldner and the mountains, took up a position along the base of the mountains near the village of Dermendere.

Wilhelminoff followed him along the base of the mountains; Schildner-Schuldner moved along the railroad so as to get around his right flank; and Shouvaloff followed along the railroad across the rice-swamps, and then turning by the right flank deployed in his front. But Schilder-Schuldner, after arriving at the village of Komat, halted his troops on account of their fatigue, and did not close around the Turkish right flank. Fuad meanwhile concentrated his troops near the village of Dermendere, and about 3 P.M. made a very savage attack upon Wilhelminoff's column, forming the extreme Russian right flank. These were the same troops which had repulsed the Turks so savagely at Gorni-Bugarof (near Sophia) on the 1st of January, and they repeated here the same tactics as on that day, and with almost equally good results—*i.e.*, they laid down behind the rocks on a ridge of the foot-hills and let the Turks approach to within 100 yards, and then received them with carefully aimed volley-firing. The Turks made three attacks, and were each time repulsed, and finally retired leaving 600 dead on the field, while the Russian loss was only about 60 in all.

Fuad's purpose in this attack was evidently to divert the attention of the Russians, and cause them to send troops to the aid of their right flank by weakening their left, and then to hasten to rejoin the rest of Suleiman's army on the Stanimaka road. But he did not succeed. Two regiments were indeed sent by Shouvaloff to Wilhelminoff's aid, but Schilder-Schuldner's column was not weakened, nor that of Krüdener.

BATTLE OF PHILIPPOPOLIS

But Schilder-Schuldner did fail to get around Fuad's right flank on the 16th, and therefore during the night Fuad again moved along the base of the mountains about four miles, taking up a new position near the village of Beleznitza.

Meanwhile, on the morning of this same day (January 16th), Gourko having gone in person to Philippopolis, and finding that it would be impossible to construct quickly a bridge over the river in place of the one which had been burned by the Turks, immediately sent the 3rd Division of the Guard down the river three or four miles to the nearest ford, and there had them ferried over the river on the cavalry horses of the 2nd Brigade of the Cavalry Division of the Guard. From there this division advanced at once to the south toward the Stanimaka road, by which Suleiman had retreated the previous day.

About 4 P.M. the 1st Brigade of this division approached this road near the village of Karagatch, five miles from Philippopolis. This village was occupied by a considerable force of Turks, the rear of Suleiman's force, with 18 guns. The Russians immediately moved forward to the attack, and carried the village with a loss of about 260 men, capturing all of the 18 guns. The Turks in turn, reinforced in numbers, attacked the Russians and tried to regain the position, but without success. The 2nd Brigade of this division, however, had been delayed at the crossing of the Maritza, and did not arrive by nightfall. Owing to the weakness of his force and his exposed position (Suleiman's main force being only a few miles farther ahead toward Stanimaka), the chief of this brigade thought it prudent to withdraw his troops and the 18 captured guns during the night a few miles back to the village of Ahlan, where he was rejoined by the 2nd Brigade.

Suleiman, however, continued his retreat, leaving Fuad to extricate himself the best way he could. By his retreat to Beleznitza during the night of the 15th and 16th, the latter had joined his troops to that portion of Suleiman's rear guard which had been cut off at Karagatch.

Sending his cavalry to follow Suleiman, Gourko prepared

to close in his whole force round Fuad, Wilhelminoff on the right near Markova, Shouvaloff and Schilder-Schuldner in the centre near Beleznitza, and Dandeville (3rd Division Guard) on the left near Karagatch.

Fuad fought with his back to the mountains throughout the whole of this day, January 17th. In the morning he concentrated his troops on the right in one final effort to drive back the Russians in that quarter, and open his way to the Stanimaka road; but his troops were repulsed, and, attacked in turn by the Russians, they lost more of their artillery. About 3 P.M. Schilder-Schuldner's troops moved forward to the attack in front of Tchiftlik, at the same time that Wilhelminoff's column advanced along the base of the mountains against the Turkish left flank at Markova. The Turks were incapable of further resistance, and, abandoning everything, they dispersed in small bands, climbing up the mountains through the snow. The Russians followed them till nightfall, and then gave up the pursuit on account of the impracticable nature of the country and the dispersion of the enemy.

The next day Gourko reassembled his troops in the vicinity of Philippopolis, sending in pursuit of the enemy two cavalry columns: 1. The Caucasian Brigade of Cossacks, which followed Fuad's detachment, cutting down more or less of the fugitives, and finally making its way through blind mountain paths to the other side of the mountains, and arriving at Demotika (south of Adrianople) on the 27th; 2. The Cavalry of the Guard and a brigade of Don Cossacks, which followed Suleiman's detachment through Stanimaka, and on the 19th captured 40 guns which were halted at a very steep hill under escort of five battalions of infantry, which the cavalry dispersed after a short engagement.

The result of Gourko's movement from Sophia to Philippopolis was the destruction of Suleiman Pasha's army of 50,000 to 60,000 men. The Russians captured 114 guns in all (96 of them in open fight), about 2000 prisoners, all the baggage, several thousand muskets, great quantities of ammunition, implements, &c., &c. The Turks lost in the series of engagements around Philippopolis very nearly

BATTLE OF PHILIPPOPOLIS

5000 men, and retreated in scattered disorganised bands through the wild Rhodope Mountains, their numbers diminishing daily by desertions, freezing, starvation, &c. About the 28th of January this disorganised force began to assemble on the shore of the Ægean near Enos, where a fleet of transports was in waiting for them under command of Manthorpe Bey, an ex-officer of the British Navy. About 40,000 men were transported in this fleet to Gallipoli and Constantinople. Suleiman was placed in arrest and ordered for trial by court martial.*

Gourko's losses between Sophia and Philippopolis were in all as follows:

	Officers.	Men.
Killed	7	220
Wounded	34	989
Total	41	1209

We have now followed the first two stages of Gourko's movements during the winter, viz., from Orkhanie to Sophia, and from Sophia to Philippopolis. Direct communications were now opened with the Headquarters and the troops at Shipka; and Gourko's army became simply the right wing of the advancing Russian army, all the parts of which were within supporting distance. Before following this further advance, it is necessary to explain the passage of the Balkans by the other columns, which had meanwhile taken place.

* The sentence of the court-martial which tried Suleiman was delivered in December, 1878. It was complete degradation and confinement in a fortress for fifteen years.

CHAPTER XI

CAPTURE OF THE TURKISH ARMY AT SHIPKA PASS

GOURKO'S movement over the Balkans by way of Sophia merely formed part, as already explained, of the general plan of advance determined upon just after the fall of Plevna. The other portions of this plan were the forcing of the Shipka Pass and the passage of a small force over the Trojan Pass.

The latter column, under General Kartzoff, consisted only of two regiments of the 3rd Division, reinforced by one battalion of the 3rd Rifle Brigade and two regiments of Don Cossacks (24th and 30th). The Balkans in the vicinity of the Trojan hill are higher than at almost any other part of them, and there is nothing but rude wood-roads leading over the mountains. The Turks had two or three small redoubts, and perhaps 2000 men defending these roads—about the same force as at Slatitza. On the 4th of January Kartzoff began the ascent of the mountains, taking only eight guns with him; but each of these was dismounted and placed on a sledge, and required twenty-four yoke of buffaloes, a company of infantry, and a sotnia of Cossacks to draw it up the mountain. His troops were divided into three detachments of about nine companies, or 1500 men each. They reached the summit of the mountains on the afternoon of the 5th, and made a reconnaissance of the redoubt. The next two days were passed in reconnoitring a route on the east of the redoubt by which it could be turned, and in hauling at the artillery. On the 7th the redoubt was bombarded in front, while a column of infantry passed around it on the east, and descended the mountain in its rear; at the same time another column of infantry

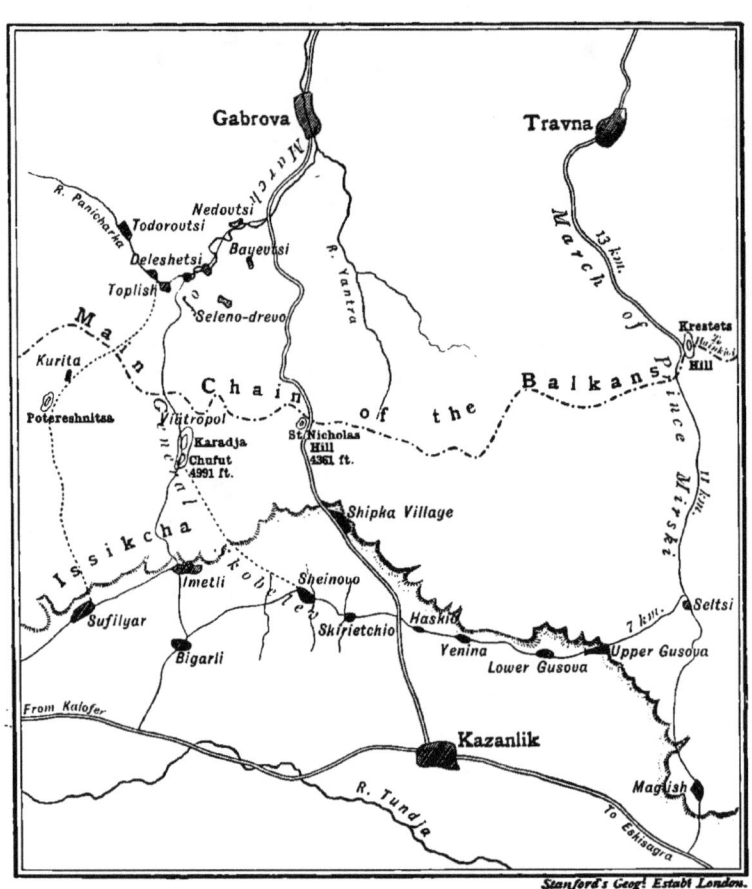

attacked it in front. The Turks fled and dispersed in the Little Balkans. The Russian losses were less than 100 men.

Two days later the other portion of this 3rd Division, which had crossed the Balkans with Gourko, and had subsequently been sent by Slatitza to rejoin Kartzoff's command, arrived at Slatitza. Finding the Turkish works there abandoned, it moved on and joined Kartzoff near Karlovo, and on the 14th the whole of the 3rd Division moved down by the high-road toward Philippopolis, and opened communication with the troops of Gourko, by whom it was directed along the roads north of the Maritza toward Haskioi.

SHIPKA

At Shipka Pass, where the Russians had now for over five months been defending with such gallantry the positions captured in the early part of the campaign, the passage was effected in a very brilliant manner.

The arrival of General Skobeleff with the 16th and 30th Divisions and the 3rd and 4th Rifle Brigades at Gabrova, in the first days of January, placed a force of 74 battalions or about 56,000 infantry, besides artillery and cavalry, at Radetzky's disposition; but of these troops the 24th Division, which had arrived on the heights of Shipka during the latter part of November to relieve for a short time the 14th Division, had in a subsequent snow-storm and cold snap lost a good many hundreds of men from freezing, and had in fact been wholly broken down by the cold. On the 25th of December this division had 6013 men unfit for duty from frost-bites and sickness brought on by the terrible exposure. It had to be withdrawn to Gabrova to refit, and was for the moment practically *hors de combat*. The rest of his troops, however, were in good order.

Radetzky's plan for forcing the passage was to divide his troops into three columns, one of which, under his own orders, was to remain in the works at the summit of the pass, while the other two were to pass on either flank, cross the mountain, and attack the pass from the rear (south), simultaneously with the attack from the north. Radetzky's detachment consisted of the 14th Infantry Division and the 35th Regiment of the 9th Division. The column of the right, under Skobeleff, consisted of the 16th Division, the 3rd Rifle Brigade (3 battalions), 7 Bulgarian battalions, the 9th Don Cossacks, 6 mountain guns, and 6 4-pdrs.—in all, 22 battalions, 6 squadrons, and 12 guns; it was to pass over the trail which leads from the village of Zelenodrevo to the top of the mountains (only about two miles and a half from the left flank of the Turks on the Bald Mountain), and thence descends to the village of Imetli in the Tundja valley; here the detachment was to turn to the left and attack the works defending the village of Shipka. The column of the left, under Prince Mirsky, consisted of the 33rd, 34th, and 36th Regiments of the 9th Division, the 30th Division, the 4th Rifle Brigrade, one Bulgarian battalion, the 23rd Don Cossack Regiment, 6 mountain guns, 8 4-pdrs., 8 9-pdrs.—in all, 26 battalions, 6 squadrons, and 22 guns. It was to leave the village of Travna and follow the trail over the Selky hill, debouching in the Tundja valley at the village of Gusevo, then turn to the right, and, joining hands with Skobeleff, attack the works defending the village of Shipka.

The movement was fixed to begin on the morning of the 5th of January, and it was calculated that the columns would arrive in the valley on the evening of the 7th, and attack on the morning of the 8th.

In both columns the guns were unlimbered and arranged to be drawn on sledges; but it was soon found impossible to get them up the mountain, even in this mannner, and they were all left behind except the little mountain guns, one battery of which was with each column. The snow on the paths which the columns had to follow was in many places TEN FEET DEEP.

From Mount St. Nicholas, where Radetzky posted himself, the villages where the two columns were to debouch into the valley could be plainly seen.

The two columns began their march on the 5th, Mirsky in

the morning and Skobeleff in the evening, the former having to pass nearly twice the distance of the latter. Mirsky met no opposition in the mountains, and on the 7th descended into the valley at Gusevo, driving the Turkish outpost away from that village, and sent one brigade of the 30th Division to occupy the village of Maglis, four miles east of Gusevo, to protect his left flank and rear. Skobeleff met with resistance in descending the mountain on the 7th, the Turks having hastily occupied a line of trenches on a ridge commanding the trail which Skobeleff was following. In order to dislodge the Turks from this place he was considerably delayed, and was only able to occupy the village of Imetli with an advance guard on the 7th.

On the morning of the 8th, the day calculated for the attacks, Radetzky watched eagerly on Mount St. Nicholas for the appearance of the other two columns in the valley. About 10 A.M. Mirsky's troops were seen coming out of the mountains near Gusevo; and deploying about noon, they moved forward to the attack in the direction of Shipka village. Skobeleff's troops were not in sight, but a cannonade was heard in the mountains in his direction, where he was, in fact, still fighting with the Turks in the position half way down the slope. About noon also arrived a messenger from Skobeleff explaining the difficulties that he had met. Radetzky sent word back to him to concentrate his column in the valley and attack Shipka from the rear on the morning of the 9th, and if possible to open communications with Mirsky, and attack in conjunction with him. He also informed Skobeleff that the 1st Cavalry Division had been sent over his trail to assist him. Mirsky meanwhile heard the cannonade off on his left, but saw no Russian troops. Finally the cannonade died away, and still no troops were in sight. He was evidently in a bad position to attack alone, with his left flank out in the air; but during the previous night he had received a precise order from Radetzky to attack on this morning. He therefore moved forward with the 4th Rifle Brigade deployed as skirmishers, supported by the little mountain battery and the 33d Regiment. In his second line were the 34th, 36th, and 117th Regiments. The 120th remained with the baggage at Gusevo, and the 118th and 119th, which had occupied Maglis on his left flank the previous night, were ordered to move forward to Kazanlyk.

After a short but hot fight his troops carried the villages of Janina and Haskioi. But beyond Haskioi was a small range of hills stretching across the road, covered with several tiers of rifle-pits. Here Mirsky's troops were brought to a halt by a very hot fire, and, the colonel of the 33rd Regiment being severely wounded about this time, the line began to waver.

The 36th Regiment was then sent forward to the support of the 33rd, which held the right of the line, and the 34th to the support of the Rifle Brigade, on its left. One battalion of the 117th was sent off in the direction of Kazanlyk to guard the left flank, and only the other two battalions of the regiment remained in reserve. The little mountain battery advanced to within about 700 yards of the Turkish position, and sent a lucky shot which exploded one of the Turkish caissons. The Russians then moved forward with a rush in spite of the fire of the Turks, and carried the line of trenches, capturing three guns and about 100 prisoners.

They thus came in front of the last line of defence of the Turks, a series of redoubts on the hills just south of Shipka village; but darkness was coming on, the troops were tired out, and their ammunition was almost exhausted. It was impossible to try to carry these redoubts that night. The Turks, however, passed to the attack, and rushed forward upon the Russians with considerable impetuosity, but were driven back by the deliberate volley-firing of the latter.

Although Mirsky was informed early in the evening that the 118th and 119th Regiments had entered Kazanlyk without finding any enemy, yet his position was anything but comfortable. His left flank was in the air, at his back was a high range of mountains over which it would be almost impossible to retreat, and in his front, only 200 yards off, was the enemy in a position which he felt he could not carry. He sent a report to Radetzky explaining his critical situation, stating that he had fought all day with superior numbers, had sustained very great losses, was nearly at the end of his ammunition, and unless he could be reinforced he must begin to retreat. Radetzky sent word back to him to hold on for another twenty-four hours: that Skobeleff would come to his relief on his left flank; and that he (Radetzky) would try to operate a diversion by attacking the Turks in front the next morning. The next morning, unfortunately, there was a tempest of wind, filling the air with blinding snow and a dense fog of particles of frozen mist. Radetzky could see nothing of what was going on in the valley, but through the fog came the sounds of heavy artillery and infantry fire, indicating that the Turks had begun to attack Mirsky. Radetzky at once made his preparations for attack, in the hope of relieving the pressure on Mirsky. He sent forward the 55th and 56th Regiments and part of the 35th along the high road and on its right against the Turkish trenches in front of Mount St. Nicholas. The ground was extremely unfavourable for attack, and in the dense fog it was impossible to see what was going on at a distance of ten yards away. Still these troops, between noon and 2 P.M., carried the first two lines of Turkish trenches in open assault, but with enormous losses—over 1700 men. Having gained these positions, the troops remained there, unable to advance, until news arrived from Skobeleff during the afternoon announcing the surrender of the whole Turkish army.

Meawhile, in the valley the fog was not so dense. The Turks had early in the morning opened an attack on Mirsky's right flank, but had not made any impression upon it. They then made an attack upon his left flank, without any better success. Mirsky then riposted with his left, and carried a second Turkish redoubt (capturing two guns in it), and also the village of Shipka. This cut off this portion of the Turks from the Kazanlyk road, but they still held a line of redoubts behind Shipka village. While Mirsky's troops were halted in front of this and a lull had succeeded in the battle in their front, they heard loud cheering off on their left at the village of Shenovo. It was the attack of Skobeleff's troops—the most brilliant assault of the whole war, deciding the day and the fate of the entire Turkish army of Shipka.

Skobeleff's column, as already remarked, had met with opposition in descending the southern slope of the mountain, the Turks having hastily occupied on the 7th a ridge northeast of the village of Imetli, from which they took his line of march in flank. This completely stopped the march of his column late in the afternoon, and Skobeleff, arriving in person at its head, found the men lying down and receiving the fire of the enemy, but without replying to it. On asking an explanation, the men replied that it was of no use to fire, for their guns would not reach the position of the Turks—about 1500 yards off across a ravine. While he was talking his chief of staff was very badly wounded in the shoulder. Skobeleff immediately ordered up a company of the 63rd Regiment, which he had armed before leaving Plevna with the Peabody-Martini guns captured from the Turks. They had hardly opened fire before the Turks ceased their fire and retired behind the crest of their ridge. Darkness, however, now set in, and stopped the fighting. The Russians remained in their positions, scattered along the trail in the snow during the night.

Early the next morning the two regiments in the lead, the 63rd and 64th, resumed their march, and by 9 A.M. had reached the village of Imetli, and found that the Turks had occupied a hill on the south-east of that village. The 64th Regiment attacked this hill and drove them out.

About 11 A.M. Skobeleff received word from the pickets left in observation on the top of the mountain that Mirsky's detachment was moving forward to the attack of Shipka village, and the firing was also heard from that direction; but Skobeleff did not credit the report, thinking that his men had mistaken a column of Turks for Russians, and as for the firing, it seemed to come from the direction of Mount St. Nicholas. Moreover, in reply to his report that he could not get his men together in the valley in time to attack on the 8th, Skobeleff had received orders from Radetzky to attack on the 9th, and *positively not to attack before all his men were assembled in the valley.* Having therefore no direct communication with Mirsky (who had only sent two sotnias of Cossacks to open communication with him, and which had not penetrated beyond Kazanlyk), and having no certain information that Mirsky was actually engaged, Skobeleff stuck strictly to his orders, and kept his two regiments at Imetli until the rest of his troops could arrive. It thus happened that Mirsky had to sustain the fight of the 8th unsupported, as has already been described.

During the afternoon the 61st Regiment got down the mountain to Imetli, and then Skobeleff sent forward the 63rd and 64th a short distance toward Shenovo. But all his troops not yet being over the mountains, they were not allowed to attack Shenovo. During the night the Rifle Brigade and the Bulgarian Legion were also assembled at Imetli, but word was received from the 62nd Regiment that they could not drag the artillery up the hill. Skobeleff sent word to them to leave the guns behind and march on during the night, so as to be at Imetli at all hazards in the morning.

Before daylight on the 9th his troops at Imetli were under arms, but Skobeleff waited still for the 62nd Regiment. As it began to descend the mountain, so that he was sure of having it as a reserve, about 10 A.M. Skobeleff sent forward a portion of the 63rd Regiment to clear the Turks out of a hill on their right flank (west of Shenovo), which threatened his left; this they accomplished with considerable loss. At the same time Skobeleff sent a portion of his cavalry on his right, and they soon opened communication with Mirsky's detachment.

Everything being at last in readiness, Skobeleff formed his troops for the assault of the Shenovo redoubts. In his first line were the 63rd Regiment and the Bulgarian Legion; behind them the 61st and 64th and the Rifle Brigade. With all the bands playing, these troops moved forward to the assault without breaking their line or firing a shot. They lost heavily, even in the bands, but still they moved on, until, on nearing the redoubts, they broke into a run with a wild hurrah and rushed at the Turkish works. There was then a little hesitation in the 63rd Regiment, until its colonel arrived among the men in the very front line, and by his personal bravery carried the regiment forward with him.

The Russians entered the redoubts, and then suddenly the hurrahing and noise of the firing were succeeded by a painful, deadly silence, lasting for some minutes, during which a fierce hand-to-hand fight with the bayonet took place. The Russians won, and six Turkish battalions laid down their arms in the redoubts, while the rest began fleeing toward Shipka. Just as Skobeleff was giving the orders for following them, arrived a Turkish officer seeking Skobeleff, and, in the name of Vessil Pasha, commanding the Turkish army at Shipka, surrendered the whole force. Twelve thousand men laid down their arms at Shenovo, and Skobeleff, while sending report of this to Radetzky, immediately set to work to disarm them, since the other half of the Turkish army was still in the positions on the mountains, and might refuse to obey the surrender of their chief, and, coming to the aid of that portion which was at Shipka village, might still make a very serious fight. It was not until midnight that this disarmament was completed and Skobeleff's troops were allowed to rest.

The Turkish army which thus surrendered numbered 41 battalions, containing 36,000 men in all, of whom about 6000 were sick and wounded; and with it were captured 93 guns (including 12 mortars) and 10 flags. But the Russian losses were not slight, being as follows:

	Officers.	Men.
Killed	19	1103
Wounded	116	4246
Total	135	5349

Of this loss, 1700 men were in Radetzky's, 1500 in Skobeleff's, and 2100 in Mirsky's detachment. Only 37 battalions, or about 25,000 men, had been brought actually under fire; so that the proportion of losses was about 22 per cent.

The capture of this Shipka army surpasses in boldness and brilliancy the advance of Gourko over the Balkans at

Araba-Konak. Although Radetzky's attack in front caused him terrible losses and apparently gained no result, yet without this it is possible that the Turks might have withdrawn from the mountains under cover of the fog, and, concentrating about Shipka village, have broken through between Mirsky and Skobeleff, and escaped to the south; and, although Mirsky may be blamed for opening his attack before he had established communication with Skobeleff according to the plan of battle, yet it is possible that, had he remained idle at Gusevo during the 8th, the Turks might have discovered him and begun to retreat. Finally, Skobeleff's energetic attack, as soon as he had got all his men together in the valley, was one of the most splendid assaults ever made, and renders more than doubtful the conclusion which has been hastily drawn from this war (from Plevna particularly), that successful assaults of earthworks defended by modern breech-loaders are impossible.

The Turks seem to have relied, here as at Araba-Konak, upon their conviction that the intense cold, the deep snow, and the impassable nature of the mountains, except over the road which they held, would render any such movements on the part of the Russians *wholly* impossible. Skobeleff's detachment passed over the Karadja Mountain, which is separated from the Bald Mountain (the left flank of the Turkish position) by a valley (or saddle) less than 1000 yards wide. One would have supposed that the Turks would have had a picket out on this Karadja Mountain, but such was not the case. Skobeleff's trail passed within two miles of the redoubt on the Woody Mountain, but he was not molested in any way on his march. That the Turks must have seen some portion of his men is probable, since when Skobeleff's advance guard approached Imetli on the 7th they found it strongly occupied by the Turks; but that the latter thought that the movement was anything more than a reconnaissance seems doubtful. The Russians had previously made reconnaissances in the same direction, and it was owing to these reconnaissances that the Turks had some time before constructed the line of redoubts facing south-west and south-east at Shenovo and Shipka villages.

The trenches near Haskioi, as well as those at Imetli, had been thrown up in the night after the Russian movement was discovered.

One of the remarkable features of this battle is the fact that Mirsky and Skobeleff both had to leave all their artillery behind (except the little mountain guns, which amounted to nothing), and that both of them carried the enemy's works without any "preparation of the attack by artillery."

CHAPTER XII

THE ADVANCE TO CONSTANTINOPLE—REMARKS ON THE WINTER CAMPAIGN.

IN the preceding chapters we have seen that the whole Turkish defence of the Balkans had gone down with a crash; one army of 36,000 men being captured in bulk at Shipka, and the other army of 50,000 men routed at Philippopolis and dispersed over the mountains toward the Ægean.

As soon as the news of the capture of Shipka reached the Grand Duke's headquarters he hastened forward to Gabrova, and, after crossing the mountains, established his headquarters at Kazanlyk. While the prisoners were being sent to the rear under guard of the 24th Division and the Bulgarian Legion, preparations were made for an immediate advance on Adrianople, and orders to this effect were issued on the 13th of January, viz.:

1. *Right Wing*, under General Gourko, consisting of the Guard, IX. Corps, 3rd Division, and a special cavalry detachment of 5000 men under General Skobeleff, Sr., to advance on Adrianople in two columns, the left following the high road in the valley of the Maritza, and the right crossing the spur of the mountains south of Haskioi, so as to arrive at Demotika, on the south of Adrianople, and cut off the communications between the latter place and the sea.

2. *The Centre*, consisting (*a*) of an advance guard under General Skobeleff, Jr., containing the 16th and 30th Divisions and the 3rd and 4th Rifle Brigades, preceded (*b*) by the 1st Cavalry Division, under General Stroukoff, and followed (*c*) by the Grenadier Corps under General Ganetzky. Stroukoff was to leave Kazanlyk January 13th, send one regiment to occupy Yeni-Zagra, and with the rest move forward with the

greatest rapidity through Eski-Zagra to the railway junction and the Maritza bridge at Trnova, and occupy this most important point. (At the date of this order the battle of Philippopolis had not yet been fought, and it was still possible that Suleiman might be retreating on Adrianople or receive aid from that point.) Skobeleff was to follow Stroukoff as quickly as possible, leaving Kazanlyk on the 15th, and after reaching Trnova to follow the Maritza directly to Adrianople.

Ganetzky's troops were to aid the artillery of the 16th and 30th Divisions and the VIII. Corps, as well as their own, in crossing the Shipka Pass, and then to concentrate around Kazanlyk preparatory to following Skobeleff. They were in fact the reserve of the centre.

3. *Left Wing*, VIII. Corps, under General Radetzky, to advance at once by Yeni-Zagra to Yamboli, and thence descend the valley of the Tundja to Adrianople, arriving on its north and east. The 8th Cavalry Division, which had been for some time detached in the army of the Cesarevitch, was to assemble at Tirnova, and, crossing by the Elena-Tvarditza pass, to rejoin its proper corps near Slivno.

4. The XI. Corps, under General Dellinghausen, to be assembled near Tirnova, and cross by the Elena-Tvarditza pass to Yamboli, and thence protect the left flank and rear of Radetzky's column; and also to send reconnaissances along the base of the mountains to Aidos, and there endeavour to join hands with the XIV. Corps under Zimmermann. One regiment of Radetzky's corps to be left at Yamboli until the arrival of the XI. Corps. The 24th Division, as soon as it had returned from escorting the prisoners to the Danube, was to proceed to Yamboli and form part of Dellinghausen's detachment.

5. The Cesarevitch's army, comprising all the troops north of the Balkans except those of General Zimmermann, to move forward against Rustchuk, Razgrad, and Osman-Bazar, to endeavour to gain possession of these latter places, and establish itself on the line of the Rustchuk-Varna railroad.

6. The Dobrudja detachment of General Zimmermann to

move forward and endeavour to gain possession of Bazardjik, cut the railroad between Shumla and Varna at Pravady, and thence try to open communications over the Derbend Pass with Dellinghausen at Aidos. To cover his right flank Zimmermann was to detach a portion of his force to observe Silistria.

Such were the orders of January 13th for the advance; but the armistice of January 31st, for which the Turks were already sueing, was signed before the greater part of the troops had made much progress in their movements. The columns of Gourko and Skobeleff, however, were moved forward with the greatest energy and celerity. The cavalry of the latter, under command of General Stroukoff, left Kazanlyk on the 13th and arrived in front of Trnova on the 14th. On the 15th he attacked the detachment guarding this village and the bridge, consisting of a battalion of infantry and about 5000 armed inhabitants, dispersed them, and gained possession of the bridge, the railway station, &c., and cut the wire and the track. He also captured six Krupp guns abandoned by the Turks in their flight.

Skobeleff left Kazanlyk the same day (January 15th), and, pushing his men forward by forced marches, 55 miles in 40 hours, reached Trnova during the night of the 16th-17th. He immediately sent Stroukoff in advance down the valley of the Maritza as far as Hermanli, which was occupied after driving out some bashi-bozouks. On the 18th Skobeleff moved his infantry to Hermanli and his cavalry to Mustapha Pasha. On the 19th he learned of the approach from Haskioi to Hermanli of an immense train of fugitives escorted by several battalions of Turkish infantry, and he therefore sent the 63rd Regiment and the 11th Rifle Battalion to cut them off on the west of Hermanli. This detachment on its approach was attacked by the Turkish escort, as well as by the armed fugitives. A considerable affair took place, causing a loss of over 50 men to the Russians, and resulting in the defeat of the escort and their flight toward the mountains, followed by the able-bodied portion of the immense caravan (over 20,000 waggons, containing 200,000 people), who left the old, the sick, and the babes to perish in the snow. The train was so many miles in length that the Russians could not guard it, and the greater part of it was plundered by the Bulgarians of the neighbouring villages, who also massacred the helpless Turks who had not strength enough to flee to the mountains.

On the same day (January 19th) Stroukoff was at Mustapha Pasha, and in the evening received word by Bulgarian messengers from Adrianople that the wildest panic prevailed in that city, and that the Turkish troops had abandoned it and retreated in the direction of Constantinople, after blowing up the powder magazines; and that the Turkish population was also in flight from that city, and from all the surrounding villages. At daylight on the 20th Stroukoff moved forward with his cavalry division, occupied Adrianople, restored order, and installed a temporary government. On the 22nd Skobeleff entered Adrianople with his infantry, and immediately sent Stroukoff forward in the direction of Constantinople.

The ancient capital of Turkey and the second city in the empire thus fell without a blow. It was defended by a well-planned and extensive series of earthworks on the surrounding hills, which, however, were not fully completed. Its garrison was about 10,000 men under command of Achmed Eyoub Pasha.

Meanwhile the right wing, under Gourko, had remained at Philippopolis from the 18th to the 21st of January, during which time the troops rested, partly repaired their clothing, and received a fresh supply of rations. On the 22nd, leaving a brigade to occupy Philippopolis, Gourko began his march toward Adrianople. That town having been occupied on the same day by the troops of Skobeleff (of which Gourko received news on the 23rd), there was no necessity for Gourko's troops to go to Demotika. They therefore simply continued their march by the high road to Adrianople, and were all concentrated there by the 27th, Gourko himself having entered on the 25th. The Grand Duke and his headquarters also arrived at Adrianople on the 26th.

Negotiations were meanwhile going on for an armistice but the Turks demurred to the terms, and all the preparations were therefore taken for marching forward at once upon

Constantinople. For this purpose the following dispositions were made:

1. The advance guard, under Skobeleff, to advance along the line of the railroad, reconnoitre the line of Turkish defence at Buyuk-Tchekmedje, select its weakest point, and assault it with the utmost energy.

2. The right wing, under Gourko, to advance to Rodosto on the sea-coast, whence it could be used against Gallipoli or Constantinople according to circumstances. The 3rd Division to go to Enos, at the mouth of the Maritza, and prevent any landing at that point.

3. The left wing, under Radetzky, to follow the northern road to Constantinople, starting from Kirk-Kilissa, where it had already arrived on the 26th.

4. The Grenadier Corps, under Ganetzky, to remain in the vicinity of Adrianople as reserve until further developments.

On the 31st of January this movement had so far progressed that Stroukoff, with the cavalry, forming the advance guard of Skobeleff's column, was at Tchorlu, which place it had captured after a cavalry skirmish (the last shot of the war) on the 29th. Skobeleff with the bulk of his troops was at Lule-Bourgas (30 miles in rear of Tchorlu), the 3rd Division at Enos, Radetzky at Kirk-Kilissa, and Gourko's troops just moving out from Adrianople. Late that night (January 31st) the Turkish commissioners signed the armistice, having received authority for that purpose from Constantinople.

The terms of this instrument are somewhat remarkable, and show that the Turks at last despaired of receiving active assistance from England, without the *hope* of which they would never have undertaken the war, and had determined to throw themselves wholly upon the mercy of the Russians. They accepted definitely the preliminary conditions of peace, as follows: 1. The erection of Bulgaria into " an autonomous tributary principality, with a national Christian Government and a native militia." 2. The independence of Montenegro, with an increase of territory. 3. The independence of Roumania and Servia, with a territorial indemnity. 4. The introduction of administrative reforms into Bosnia and Herzegovina. 5. An indemnity in money to Russia for the expenses of the war.

The armistice then specified that the Turks should immediately surrender the Danube fortresses of Widdin, Rustchuk, and Silistria, with the privilege of withdrawing their material of war, or selling it to the Russians; they should also evacuate Belgradjik, Razgrad, and Bazardjik. The fortifications of the line of Buyuk-Tchekmedje) the last line of defence of Constantinople) should be evacuated by the Turks, but not occupied by the Russians; the Turks should retire behind the line of Kuyuk-Tchekmedje,* and the Russians advance to the line of Tchataldja, and the space between the two forces (about ten miles) should be a neutral zone. The Russians should occupy the towns of Bourgas and Midia on the Black Sea coast, and have the privilege of revictualling their army through these harbours. The Turks were to raise the blockade of the Black Sea ports.

The position of Buyuk-Tchekmedje is as remarkable in natural military strength as is Constantinople itself in geographical situation. The peninsula (between the Black Sea and the Sea of Marmora) is here but twenty miles wide, and twelve miles of this space is occupied by broad lakes extending up inland from either shore. Of the remaining eight miles, at least half is filled with impassable or difficult swamps, and the remaining half with almost impenetrable thickets. Behind this line of lakes, swamps, marshes, and thickets, runs a continuous ridge from sea to sea, from 400 to 700 feet in height; and on this ridge the Turks had in process of construction not less than thirty large redoubts, besides outlying trenches and rifle-pits, the greater part of them concentrated in the centre of the line, and disposed irregularly according to the nature of the ground in three lines. These redoubts were only half finished, but they still afforded complete protection for infantry; they would have mounted about 150 siege-guns and as many more field-guns,

---

* The two villages of Buyuk- and Kuyuk-Tchekmedje are at the mouths of small streams emptying into the Sea of Marmora, and respectively 25 and 10 miles from Constantinople.

and their proper garrison would have been 60,000 to 75,000 men. With such a garrison—since the flanks of the line rested on the sea, and could not be turned or invested—these lines might fairly be called impregnable. The force actually in them consisted of about 30,000 men, made up of the wrecks of Suleiman's army, which had been brought by sea from Enos, of Achmed Eyoub's division, which had retreated from Adrianople, and of some reserves which had been at Constantinople during the war—the whole under the command of Ghazi Moukhtar Pasha, who had lately returned from Asia, where he had lost his whole army. Yet such was the natural strength of this position, taking into account the shortness of the line, which allowed the men to be within easy supporting distance of each other, that 30,000 men here constituted a more formidable adversary than 60,000 in the line of works held by Osman at Plevna. But the armistice gave these away with a stroke of the pen to the Russians.

Meanwhile railway communication had been established along the Constantinople-Adrianople railroad, and negotiations were immediately opened at the latter place for the conclusion of a treaty of peace. Skobeleff's whole column was concentrated in front of Tchataldja, on the line marking the "neutral zone" of the armistice; Gourko moved on to Tchorlu and Rodosto; Radetzky was just behind him and on his left flank; Ganetzky's Grenadiers were at Adrianople and Demotika; Dellinghausen's detachment went to occupy the Black Sea ports. On the north of the Balkans, Todleben (who had succeeded the Cesarevitch in his command, the latter having departed for Russia upon the conclusion of the armistice) entered Rustchuk at the head of his troops on the 20th of February without having the trouble of besieging it. Zimmermann occupied Silistria and Bazardjik.

But on the 12th of February the British fleet in the Ægean passed through the Dardanelles and proceeded toward Constantinople, the British Government alleging that this was necessary to protect the lives and property of their subjects at Constantinople. The British Ambassador had asked, in accordance with the Treaty of Paris, the permission of the Porte for this proceeding, but had been refused; the

British then availed themselves of a permission granted under other circumstances some months previously, and their fleet passed through the Straits without regard to the Treaty of Paris. The Turkish Government remonstrated, but did not support their remonstrance by force; which was a prudent proceeding, since the four large ironclads (*Alexandra, Devastation, Sultan,* and *Achilles*), forming the main strength of the British fleet, were quite strong enough to have lain alongside the Turkish batteries and demolished them.

As soon as news of this movement on the part of the English was received at St. Petersburg, the Emperor telegraphed to the Grand Duke Nicholas, authorising him to enter Constantinople with a part of his troops; and at the same time Prince Gortchakoff addressed a note to the Powers explaining to them that the Russian troops entered Constantinople for the same purpose that the British fleet arrived there, viz., the protection of the lives and property of the Christians inhabiting that city. It was, however, a fact, notorious to every one in Constantinople, that no disturbance either existed or was threatened there, and that life and property were then no more insecure in that city of religious fanatics than at any other time.

Upon the receipt of this telegram the Grand Duke immediately opened negotiations with the Sultan for occupying peacefully a portion of the environs of Constantinople with his troops; and in a few days a verbal agreement (with memorandum) was made, by which the armistice of January 31st was so far modified as to permit the Russians to occupy the village of San Stefano, on the Sea of Marmora, about six miles from the walls of Constantinople, and also to station troops in certain villages on its left (north).

The Turkish troops withdrew therefore to the immediate vicinity of Constantinople, and on the 23rd of February the Grand Duke and Staff, accompanied by a regiment of Cossacks and his body-guard, left Adrianople by train and came down to San Stefano, where they arrived on the afternoon of the 24th. On the same day arrived the Preobrazhensky Regiment of the Guard, which had marched down from Rodosto. More troops soon arrived, and during the month of March the headquarters of the 1st and 2nd Divisions of the Guard were at San Stefano, of the 3rd Division at Kuyuk-Tchekmedje. Skobeleff's headquarters were at St. George, twelve miles north of San Stefano, and Radetzky's at Tchataldja.

At this time (the middle of March) there were but about 30,000 Turks in front of the Russian army, which could have entered Constantinople without any difficulty, from their positions at San Stefano and St. George. Such was, however, far from being the case at the latter part of May, when the Turks had succeeded in assembling an army of 100,000 men, and in erecting a series of strong earth-works around the city, from Makrikioi on the Sea of Marmora, to the Belgrade forest, between the Bosphorus and the Black Sea.

On the 3rd of March, at 5 P.M., was signed the Treaty of San Stefano, upon the basis of the terms of peace above stated.

REMARKS ON THE WINTER CAMPAIGN

The Russian Campaign of 1877-78, begun with the plan of crossing the Danube, masking the fortresses in the Quadrilateral, crushing the Turkish force in the field, and marching over the Balkans to Adrianople, was brought to a sudden halt immediately after the first part of the plan—the crossing of the Danube—had been accomplished by two causes: first, the total inadequacy of the forces with which the campaign was begun; and, second, the opportune arrival of Osman Pasha's army on the right flank of the invaders. Until this obstacle could be removed no further advance was possible, and therefore for five months the campaign was paralysed, and no forward progress was made.

I have endeavoured in the preceding pages to narrate these circumstances as faithfully and accurately as possible; and the mistakes which caused them—and which the Russians most freely acknowledged—are patent to any one who examines the facts. The overweening confidence and contempt for their enemy which induced the Russians to open the campaign with half the force which was found necessary to conclude it; the lack of practical experience at the beginning of the war, which resulted in such ignorant attacks, without reconnaissances, as that of Schilder-Schuldner at Plevna on July 20th; the dispersion of the army into detachments scattered over an enormous extent of territory; the assault of entrenched camps with forces inferior to those of the defenders; the lack of tactical *ensemble* in the assaults—these are some of the faults which characterised the first two stages of the war, and brought delay in the progress of the struggle, and death to many a brave, willing man.

But once this obstacle of Plevna removed by the capture of Osman's army, the whole character of the campaign changed; and among the wars of this century, since those of the great Napoleon, we will seek in vain an instance of a movement more bold in conception, more energetic in execution, more overwhelmingly successful in its results, than the passage of the Balkans during the succeeding winter; and Russia owes a lasting debt of gratitude to the Grand Duke Nicholas, who determined that there *should be* a winter campaign; to Generals Gourko, Radetzky, and Skobeleff, who conducted it; and, above all, to the patience and willing endurance of the Russian soldier, which alone made it possible.

Beginning with the fall of Plevna on the 10th of December, it ended with the conclusion of the Armistice of Adrianople on the 31st of January; and in these fifty-one days the Russian armies had marched over 400 miles; had crossed a lofty range of mountains, where the snow was from three to ten feet deep, and the temperature as low as $-10°$ F.; had fought three series of battles, lasting from two to four days each, and resulting in the complete capture of one Turkish army of nearly 40,000 men, and the dispersion of another of over 50,000; had captured 213 guns, and small arms, baggage, tents, and supplies of all kinds, including cartridges and rations by the millions; and, finally, had been able to dictate such terms of peace to the conquered as to remove them permanently from the list of *independent* military nations. And this the Russians had accomplished with the loss of less than 20,000 men, of whom about half fell in battle, and the other half succumbed to the rigours of the season and climate.

Even after all criticism has been made upon the faults of the Russians at the beginning of the war and around Plevna, still the campaign as a whole must be judged to be the equal in brilliancy and the solidity of its results of any in recent history.

In the Franco-German War of 1870—the military marvel of modern times—the Prussians were as superior in numbers to the French as were the Russians at the close of this to the Turks, and the individual courage of the Turks is not surpassed by that of the French. By their skilful operations the Germans shut up Bazaine in Metz, captured MacMahon at Sedan (the counterparts of Plevna and Shipka), and then marched on Paris, the capital; which surrendered on the 28th of January, 1871, six months and nine days after the declaration of war. In the Russo-Turkish Campaign the Armistice of Adrianople was signed on the 31st of January, nine months and seven days after the declaration of war. In both cases the conquered nation lay absolutely at the mercy of the conqueror. France, owing to her wonderful vitality; to her resources both in agriculture and manufactures; to the skill, frugality, and industry of the great mass of her people, has astonished the world by regaining in the course of a few years her position among the first nations of the earth. Turkey, having none of these resources, and being a heterogeneous collection of conflicting nationalities and creeds, which the dominant race has never been able—if it has attempted—to assimilate, and having her national vitality destroyed by the degeneracy of the ruling class, seems destined never to rise again; but to be protected and propped up for a certain period by other nations having supposed interests in her maintenance, until this outside support shall have been proved wholly and incontestably to be ineffectual, when she will be succeeded by some other form of government for the countries now under her rule. As an *independent* Government, Turkey in Europe has ceased to exist, though the Sultan may yet live for many years on the European side of the Bosphorus. And this is the result of the campaign of 1877-78.

Of other wars since the long peace, those of 1848 and 1859 are in no way remarkable in a military sense. The Crimean War was mainly a long siege—the most famous perhaps of authentic sieges—which certainly added little to the military fame of the assailants, though it resulted in political humiliation for a certain period to the nation of the defenders.

In the Austrian war of 1866, one great battle sufficed to prove to the Austrians that their wisest course lay in making peace, and the short duration of the campaign prevents any comparison with those of 1870 and 1877-78.

Our own war from 1861 to 1865 is also difficult to compare with those in Europe, since the two combatants were of the same race, and their fighting qualities were so nearly equal, the theatre of war was so enormously extended and so difficult in general for military operations, and there were at the outset no trained armies of any magnitude. Such rapid and conclusive military movements as those in France and Turkey were therefore not to be expected. Grant's Vicksburg campaign will take its place in history alongside of Napoleon's beautiful campaign of 1796, for its boldness and success; Sherman's Atlanta campaign and march to the sea, and the combined movements of Grant and Sherman in the spring of 1865, will always stand out as magnificent examples of the skilful handling of large bodies of men; while, on the other hand, Lee's long defence of Richmond has placed his name for ever among the list of great soldiers. But it was a war of chequered successes and reverses for both sides, and it was finished, not by one bold movement, but by the absolute crushing of the military strength of the weaker by the stronger party.

It was the winter campaign of the Russians which destroyed the military strength of Turkey, and let us now turn to details and examine the means by which the Russians were able to overcome the difficulties which in this season usually bring military operations to a standstill.

The great and pre-eminent cause of their success lay in the almost boundless patience and endurance of the Russian soldier. From the time the movement was well under way the men never saw their knapsacks, which remained north of the Balkans, till some time after the armistice. They marched and fought and slept in snow and ice, and forded rivers with the thermometer at zero. They had no blankets, and the frozen ground precluded all idea of tents; the half-worn-out shelter-tents which the men had used during the summer were now cut up to tie around their boots, which were approaching dissolution; and, although an effort was made to shelter the men in the huts in the villages, yet always at least half of them had to sleep out in the open air without shelter. Their clothing at night was the same as in the day, and it differed from that of the summer only in the addition of an overcoat, woollen jacket, and a " bashlik " or woollen muffler for the head. Their food was a pound of hard bread and a pound and a half of tough stringy beef, driven along the road; they were forced to carry six and even eight days' rations on their backs (in addition to an extra supply of cartridges in their pockets); there was more than one instance where the men fought, and fought well, not only without breakfast, but without having tasted food in twenty-four hours. Yet, in face of these unusual privations and hardships, there was not a single case of insubordination; the men were usually in good spirits, and the number of stragglers on the march was far less than during the heat of the preceding summer.

The ordinary, and usually insurmountable, difficulties of a winter campaign may be classed under three heads:

1. The supply of food for men and animals;
2. The supply and transportation of material—ammunition, clothing, camp equipage, &c.;
3. The sickness and suffering among the men and animals.

I will endeavour to explain how all these were overcome or done away in the present instance.

First, as to food. Northern Bulgaria was at the beginning of winter practically exhausted of its supplies of forage and breadstuffs beyond the immediate wants of its inhabitants. Of cattle and sheep, however, there was still a certain quantity available. These were bought by the various colonels from the regimental commissariat fund ("soup money") at whatever price they could bargain for; but the maximum price was fixed at 20 roubles gold ($15.60) per head for cattle of a weight of 300 to 350 lbs., and 1½ silver roubles ($1.10) per head for sheep weighing 30 to 40 lbs. If the peasants refused to sell for less, the colonels were authorised to take by force at these prices, which were from one-quarter to one-third greater than current prices before the war (many regiments in fact succeeded, especially at first, in buying at much cheaper rates), and the cash was always paid down when the cattle were taken. This inspired great confidence among the peasants, and instead of attempting to conceal their flocks and herds, they brought them to the Russians for sale. Of hard bread and a certain kind of desiccated or "conserved" food for horses, a considerable supply had been accumulated during the summer and autumn in the depot at Sistova. But the Danube bridges were all either carried away in the storm of December 18th to 23rd, or taken up on account of the ice, and there was then no communication across the river except by a few steam-tugs acting as ferry-boats. Early in January the river froze solid, and carts began to pass on the ice; but this was always more or less dangerous, and it broke up in February. During the time of the active operations, therefore (December 15th to January 25th), it may be said that there was no communication across the Danube, and the only resource of the Russians in the way of base of provisions was therefore the depot at Sistova. But from this they drew their hard bread only; for the rest they lived on the country and on the supplies captured from the Turks. By the celerity and boldness of their movements, war was in truth made to feed war. At Orkhanie was captured 1000 tons of rations, at Sophia 4000 tons, at Kazanlyk 1000 tons. They consisted principally of flour, rice, barley, beans, salt, oats, and a small amount of coffee, sugar, hard bread, and salt meat. But these articles were not portable, and they were enjoyed by the garrisons left behind to guard them; but the troops moving so rapidly in advance must have hard bread, and of this there was unfortunately but a small quantity in the Turkish depots, and it had to be brought, as just stated, from Sistova. For the other articles of the ration—such as tea, sugar, spirits of wine, vinegar, gruel, cabbage, &c.—the men simply had to do without them. The campaign was made on hard bread and the cattle driven along on the hoof —nothing more. Skobeleff's men on the march between Adrianople and Tchataldja were for a part of the time without hard bread even; they were only kept from starving by the extraordinary energy and administrative capacity shown by their young chief in organising bakeries in every village along the line of his march, and making the peasants bake soft bread enough to last for a day or two days at a time; thus tiding over the difficulty until the armistice brought his march to a halt and enabled him to take other measures.

The country south of the Balkans, particularly the valleys of Sophia and of the Maritza, is *most abundantly* rich in cattle and sheep, grains and rough forage. The Turks had need of this up to the last moment for themselves, and then it was too late to destroy it thoroughly. They set fire to nearly every village on the line of their retreat; but the houses and stacks were covered with snow, and the Russians were so close upon their heels that they arrived in time to put out the fires before they had made much progress. What would have happened had the Turks laid waste their country as the Russians did theirs in 1812, is of course a mere matter of conjecture. The fact as it actually occurred is that the Russians in 1877–78 overcame the difficulty of food supply by drawing their hard bread from depots previously accumulated on the southern bank of the Danube, and for the rest lived on the country and the supplies captured from the Turks.

Secondly, as to material. All efforts to supply tents or clothing were abandoned, if indeed they were ever contemplated. The men wore the same clothing which they had brought into the campaign and had worn all through the summer and autumn. Their knapsacks were all left behind with the company waggons on the north of the Balkans, and in fact there was not much in them. A little clothing was captured from the Turks at Orkhanie, but not more than enough for one or two regiments. The Turkish dead after every fight were stripped of their clothing for immediate use, but this also afforded very little. Whenever a day's halt was made the men did what they could to patch up their clothing, but at the close of the campaign most of them presented a sorry appearance, with overcoats and trousers burnt by bivouac fires, and gaping boots wrapped up in gunny-sacks and pieces of canvas.

For ammunition the artillery was able to take care of itself without other means of transport. The artillery park nearest the Danube received its ammunition (before the bridges were destroyed) from the railroad which was built up to Zimnitza; it transported this to the next park, and so on until it reached the battery at the front. For Gourko's column, for instance, there were parks at Sistova, Gorni-Dubnik, Orkhanie, and Sophia. Moreover, the artillery was very numerous, its normal strength being 4 guns to 1000 men; and as the number of men was constantly diminishing, while the number of guns remained the same, it was practically between 6 and 7 pieces to 1000 men. This was more than necessary; and in Gourko's column half the artillery was left on the north of the Balkans, and did not rejoin the troops until long after they had reached San Stefano.

Skobeleff and Mirsky, as we have seen, crossed the Balkans at Shipka without any artillery, and Skobeleff began his forward march with only about 2 pieces for 1000 men, leaving the rest to rejoin him when it could.

The infantry ammunition consisted of 48 rounds for the Krenk system, or 60 rounds for the Berdan, carried in two cartridge-boxes; in addition to this, the men carried about 30 to 40 rounds in their pockets, and 100 rounds per man additional accompanied the troops on pack-horses. This gave nearly 200 rounds per man immediately disposable;

this was not all used. To provide against emergencies, however, several trains of intendance waggons loaded with cartridges were on the road between Sistova and the Balkans, but the armistice came before they were needed.

Many millions of cartridges were captured from the Turks, but they were of calibre ·45 (Peabody-Martini), whereas the Russian Berdan was calibre ·42 and the Krenk calibre ·60. They were therefore of no use. Skobeleff got permission on the fall of Plevna to arm one of his regiments with captured Peabody-Martini guns, but there was no time in the midst of the campaign to make any extensive changes of armament of that nature, and it would have been imprudent, at least, to count upon the capture of Turkish ammunition as a certainty.

Lastly, as to the health of the men and horses. Gourko lost about 2000 men, *hors de combat* from freezing during the storm of December 18th–23rd, before his movement began. During the movement Dandeville's column lost about 1000 more. At Shipka the 24th Division lost over 6000 men (80 per cent. of its strength) during the same storm, and was for the moment completely disorganised and useless. After the march was fairly begun there were several hundreds more or less who gave way under the cold or were frozen, but the number was not very great— not so much greater than the sunstroke and diarrhœa cases in the terrible heat of summer, as to be particularly noticeable. Once well in the valley of the Maritza, the climate was not so severe, though still cold enough and accompanied with plenty of snow. But for the moment there was not much sickness. In this march, however, bad food and the lack of change of clothing laid the seeds of the typhus and typhoid fevers which broke out at San Stefano in the following month of May, with such terrible malignity that at one time 50,000 men, 45 per cent. of the whole force stationed thereabout, were in the hospitals.

As for the animals, the cavalry being always in advance, found plenty of forage, and managed to keep in pretty fair condition; but the artillery horses, than which I never saw a finer looking lot of animals as they passed in review at

Gorni-Studen in October, were a sad-looking lot of skeletons when they arrived at San Stefano the next February, even although only the best horses had been selected for the march, the rest having been left with the guns which remained north of the Balkans. Their march had been a very hard one, the roads being almost everywhere covered with smooth ice, on which they fell and hurt themselves a great deal; being always with the infantry, they nearly always found the forage in the various villages eaten up by the cavalry which had preceded them; and it was suspected that no small portion of their desiccated food had found its way into the mouths of the hungry gunners. All the baggage-waggons were left behind the Balkans, the officers' baggage in very limited quantities being taken along on a few pack-horses. The men had no baggage except what they could stow away in the pockets of their overcoats; their rations they carried on their backs.

The only vehicles which kept up with the troops were a few hospital ambulances, in which the wounded of each affair were carried to the nearest village and left there until they could be collected by the sanitary department and transported in country carts to the large hospitals at Sophia, Philippopolis, Adrianople, Kazanlyk, &c.

In brief, then, it may be said that the natural difficulties of a winter campaign were overcome by the extraordinary patience and physical endurance of the men, by the untiring energy of their commanders, Gourko and Skobeleff, and by the fact that all impedimenta were left behind; and that, in spite of the inclement season, the men were deprived of everything but the very minimum of food necessary for life, and of arms and ammunition for warfare.

INDEX

ADRIANOPLE, capture of, 244
Alexander, Emperor of Russia,
    declares war, 1
    establishes headquarters at
        Biela, 29
    orders reinforcements, 71
    arrival at Plevna, 104, 131
Araba Konak Pass, capture of, 169,
    201
Armistice, signature of, 243
Army of the South, organisation
    of, 9
    concentration in Roumania, 12
    naval operations on the Dan-
        ube, 14
    passage of the Danube, 18
    plan of campaign, 6
Ayazlar, Battle of, 87

BULGARIA, campaign in, 1–258
    theatre of operations in, 4, 32

CERKOVNA, Battle of, 91
Charles, Prince of Roumania,
    orders his troops to cross the
        Danube, 72, 94
    arrives at Plevna, and assigned
        to command of "West
        Army," 103
Constantinople, advance to, 241,
    248

DANUBE, passage of the, 19
Dardanelles, passage of, by the
    English fleet, 247

Dobrudja, line of advance, 18, 30
    operations in the, 165, 205,
        207, 242

EGYPTIAN troops at Battle of Cer-
    kovna, 92
Elena, Battle of, 161
Eski-Zagra, combat of, 47
Etropol, capture of, 169

GALATZ, passage of the Danube at,
    18
Gorni-Dubnik, Battle of, 148
Gourko, General, first expedition
    over the Balkans, 27–49
    ordered to Plevna, 141
    advance to Orkhanie, 167
    passage of the Balkans near
        Sophia, 201
    advance to Philippopolis, 219
    advance to Constantinople, 241
Grivitza redoubt, assault of, 57,
    114, 144

KARAHASSANKIOI, Battle of, 87
Kars, siege of in 1855, 197
Katzelevo, Battle of, 88
Krilof, General, cavalry operation
    near Plevna, 137
Krüdener, General, capture of
    Nikopolis, 51
    attack at Plevna, 57

LOM, operations on the, 84, 159,
    164

INDEX

Lovtcha, Battle of, 96

MARITZA, valley of the, 219
Mehemet Ali Pasha, advance on Lom, 84
    relieved from command, 93
    ordered to Sophia, 167
Metchka, Battle of, 162

NAVAL operations on the Danube, 14, 166
Nicholas, Grand Duke, commanding the Russian army, crosses the frontier, 12
    passage of the Danube, 19
    orders the attack of Plevna, 54, 58
    commands in person at Plevna, 104, 126
    gives orders for the winter campaign, 204
    arrives at San Stefano, 248
Nikopolis, capture of, 50

ORKHANIE, capture of, 171
Osman Pasha arrives at Plevna, 54
    defeats the Russian attacks, 55, 57, 107
    attacks the Russians, 96, 179
    defeated and captured, 190
    remarks on the siege of Plevna, 195

PARIS, siege of, 197, 200
Pelishat, Battle of, 96
Philippopolis, Battle of, 224
Plevna, Battle of, July 20, 55
    July 30, 58
    September 11, 112
    investment of, 136, 156
    fall of, 177, 197
Pravetz, Battle of, 169

RADETZKY, General, defence of Shipka Pass, 76, 157, 230
Radetzky, General, advance to Constantinople, 241
Reinforcements, arrival of in Bulgaria, 72
Richmond, siege of, 197, 199
Roumanian troops, strength of, 95
    attack at Plevna by, 114, 144
    capture of Rahova by, 175
Rustchuk surrendered to the Russians, 247

SAN STEFANO, arrival of Russian troops at, 248
    treaty of, 248
Sevastopol, siege of, 197, 198
Sieges, tabular statement of, 197
Shipka Pass, capture of, 38
    battles at, 82, 158
    capture of Turkish Army at, 231, 237
Skobeleff, General, attacks at Plevna, 64, 117, 174
    attack at Lovtcha, 101
    attack at Shenova, 236
    advance to Constantinople, 243, 248
Sophia, capture of, 215
Suleiman Pasha, arrival in Roumelia, 41
    attacks Shipka Pass, 74, 158
    ordered to command on the Lom, 159
    attacks the Russians at Metchka, 162
    ordered to Roumelia, 202, 220
    escapes from Philippopolis, 224, 227
    relieved from command, 228

TASKOSEN, Battle of, 211
Tatar-Bazardjik, capture of, 222
Telis, attack of, 153, 155
Tetevan, capture of, 168
Tirnova, capture of, 80

Todleben, General, arrival at Plevna, 141
    orders investment of Plevna, 144
    report of the capture of Plevna, 179
    enters Rustchuk, 247
Trajan's Gate, capture of, 221
Trojan Pass, capture of, 230
Treaty of Peace signed at San Stefano, 249
    conditions of, 245
Tristenik, Battle of, 162

VICKSBURG, siege of, 197, 198
Vratza, capture of, 168

WAR, declaration of, 1
War council at Constantinople, 73
Winter campaign, remarks on the, 249, 252, 258

YENI ZAGRA, combat of, 46

ZGALEVITZA, Battle of, 97

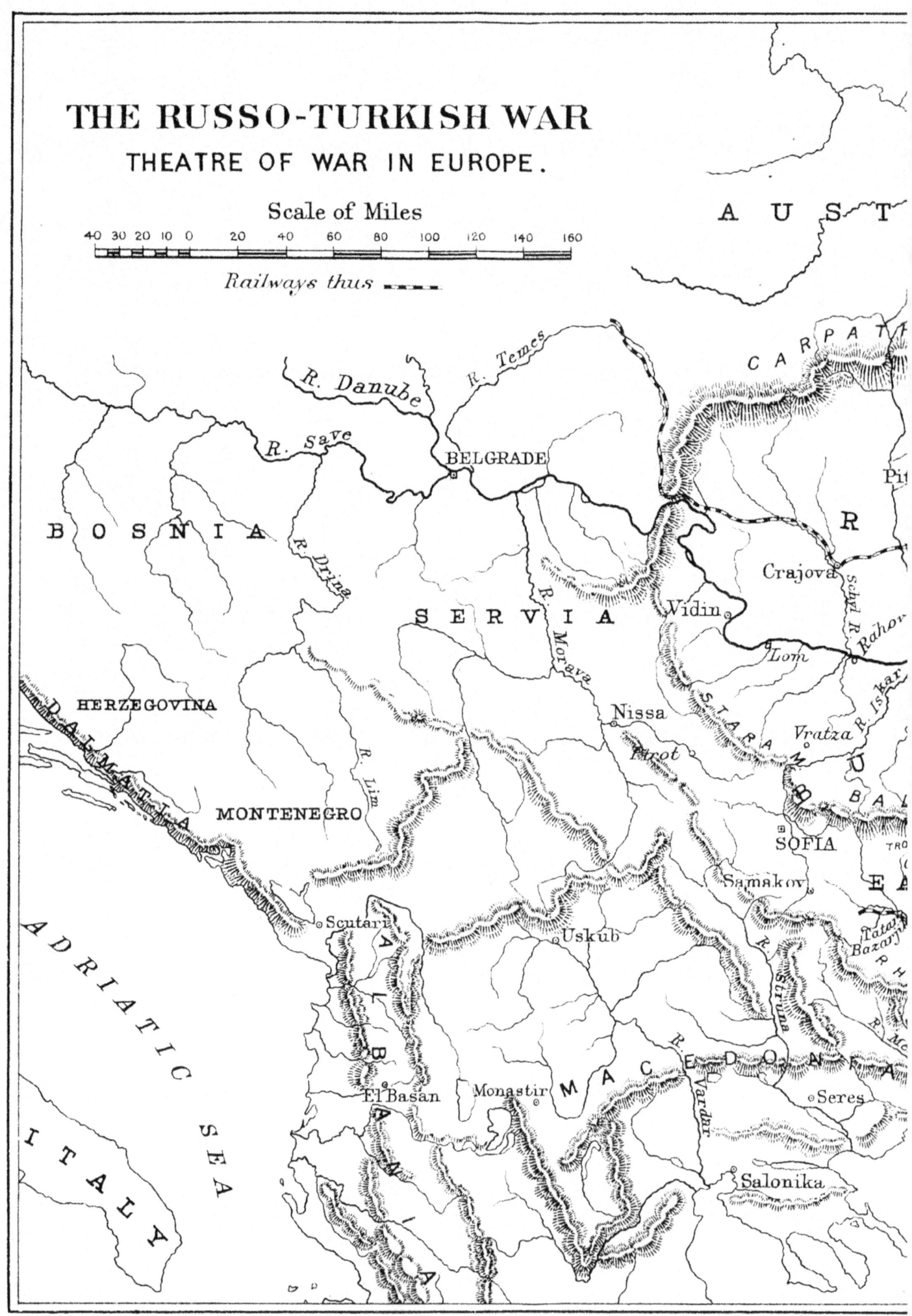

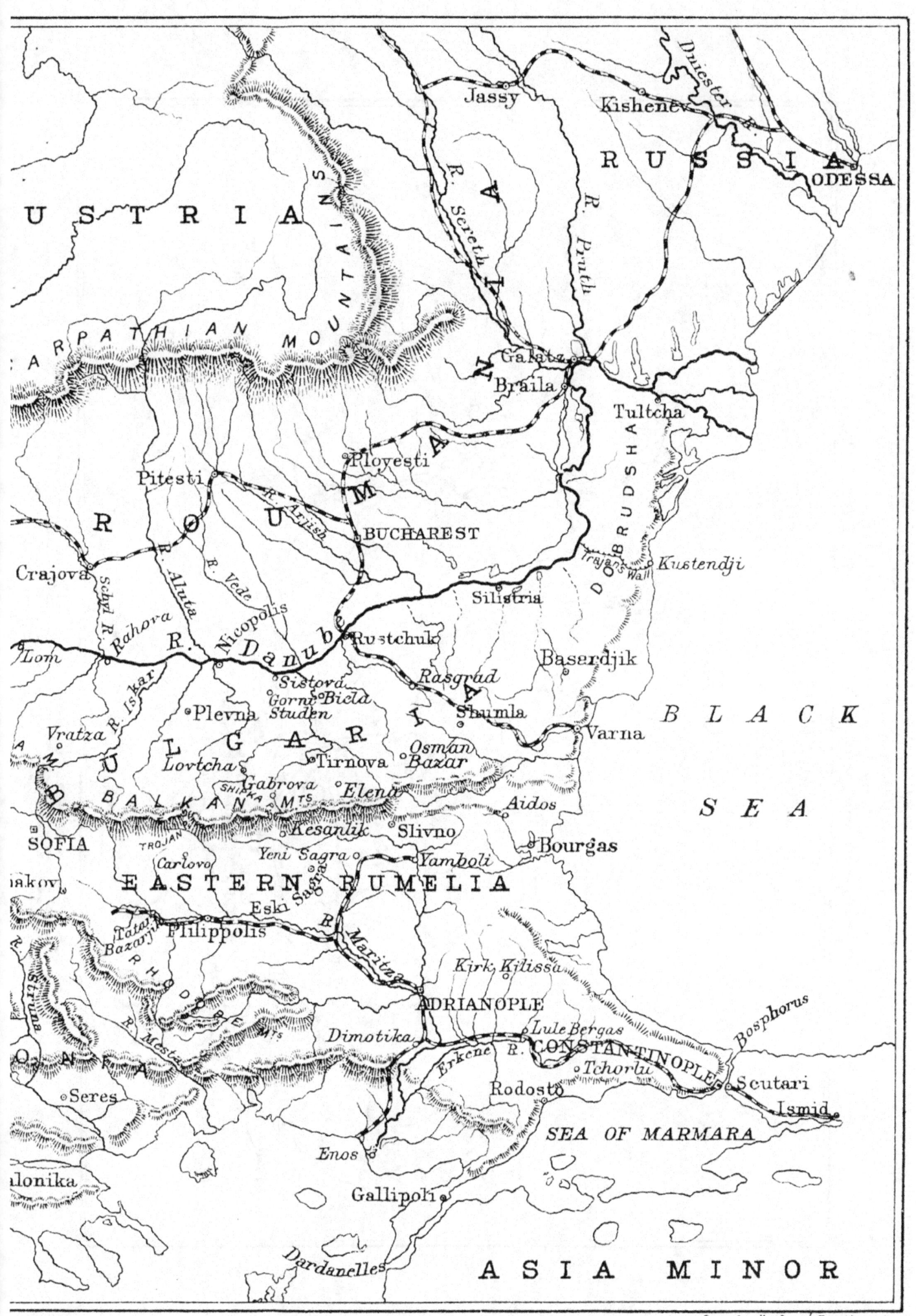

PROGRESS MAP Nº 1.

FIRST PERIOD OF THE CAMPAIGN

From the Declaration of War to the Crossing of the Danube, April 24th to June 27th, 1877

A Russian Army Corps consisting of two Infantry Divisions, two Artillery Brigades and one Cavalry Division is represented thus [ ] at commencement of a Period; and thus [ ] at its conclusion. The Roman numbers designate the Corps, the Arabic the Infantry Divisions, the Artillery and Cavalry are not shown. The Guard is indicated by letter G in place of Roman numbers. Rifle Brigade thus [ ], Grenadier Divisions thus [ ]. Turkish Troops are represented thus [ ] at beginning of a period and thus [ ] at its conclusion.

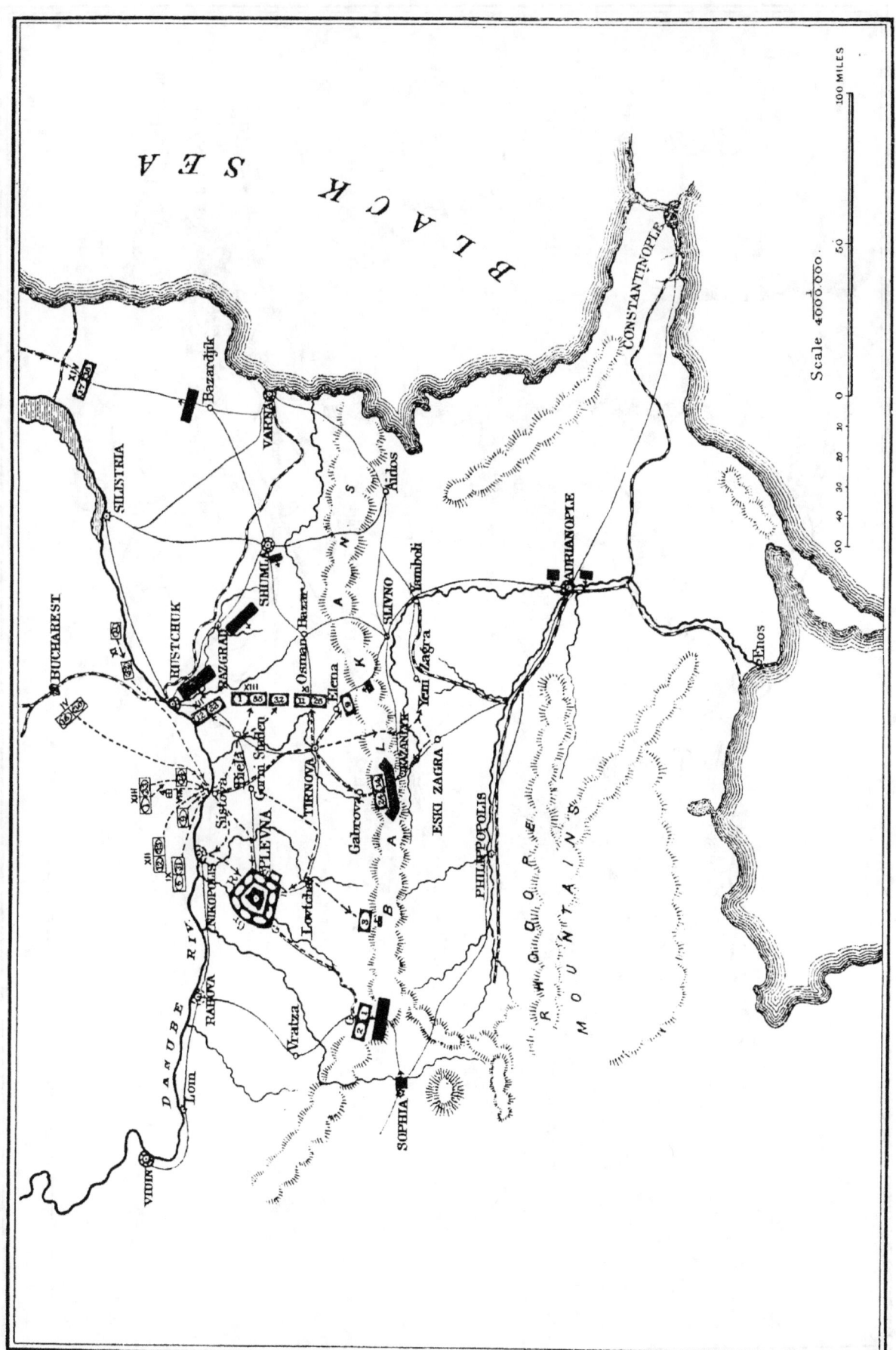

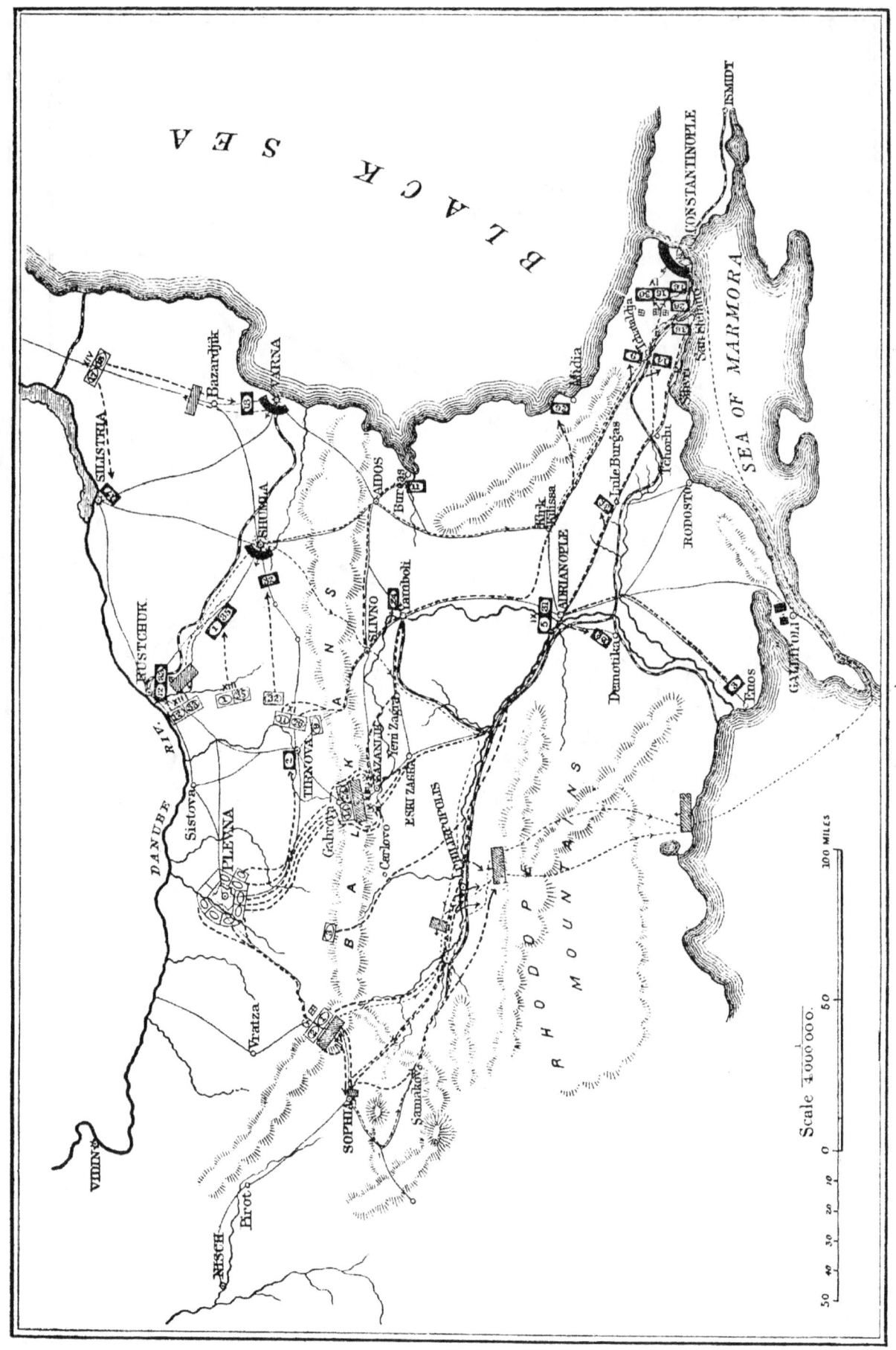

RELATIVE POSITIONS
OF
RUSSIAN & TURKISH ARMIES
AUGUST 5TH 1877

RUSSIANS		
Hd. QUARTERS AT GORNI STUDEN.		
IX C. / IV C.	35000	INFY. – in front of PLEVNA
XII C. / XIII C.	42000	„ – on line of LOM
XI C.	20000	„ – in front of OSMAN RAZAR
VIII C. / 4.R.B. / Bulg. Legion	23000	„ at Shipka Pass, GABROVA / ELENA / SELVI / TIRNOVA
	120000	
	35000	Roumanians opposite NIKOPOLIS

TURKS.		
Osman Pasha	50000	INFY. PLEVNA
Suleiman Pasha	40000	„ YENI ZAGRA
Mehemet Ali Pasha	65000	„ RAZGRAD
„ „ „	10000	„ SHUMLA
„ „ „	10000	„ RUSTCHUK
„ „ „	8000	„ OSMAN RAZAR
Adit Pasha	12000	„ LOVTCHA
	195000	

10 5 0 10 20 30 40 50 MILES

Scale $\frac{1}{1350.000}$

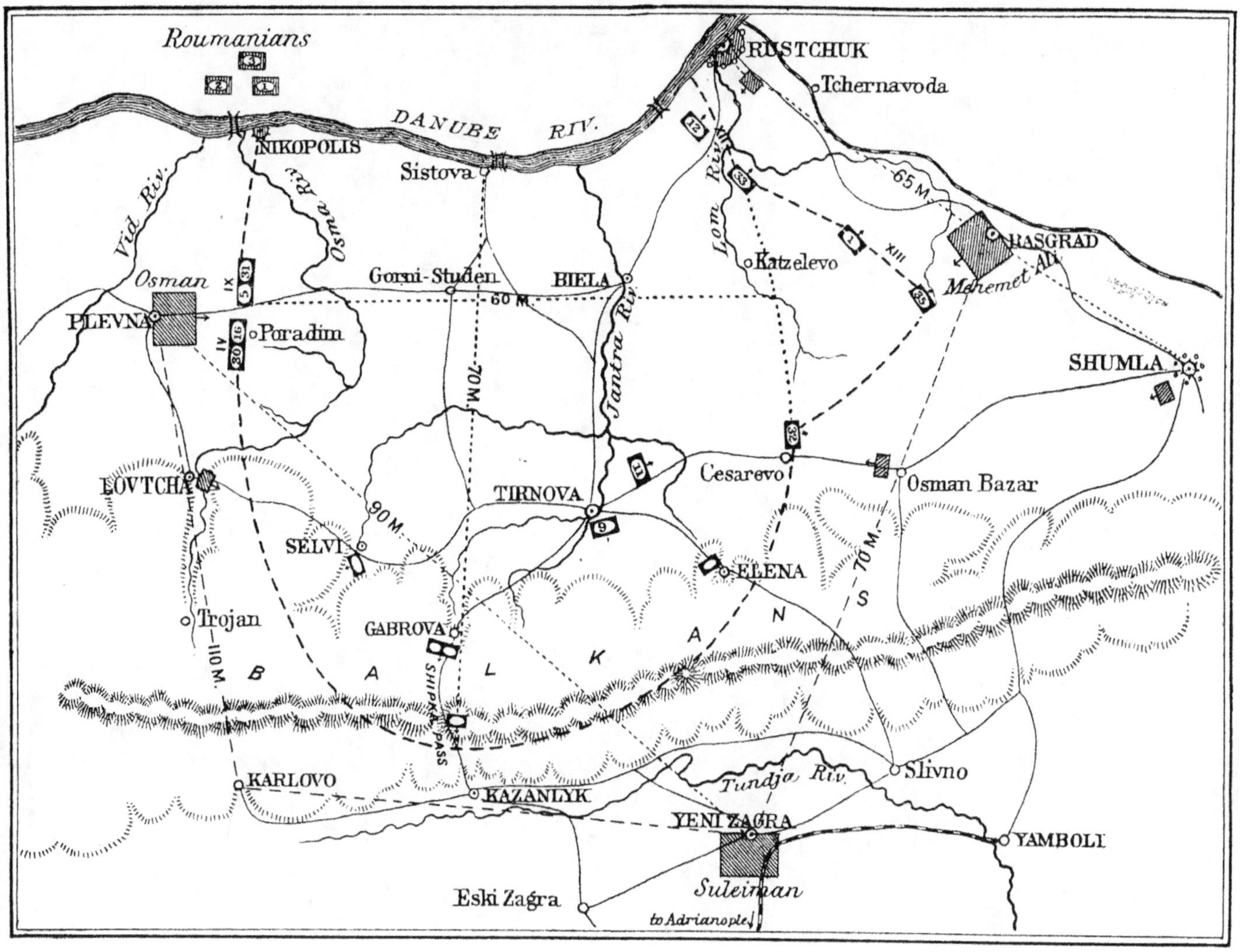

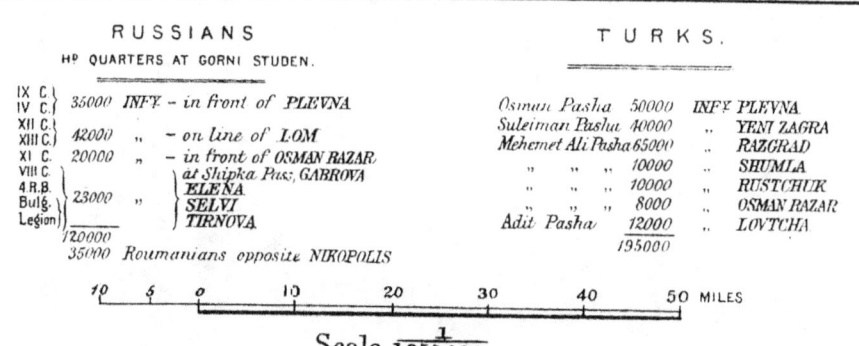

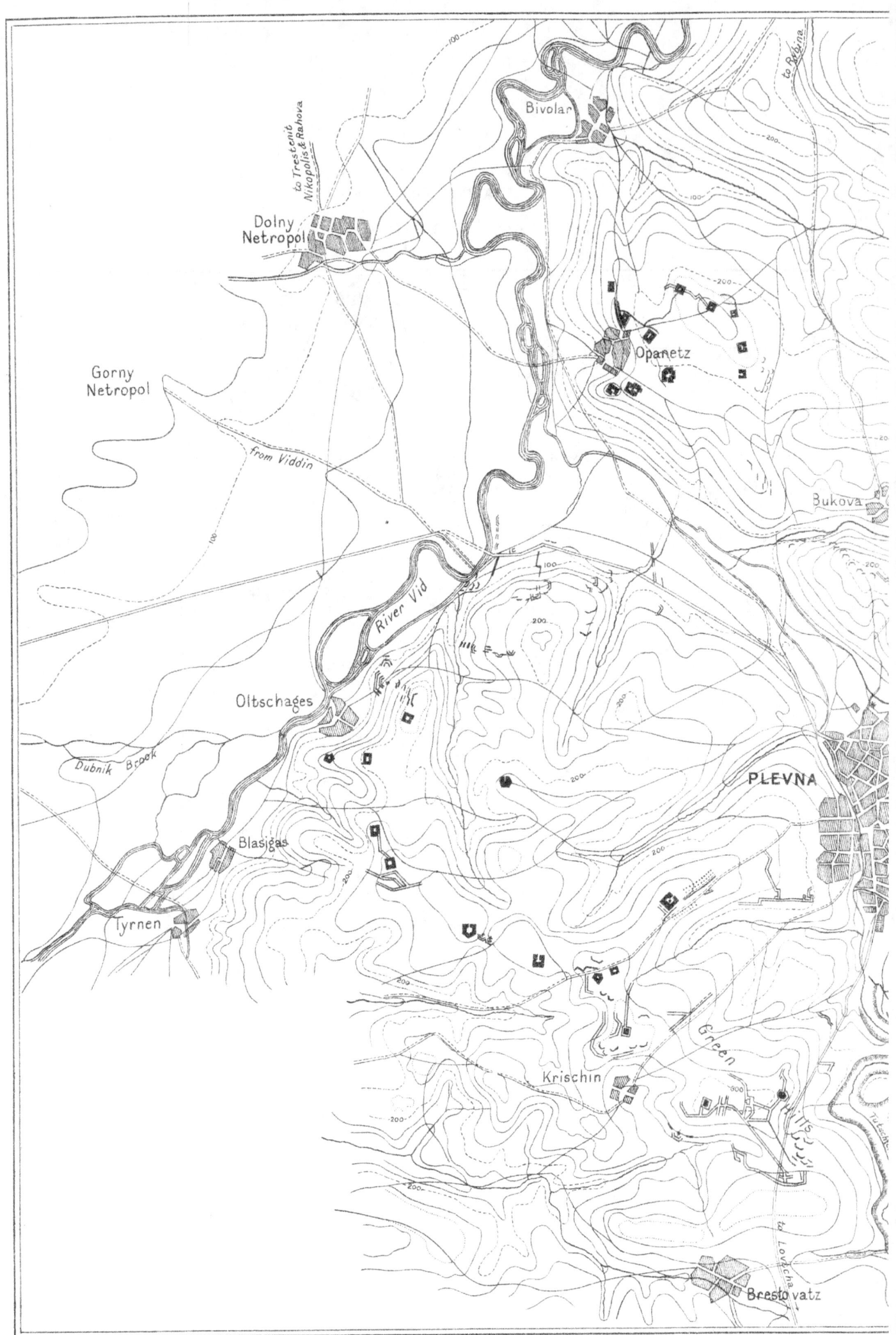